The Wire
Re-Up

The Guardian Guide to the greatest TV show ever made

The Wire Re-Up

Edited by Steve Busfield and Paul Owen

guardianbooks

Published by Guardian Books 2009

4 6 8 10 9 7 5 3

Copyright © Guardian News and Media Ltd 2009

First published in Great Britain in 2009 by
Guardian Books
Kings Place, 90 York Way
London N1 9GU

www.guardianbooks.co.uk

A CIP catalogue record for this book
is available from the British Library

ISBN 978-0-85265-221-3

Typeset by seagulls.net

Printed and bound in Great Britain by CPI Bookmarque, Croydon

Contents

Foreword

I don't need to tell you how epic, engrossing, detailed, emotional, ambitious, etc The Wire is, because that's why you are reading this book. But I do need to tell you a little about the history of The Wire in the UK for you to understand this book.

While The Wire was first broadcast in the US in 2002, it was not aired on a terrestrial TV station in the UK until 2009. In the intervening period the five series were broadcast in the US and became a cult hit in the UK via downloads, DVD box sets and fringe digital channel FX. The full five-season box set only finally arrived last Christmas.

I first became aware of David Simon's masterpiece thanks to the championing of a small but vocal band of MediaGuardian readers who at the end of 2006 corralled enough votes to make The Wire the seventh most popular programme of the year in our annual vote, despite its lack of a major broadcaster or mass viewership. (The following year it was fifth and last year it finally toppled Dr Who.)

As soon as I watched it I realised that they were right. Although, obviously, rather than being the seventh best show of 2006 it was in fact the best of this century, if not the greatest TV programme ever made (© Joe Doone, or is it Charlie Brooker?). But I then encountered a common problem. No one else I knew was watching the show at the same time as I was. When encountering another Wire-ite, the first question was always: "Where are you up to?" Fear of spoilers was a conversation killer.

So, when the fifth and final season aired I knew what to do. I liveblogged it and the readers of the MediaGuardian blog, Organ Grinder, became my companions on a rollercoaster ride.

And then the show finished. And we were distraught. There was a big empty space in our lives. And, because of all of the above, we had never really satisfied our need for Wire conversations. The answer was obvious. The Wire is a sprawling, "Dickensian" novel in TV format, so why not start an online book club? And so we started blogging again, from the beginning and called it the Wire re-up.

Thus, this book came about. The structure is simple: a bit of preamble and then an episode-by-episode guide interspersed with interviews and blogs with and about the writers, actors, and characters. But there are also some oddities within this format. Seasons one to four were written with the benefit of hindsight and foreknowledge. Season five was written afresh without that background. Nevertheless, I would say the comments on that season are as perceptive as those written for the other seasons.

And it was the fantastic wit, wisdom and insight of the readership/commenters that really made this book. I felt like Carver watching Randy walk away when the publisher told us that we would have to shave off 150,000 words from the first draft. To those commenters whose wise words failed to make the final cut, we apologise. It wasn't because they were not fascinating, intelligent, illuminating, funny. It was the failings of this format. (Much as some would argue of the ten-part final series of The Wire.) The comments were certainly the best part of my blogposts.

The other thing that you will notice as you read is that there are no reader comments in series three and four. That is because we had not reached those series in our online book club by the time we produced this book. But, fear not, that merely means that, should you wish, you can go and join that debate and add your own comments, weekly at guardian.co.uk/wire-re-up. There you can also find the much fuller debate from series one, two and five. I have a fond hope that one day the educational authorities will decide that The Wire is a work worth studying and we can turn this book into a big, thick textbook complete with all the missing words, plus those from series three and four.

So, whether you have loved The Wire for seven years or just become obsessed via the BBC or an HBO box set this year, this book is for you.

A few thank yous. To Lisa for immediately deciding that this was a book worth doing; to the grandparents for giving me the time and space this summer to finish it; to David Simon and co for their vision and talent; to the Organ Grinder readers and commenters who make the weekly blog such a joy; to Paul Owen who insisted that we blog every single episode; and to our fellow Guardianistas.

Finally: McNulty (well, Dominic West really) we still need to finish that game of table footy – 5-5 was no way to leave it.

Steve Busfield

Why The Wire is the greatest TV show ever made

Nine reasons why The Wire is the greatest

JON WILDE

1. No other television drama comes close to the scope of its ambition. As co-creator and executive producer David Simon says: "Our model when we started doing The Wire wasn't other television shows. The standard we were looking at was Balzac's Paris or Dickens's London, or Tolstoy's Moscow." Over four seasons, the show has never flinched from that ambition and managed to realise it consummately. Salon.com got it spot on when they described the show as "a Homeric epic of modern America".

2. The Wire's consistency is nothing short of staggering. The Shield lost the plot in season four. Deadwood ran aground midway through series three. Even The Sopranos experienced dips in two and six. The Wire has not faltered for a moment in seasons that have tackled the pointlessness of the war on drugs, the bureaucracy and corruption that infest both the police force and drug-dealing gangs, class war against the labour unions, and the city's dysfunctional public schools system.

3. The casting is spot-on. Dispensing with big-name stars and celebrity guesting, the show opts for unknown actors and is all the better for it. For added realism, a good many of the street characters have real-life criminal records as long as your arm – including Felicia Pearson (Snoop), who was dealing drugs at 12 and was imprisoned at 14.

4. You would need a swinging brick in place of a heart not to care deeply about the fate of the characters. You don't just side with flawed cops like Jimmy McNulty, Bunk Moreland and Thomas Hauk. Equally, if not more so, you root for street urchins like Bodie Broadus, along with bad-ass entrepreneur Stringer Bell.

5. It's the greatest ever cop show that isn't actually a cop show. We spend as much time with the junkies, the pimps, the murderers and the frightened street kids as we do with the law. The Wire is a dense, novelistic drama about those on both sides on the law caught up in the whirlpool of an entropic, near-suicidal society where dark reality is fast outpacing hope.

6. The writing is immense and never misses a beat. Creators David Simon and Ed Burns are supremely qualified to depict life in one of America's poorest and most violent cities, being a former crime reporter and former homicide/narcotics cop respectively. They are ably abetted by some of America's finest crime writers including Richard Price, George Pelecanos and Dennis Lehane.

7. Like all great drama, it succeeds in making its location something like a central character. Not to be confused with the fruitcakey world of John Waters's movies or the sentimental place depicted in the work of Barry Levinson, The Wire's Baltimore is a city in its death throes, fighting to hang on to its very soul. Never pretty, never less than compelling.

8. It features Bubbles, the most sympathetic character ever to appear in a TV drama. Expertly played by the mighty Andre Royo, Bubbles breaks your heart every time he appears on screen, always about to clean up, clawing his way through Baltimore's meanest streets, precariously holding onto his last scrap of dignity. I weep just thinking of him wheeling around his portable supermarket – a trolley piled with cheap toilet rolls and knock-off white T-shirts. More than any other character, Bubbles encapsulates the humanity at the heart of the show.

9. The Wire is a guaranteed way to win friends and influence people. Evangelistically recommend it to complete strangers and it's a cast-iron guarantee they'll become your lifelong disciples. Just don't go lending out your DVD box sets. Anyone who borrows it will want to hang on to it as much as you'll be longing for its return.

A panel of top crime writers explain

IRVINE WELSH

It's the best thing on TV. By far. Nothing's close to it. A lot of things interest me about the programme: the huge ensemble cast and the fact that there are no stars, the sheer honesty of the writing. It makes just about all of the writing on British TV look absolutely shit. We don't know what to do with quality. We wouldn't recognise it if it bit us in the arse. All of the HBO stuff shows up how poor and puerile we are, and how our TV people completely patronise the public. Guys in housing estates in Britain go crazy about The Sopranos but programmers assume they just want shit like The Bill. A real revolution in programming is required in British television.

It's significant that none of the writers on The Wire came up through TV and that quite a few are crime novelists. There's a big difference between a proper writer and someone who's learned how to write scripts. We've got a big culture now of screenwriting and telling people how to structure things. Anyone can learn to write a three-act script but what they don't tell people is how to tell stories. The guys on The Wire are proper storytellers.

Of course you get good novelists who can't do scripts. F Scott Fitzgerald was one of the great writers of all time but he couldn't cut it in Hollywood. He couldn't get down to the crass discipline of doing three-act structures and plot points and foreshadowing. I had dinner with David Simon [the show's creator] a few weeks back and I was asking him how they managed it. He's just so careful about selecting the writers. That's the most important thing to him. It's very, very hard to get a job writing on The Wire.

Simon has created a whole alternative Baltimore in the show. If you take a train from New York to Washington, D.C., you pass through the city and you can see all these places. Large swathes of north Baltimore are [made up of] all these beautiful small old Victorian houses that are completely derelict and overrun. You can see the kids standing on the street corners. Basically the whole of north Baltimore and parts of the south are like a big empty derelict film set for The Wire. It's like an alternative universe, with the politics and the school boards, but it's very close to the reality of the city in many ways. They use great local actors too. The guy who plays Proposition Joe [Robert F Chew] is a well-known theatre actor who trains all the young kids. The whole thing is very much a local industry.

I find the character of Omar particularly interesting. He's an outsider's outsider, this Robin Hood-type of guy who steals from the drug lords as well as the police. He's an isolated figure, completely against everybody, and one of the few homosexual characters in the show, but he always seems to be one up. The guys in the police department and even the smooth characters like Proposition Joe are always a hop behind him.

Simon is normally very brutal about killing his darlings but Omar seems to have a different set of rules. Looking at the writing of The Wire, he's right out of kilter with the other characters. He is this hyper-real, fantastical character – a sort of mysterious phantom, almost super-powered – whereas the others are all very realistic. If he were a realistic character he would have been dead a long time ago. It's a tribute to the writing that this never hits a false register. It works as grammar, adding something rather than weakening the plausibility of the show.

My advice to anyone watching The Wire for the first time is to stick it out. The first two episodes in season one are actually pretty sketchy. They're a bit rough and ham-fisted, and it doesn't look as great as it actually becomes, but it kicks in around episode three, and when it starts to pull together it's really fantastic.

Irvine Welsh's novels include Trainspotting, Filth, Porno, and Crime

MICHAEL CONNELLY

If you look at The Wire in shorthand, it's a story about drug dealers and the cops trying to catch them. That just doesn't sound interesting. But somehow they got inside these people and their neighbourhoods and the bureaucracies they work in to a unique degree. I have never seen anything like it on TV before. I've watched The Wire from the first night it aired, largely because I have a friend, George Pelecanos, who is a writer on the show. Also, David Simon and I come from a similar background: we were both police reporters on a newspaper.

I know in particular about the difficulty of moving from writing a book to a screenplay and how completely different they are. In a book you can explore what's going on in someone's head but you can never do that in a script. Instead you go for broad demonstrations of character, which often means that bad guys are all bad and good guys are all good. That's what you see most of the time in TV and movies but you don't see that in The Wire. The achievement of the series is that it has captured the humanity of every individual in it, whether they are a good person by trade or a bad person. In some cases it goes further by showing the nobility of the characters, be they drug dealers or even killers.

It's a fabulous accomplishment that the writers on the show, like Pelecanos and Dennis Lehane and Richard Price, have somehow been able to stay away from the stereotypical script. I had the opportunity to sit next to Simon at Lehane's wedding earlier this year and I asked him how they managed to do it so well. He said: "It's my show but I trust these writers. I love their books. I love other scripts they've written. So I allow them to do their thing. I trust that they're good storytellers and they know what's important." He provides the framework and the beat points – what has to happen in each episode – and he lets them wing it.

HBO deserves a lot of credit too. In the early years the ratings were pretty lean but the channel believed in the show and let Simon do his thing – pretty rare in TV, in America at least. They didn't have the ratings of The Sopranos. Maybe they could have had if they'd made the show more simplistic and focused on a core group of five or six mobsters, but this thing is all over the place. It's risky. I applaud that. I like to work for my entertainment. I like to put two and two together. I don't like to have everything handed to me on a plate.

There's a sub-theme in the final season about the declining newspaper business in the US that is so important and so accurate. I loved all the seasons but this one connected with me the most because that's where I came from, and because I also happen to be writing a novel about a newspaper reporter.

If you read a good book you get glued to your chair and have a visceral reaction to it. This was happening every week on The Wire.

Michael Connelly is author of the acclaimed Harry Bosch series

I didn't watch The Wire till around halfway through series two, delayed by the fact that I'm one of those people who steadfastly ignore things that everyone tells them will appeal to them ("snobs", I think, is the technical name). When I did succumb it took a little while to get my ear tuned in enough to start picking up the dialogue, but not much longer to realise that this was remarkable TV, a crime series that actually aspired to tell the truth about the way we live now rather than simply bamboozle us with an insanely complex whodunit or entertain us with "ironic" brutality. And, to be honest, I was kind of annoyed.

Why annoyed? Because here was a TV show, a product of the most commercial industry you can imagine, and it was taking bigger risks than anything I'd lately encountered in the world of fiction, especially anything in crime fiction. That was saddening for me as I'd spent a fair bit of time over the past couple of decades championing crime fiction as the one art form that really tells it like it is.

Some time in the 1980s it struck me that mainstream contemporary fiction was doing a woeful job of reflecting what was going on in our modern-day cities. Meanwhile, in the world of crime fiction, writers like Elmore Leonard, James Lee Burke, Sara Paretsky and the late, great George V Higgins were turning out books that married social realism to energetic storytelling. They, and others who followed in their footsteps, such as Walter Mosley and George Pelecanos, successfully conveyed the notion that out there on the streets was a world that Miss Marple and Hill Street Blues were never going to set right, a world that Amis and McEwan, or McInerney and Ellis, barely seemed to realise existed.

I was so enthused by this notion that I wrote a book called Into the Badlands in which I roamed America, talked to its great crime novelists, and fleshed out my case. And for the next decade or so I suppose I mostly still believed in it. But as I went on reviewing crime fiction in the noughties, I felt an increasing sense of disappointment at the prevailing lack of ambition to do anything more than entertain. Everything people always used to say about crime fiction – isn't it just a formula? – seemed to be true. There was a plague of serial killers, pathologists and profilers, cops with bad marriages and drink problems. Lumbering plots with saccharine endings. I couldn't deny it any longer: the world of crime fiction had ceased to interest me.

Then I watched The Wire. And there was everything I'd liked in the work of Higgins or Leonard or Pelecanos: the inventive dialogue, the characters etched in shades of grey, the prevailing mood of moral ambiguity and profound cynicism as to the motives and efficacy of the forces of law and order. There, in particular, was the sustained attack on the war on drugs – a war that makes the Iraq adventure look well thought out – that neither our newspapers nor our novelists (with the shining exception of Richard Price) seemed able to make. There, in a nutshell, was the revival of American social realism: the Steinbeck/Hammett/Algren tradition that seemed to have been lost in a welter of postmodernism, postcolonialism and pure unadulterated schlock.

So I watched The Wire, and watched it some more, and nodded my head in respect as it widened its brief to take on education and politics, becoming positively Zola-esque in its detailing of the ways in which the rich and the powerful fail and exploit and madden the poor and the powerless and – in Baltimore at least – the black.

My one consolation, I suppose, in finding a TV series that is so much better than contemporary crime fiction is that much of the series is actually down to writers – not screenplay writers but book writers. Its progenitor, David Simon, made his name with a wonderful non-fiction account of policing in Baltimore called Homicide. And the show's regular writers include the aforementioned George Pelecanos and Richard Price, as well as Dennis Lehane.

Which is perhaps why, for me, The Wire is so satisfying. It's got all the advantages of a great series of crime novels, plus moving pictures – and for once there's no one telling the writer that it'll only sell if they stick a serial killer in the middle of it.

John Williams is best known for his Cardiff thriller trilogy

MARK BILLINGHAM

To seek out novelists as members of a show's writing team is extremely rare, but just such a forward-thinking policy – specifically the use of a triumvirate of America's finest urban crime novelists – has played a major part in making The Wire into the most acclaimed and groundbreaking TV drama in decades. George Pelecanos, Dennis Lehane and Richard Price are the perfect writers for a show that is anything but a conventional crime series. As with their critically lauded novels, The Wire is able to deliver the genre goods while at the same time painting a deftly nuanced portrait of a city – in this case Baltimore – where the social fabric has been systematically degraded by those entrusted with its welfare.

With what David Simon has called a "murderers' row" of writers on board, the show was further able to develop the novelistic approach which makes it so unique. With each episode a "chapter" in a novel that lasts a season, The Wire makes no concessions to its viewers. This is not a show you can pick up halfway through.

Pelecanos, Lehane and Price each write with the precision that can only come from a novelist's research, and their work has an enviable economy. Theirs is fat-free storytelling, with each able to nail a character in a few key lines of razor-sharp dialogue without the need for back story or clumsy exposition. Though the plot moves along quickly enough to satisfy those used to less ambitious projects, the writers have been given the freedom to let themes and story-strands develop at their own pace. Characters are brought to life during seemingly innocuous conversations in bars or in police cruisers, each relationship as important as any other in a narrative arc that is not constricted by a ticking clock or the need for action sequences.

It remains to be seen if the righteous fury of The Wire's vision has been the wake-up call it should be.

Mark Billingham is the author of the Tom Thorne series

What's all the fuss about? It's rubbish

URMEE KHAN

Partly thanks to the Guardian, The Wire is starting to lose its cult status in the UK, and an unstoppable bandwagon towards mainstream popularity is seemingly under way.

"The most critically acclaimed television show in the history of the medium." "If Dickens were alive today, he'd be writing for it." "The best TV show of the last 20 years."

In the face of such solemnity, only some species of eccentric could dislike it. My friend is obsessed with The Wire and has been for the past couple of years and I've resisted, until the Guardian put up the first episode on its website for free. So I watched it.

And you know what – I'm not surprised that the programme got rave reviews by middle-aged blokes. Because to appreciate The Wire, it really helps to be cerebral, probably middle-aged, and above all male.

Watching it, I felt utterly exhausted. Charlie Brooker makes three good points:

- You have to be patient, as it is like a novel and we are used to instant gratification from TV.

- Concentrate: don't be fazed by the slang.

- Prepare to obsess.

OK, that last one's the bit I can't deal with. I don't want to obsess about the programme because I don't actually like it, and here are the reasons why:

- It is misogynistic. All the main characters are men, apart from one woman. It is a world of men, in which many of the women are portrayed as subservient, lap-dancing gangsters' molls. The Wire is popular among men for the same reason that war films are – it is telly that makes no pretence of attracting women viewers, and, for that, reviewers celebrate it. Mums, wives, sisters, female detectives, female cops, all seem to be bizarrely absent in its first episode. The Wire is proclaimed for its grit; its supposed realism, "the most hardboiled TV show ever" said one fan. So if you're a middle-aged British bloke, denied the wars of his grandfathers, denied the elemental violence of American culture, The Wire is great; it's about men who have some kind of meaning in their lives. Charlie Brooker's comment that many men are in love with Stringer Bell is revealing: The Wire is homoerotic in its message that men's lives are lived to the fullest when they are unencumbered by women. Relationships with women that aspire to equality are always, in The Wire, a source of angst and hassle: witness McNulty's problems with access and maintenance at the hands of his unreasonable ex-wife; or the difficulties faced by Daniels and Kima at the hands of their female partners.

- For white British men, The Wire's handling of race is also part of its attraction. No city in the UK is like Baltimore, with such a massive black population. So no white British men have to negotiate the minority status faced by white men in Baltimore. The white characters in The Wire inhabit – usually – a sort of post-race world, where friendships and enmities with black men are denuded of racial tension. There are questions about how realistic this is, but for the purposes of the show, race in The Wire is a background hum rather than a dominating theme. When, in season three, a white detective kills a black colleague, under the mistaken belief he's a criminal, the "racial element" (as it's referred to) of the resulting controversy is shown as something unreasonable. In Britain, there has never been a TV drama with a majority black cast that has been critically acclaimed. This is itself a comment on television, and it helps to explain why The Wire has a shock of the new, which can sometimes gloss over its defects.

- To enjoy The Wire, you need to be desensitised to screen violence. Otherwise you simply feel drained after an hour of it. Charlie Brooker says it's like a novel – yeah right. A novel you can put down, but with The Wire you have to see it through the hour-long episode because it is so good, but it's not enjoyable. I suppose the programme is like Shakespeare: you know it's good, but do you really want to read the whole of Richard III from beginning to end?

Compared to most stuff on TV, it's even brilliant. But "greatest ever"? Sorry, but it isn't that good – and guess what? Unless you're

a middle-aged, middle-class white bloke you might not even like it!
I have said my piece, I have lit the fuse, and now I retreat.

**Urmee Khan is a journalist and Digital and media correspondent for the
Daily Telegraph**

Series One

Welcome to Baltimore

EPISODE 1 – "This America, man"

STEVE BUSFIELD

We are thrown in at the deep end. This world has been existing for years without us and we are given very little explanation about what it is all about. We are expected to just catch up.

Snot Boogie is dead ("This America, man", which says it all), D'Angelo Barksdale beats a murder rap, McNulty unleashes an internal police "shitstorm" by telling Judge Phelan that the Barksdale Crew run most of Baltimore, all the senior pOlice are annoyed, a task force has been created, D'Angelo has been demoted and the security guard who was brave enough to testify has been murdered. All in an hour, with time to introduce us to Bunk's out-of-office pastimes and Bubbles' drug procuring and taking habits.

And the simple explanation of the drug business hierarchy: D'Angelo's demotion from the towers and his threat to Wallace that if he didn't look after the money better he too would be demoted, to the role of street boy yelling "5-0" when the pOlice appear on the scene.

RUNNING TOTALS:

Murders: three (not including the 10 that McNulty flagged up to Phelan).

COMMENTS

Chris7572 Although we don't realise it at the time, episode 1 is introducing us to The Game, in all its glory, where everything is subservient to the numbers. For the drug crews it's all about the money, the corners and the towers; for the pOlice it's all about the body count and crime stats; for the politicians, it's all about the votes. As the Game is played, we get to see how it's done – in some cases ruthlessly, in some morally – by the members of the different groups. Just because you're part of one group doesn't mean you're automatically good or bad. And all this is what makes The Wire so fascinating. At different times, I found myself for and against the same character (see Stringer debate).

When the 'experiment' in series three upsets the entire balance of the Game people start behaving (well, many do) in a more constructive way. But the relief when normal services and positions are resumed is palpable almost everywhere.

PaulOwen I think McNulty is a sort of decoy character – a typical cop-show type thrown in to give the initial viewer something they recognise and understand, before the rest of the show moves on to more unfamiliar ground. (It's interesting to note how contemporary reviews focused on him.)

Suziebee Intriguing is that final scene where D realises just who has been shot, with the aid of a flashback we are actually shown who it is – was this a pilot episode? Cos in later episodes there is no way we'd be helped like that! You gotta work for it!

Carloscontrole Simon referred to it as The Pilot episode and that's the way HBO looked at it too. The flashback of Gant, the security guard, was HBO's idea in case viewers has forgotten during the previous 50-odd minutes. Simon was ambivalent about the method and states that they'll be no more flashbacks in the narrative, however he concedes that the sprawl of the story and the amount of characters introduced may have pushed his audience too far considering they were being "educated" in how to watch a series like The Wire.

There is some excellent info spilled by the commentary. For example, Carver and Herc discussing the battle against drugs. Carver says, "This ain't no war", Herc replies "Why?', "'Cos wars end". This an Ed Burns line which DS says the man deserves credit for because he fought and lost two wars in his life, Vietnam with the US military and drugs with the Baltimore POlice Department.

The character that Bubbles is based on was a real life POlice snitch, dying of Aids, that DS met. First time for three hours, second time for a further few hours and when he went back for a third he found out that he'd died. DS ended up writing his obituary in the Baltimore Sun.

SuperFurryDaniel I like how the episode seems to set up McNulty and D'Angelo as different sides of the same coin throughout the first series. They both get in trouble with their superiors and they both end up getting screwed for trying to do essentially the right thing…

Carloscontrole DS stated that the scenes of the Rawls/McNulty chew out followed by the Avon/D'moted (thanks, JoeDoone) ass-rippin' were designed to mirror each other. There's a difference between the "goodies" and the "baddies" but there's no difference in the system. D'Angelo gets The Pit and, eventually, McNutty gets The Boat (be carefully what to wish for, McN).

Still on the hierarchies theme… when Wallace gets threatened by D'Angelo about the funny money scam Wallace points out that it's not a dead president on the 10 dollar bill but Alexander Hamilton, who was a Secretary of the Treasury. At the bottom of the food chain, even when you're right, you're wrong. Looking it up, he was the first Secretary of the Treasury. I have been educated, right there. I ain't never lurned nuttin' like dat from CSI: Miami.

DJShep I first picked up on The Wire through Hip Hop Connection magazine, which described it as "the most hip hop show of all time". Da Mystery Of Chess Boxing and GZA on "Liquid Swords" were the hook that truly drew me in and I can see why hip hop journalists love this show so much. If I were to suggest recommended listening for the show I would say the "Wu-Gambino" era of mid-nineties Wu Tang should be on your playlist. Raekwon's "Only Built For Cuban Linx" was the first of their solo albums to step away from Shaolin and into the murky world of fish scales and street slang but it would be Ghostface's "Ironman" for me; not only is the street slang present and correct but you get an album that goes from the hardcore misogyny of "Wildflower" to the heart rending "All That I Got Is You".

AxxB It's funny how when you think of "The Wire" you think of the way it shows things at all levels, from the Street to City Hall, how actions have consequences up and down the ladder. But in the first episode, it really is just a show about Cops and Drug Dealers. No

Carcetti, no Omar, no Clay Davis, no dockworkers, no schoolkids, no media. So much of what The Wire is, hasn't started happening yet... but the idea that although we don't see it, somewhere out there Marlo Stanfield has maybe one corner, Carcetti's sitting on one committee...

KingKongBassett Wu Gambinos is probably more in line with the Avons, the Stringers, the Prop Joes... the high-end players. Clipse espouses the grittier two-gel-caps-and-a-coke-kicker kind of drug life. I love this Clipse couplet in particular (from the track Virginia)...

> *I reside in VA, ride in VA*
>
> *Most likely when I die, I'm gon' die in VA*

Really reminds me of Bodie's chat with Shamrock when they're in the van making an out of town pickup and Bodie says something about not understanding why anyone would ever want to leave Baltimore.

> *I'm from Virginia, where ain't shit to do but cook*
>
> *Pack it up, sell it triple-price, fuck the book*

Hell, Clipse's record label is called Re-Up Gang Records, what more do you need?

SaptarshiRay Isn't it wonderful to be able to understand what people are saying the second time around? Watching this episode again reminded me of the pain between my ears as i tried to decipher the slang/accent/jargon triple hit combo the first time I saw it.

EPISODE 2 – Ronald McDonald

PAUL OWEN

The second episode of The Wire kicks off with one of the most memorable scenes of the first series: teenage drug dealers Wallace and Poot's misguided conversation about how rich the guy who invented Chicken McNuggets must be.

The response of their boss, D'Angelo, is scathing: "You think Ronald McDonald gonna go down that basement and say, 'Hey, Mr Nugget. You the bomb. We selling chicken faster than you can tear the bone out. So I'm a write my clowny-ass name on this fat-ass cheque for you.' ... Man, the nigger who invented them things – still working in the basement for regular wage thinking of some shit to make the fries taste better."

It's similar in a way to D's celebrated chess speech; at this point the show is keen to prove that its project characters are people, not stereotypes. And Wallace does answer back; it's not only D whose intelligence is demonstrated.

Meanwhile, over at the police station, Lieutenant Daniels is starting to realise he's been stuck with a load of useless "humps" to make up his team. We are introduced to Sydnor and Freamon for the first time and remain as ignorant as Daniels that the older detective, engrossed in carving his miniature furniture, is anything other than a "cuddly housecat".

David Simon, the programme's creator, has talked about how he enjoys casting actors on both sides of the law, and it's interesting to see some of these actors in The Corner, his previous show, where Lance Reddick (Daniels), Maria Broom (his wife), and Clarke Peters (Freamon) all played drug-ravaged heroin addicts, while Corey Parker Robinson (Sydnor) featured as a puppyish young corner boy.

McNulty and Bunk bring D'Angelo down to the station, resulting in a fine piece of black comedy as they go further and further in sanctifying William Gant, the dead witness murdered by the Barksdale crew last week, Bunk even going so far as to plonk a picture of his own cute kids down in front of D and pass them off as Gant's. The outrageous witness box scene is a bit of a Wire staple – the quizzing of Cheese for shooting his "Dawg" in series three is another favourite of mine.

The episode draws to a close with a disturbing scene: Carver, Prez and Herc raising havoc in the projects. The incident is shocking for the callow detectives' indiscriminate brutality – especially Prez's, which actually seems to trouble the other two momentarily – but also for the idea that a housing estate would in effect be a no-go area for police. You get a sense of this too in the scene where Stringer and Wee-Bey's cars pull up while McNulty and Bunk are searching D'Angelo.

Last week, reader DJShep talked about viewers becoming desensitised to The Wire's portrayal of poverty and criminality. It wasn't until series four skipped a generation that I felt again the sadness and dismay I experienced when I first watched these early scenes set around that beat-up old orange sofa in the low-rise housing "pit". (Although D'Angelo's stomping ground isn't a tremendous contrast with McNulty's dishevelled, furniture-free bachelor pad, it has to be said.)

RUNNING TOTALS:

McNulty giving a fuck when it's not his turn: two (up one). He pressed Bunk to link the Gant killing to the Barksdales.

COMMENTS

KingKongBassett This is a great episode to compare the Barksdale crew with Marlo's gang. Just how much more likeable are the Barksdales than the Stanfields? Avon is in the kitchen cooking for the community, doting on his nephew's child... D'Angelo is trying to be a good dad... all right, we later come to understand that Stringer's interest in Donette isn't quite so wholesome, but still, for now, it's nothing but love in the Barksdale camp.

Oh, and this is the first episode with the hats. I love that scene with Wee-Bey, Stinkum and Little Man being given the red hat by Bubs.. the way Bey poses with it is hilarious. For a cold-blooded killer, he wasn't all bad. Imagine Bubs trying the same stunt with Chris, Snoop and Monk...

And the ending with Marla and Cedric brilliantly highlights the difference between her selfish world of politics and the brotherhood of the BPD. She says he should give Herc, Carver and Prez up... the thought never crosses his mind. Good man, that Daniels.

FrankyFlynn one of the things i love most about The Wire is the notion that people can change. in this episode we see Prez in the scene where they head into the towers and he comes across as an obnoxious fool who just wants to be accepted as "one of the boys." however when Lester takes him under his wing he shows him that its OK to stand out from the crowd.

a similar thing happens to carver in season three when bunny sits him down and tells him how it is. we see a notable change and carver becomes his own man, rather than just another sheep in the herd, running round "busting heads."

its the best handling of a change in a person i have ever seen on screen. usually one of two things happen

1) characters don't ever really change, they always revert back to type

2) there is an inexplicable immediate change that doesn't make any sense

whereas in the wire you see the reasons and the motivations for a person to change and you understand how people come to make that change.

DrinkSoddenMancunian I was wondering what people's initial reactions were upon viewing these early episodes for the first time? Looking back, I think I was thrown by how modest the ambitions of this first series were, expecting the sprawling, Dickensian beast that I had read so much about in the media. Worthy, i thought, very worthy, finely acted, certainly searingly original, but something just didn't quite click. Then, somewhere around the episode with the east v west basketball game (oh Prop Joe!) I vividly remember sitting there and thinking to myself: "Something amazing is happening here".

At first it was an abstract feeling that i couldn't quite put my finger on...I just felt like the program was important in a way that no other in its medium had been in my lifetime (I'm 23). It wasn't until season 4 (which I genuinely regard as the greatest artistic achievement of our young century) that i realised that the reason I was so immersed in this thing, so taken by it, was that throughout each season I think there is a sense that those behind the program, having set out with noble yet perhaps modest ambition, slowly realise the potential power and import of their creation and harness the opportunity to create something unforgettably powerful.

I think my age contributes a great deal to my love of the show too. Being relatively young, and having grown up believing that television, while capable of wonderful achievements, was but a lowly cultural form in comparison to cinema/literature etc, It was pretty jaw dropping to engage with something that, for me at least, re-defined what could be achieved in its medium.

With The Wire there is also the issue of how people consume the show, particularly the DVD box set. Having never had to wait another week in between getting my fix, I would be interested to hear what people who are newly experiencing The Wire in its original form are thinking. For me, the definitive way to watch such shows is through having all episodes available at the same time to binge on or watch at your own pace. I think this could be the future for television and open up new modes of storytelling, giving credence to the whole "TV novel" idea.

suziebee I'm very glad I watched it first time round once a week on FX, in between eps I thought about it a lot and absorbed what I'd seen. I also checked out the synopses on the HBO website, as let's face it we all miss things sometimes, and found it enhanced my enjoyment and increased anticipation. Admittedly it did drive poor husband mad, as a result of this was endless speculation about what would happen to peeps…usually hopelessly wrong (those i got right, like Michael going to Chris for help, made me inordinately proud though!!)

siidy I love the lightning-paced reassessments of D'Angelo that the viewer has to make in these earliest episodes. In episode one we see him as "The Accused", and then within the value system of his own peers, so that along with String and Avon, we wonder if he's a bit weak, or a bit of a liability. The early exchange with Avon seem quite immature, especially his reasoning as to why he committed the murder. Suddenly in the Pit he is placed at the top of a hierarchy, and all sorts of wisdom and nuances spill out. (Similarly we get under the skin of Wallace more when we see him at the top rather than the bottom, looking after all the little kids). Grasping D on his slip-slide of a character development is one of the poignant mysteries of the first two seasons; once his mother moves in at the end of 1 he closes down to the viewer – he's slipped away from the police sphere and that's kind of replicated in the shut-off nature of the final scenes of the season. It's out of all of our hands. Then at the beginning of Season 2 he has shut himself off from the crew, so again the viewer isn't totally allowed into his head.

Busfield Prezbo's transformation is surely testament to the redemptive powers of finding what your place in the world is supposed to be. And how the wrong career can you turn you into the wrong person. He is a green cop who becomes a bad cop because it's not what he really should be doing. Lester turns him into a smart cop, using his brain and his ability to problem solve. He breaks free of the horrible hold that his father-in-law holds over him (both career-wise and personally). He becomes a green teacher but develops an aptitude. Becomes a good teacher. One of the show's few redemptive stories. And even then you know there is the heartache ahead of thousands more kids like Dukie to come

As for Herc, he was bad old fashioned pOlice. He was a numbskull doing a numbskull job. There are plenty of those. When he leaves the pOlice what is he going to do? The wrong side of the legal divide know that those sort of characters can be bought and can help them do a job. It was, of course, as GonzoC says, a neat plot tool.

SaptarshiRay Herc is a blunt tool borne out of decades of bad police training (ironic as at the end of season 1, Lester looks on proudly as Herc tells two rookies that it takes brains to make a case... and then seemingly ignores it in season 2) but ultimately i think he is also hung out to dry. Whenever he tries to take the initiative, like with his Fuzzy Dunlop bug or the camera, it inevitably backfires but that doesn't mean the ideas themselves were so very stupid – compare taking a department camera to Lester & jimmy (two of the best detectives there are) inventing a serial killer.

I agree him basically telling levy about the wire seemed odd but then don't underestimate the power of resentment. Herc was like a loyal dog to the BPD and it takes a lot for a dog to turn against his master. And he is just about stupid enough to separate in his mind doing his buddy Carver a good turn, from screwing the force over a case, even though they are intertwined.

EPISODE 3 – Omar coming

SAPTARSHI RAY

It's the aftermath of the wrong-headed, beer-sodden, chest-beating exercise in calamity otherwise known as Herc, Carver and Prezbo's trip to the towers. Daniels is not impressed, nor is anyone in the department, nor us frankly, and, as we glimpse Valchek for the first time, appealing for clemency for his useless son-in-law, our opinion of Detective Pryzbylewski reaches the televisual equivalent of absolute zero.

As people commented last week, it is difficult to separate the characters as we see them now from what we know they will become; like the nagging, overinformed, chorus of "why?!" when watching a young Michael Jackson. So just as this time we see

Stringer in a colder light and are not so charmed by the employment of boardroom tactics on the corners, we are inclined to watch Carver and Prez through rose-tinted fingers. Herc was, is, and always will be a clusterfuck of biblical proportions.

Two of the programme's (many) iconic scenes feature in this episode: D'Angelo's chess speech and the raid on the pit, when the police "don't even know what doors to hit". In the former, D's mesmerising comparison of chess to the game transfixes Bodie and Wallace. The latter scene reveals Kima to be a police through and through, running across the pit to join in the thrashing of Bodie after he punches Detective Mahon – just as we think she's running over to stop the madness.

So what else is happening? Rawls, Burrell and Bunk play down the witness angle to the Gant murder; McNulty suggests a less enlightened man than he would call his ex-wife "a cunt"; the stripper with the Dame Edna glasses, Shardene, falls for D's patter at Orlando's; as Jimmy enquires about the legal locks to be picked to clone a pager, he and Rhonda hook up, without it being clear whether it's the first time or not – later we know it isn't, but their salacious banter is deliciously vague; Lester reveals himself to be "natural police", by procuring the first picture of Avon the detail has seen; Sydnor prepares to go undercover in the projects with a little help from Bubs ("You walkin' in the alleys in the projects, you steppin' on dead soldiers … empty vials"), Agent Fitzhugh tells Jimmy "Daniels is dirty"; and one Omar Little emerges from the shadows of Baltimore's streets.

On second viewing, it's strange to feel ambivalent towards one of the show's best-loved and most flamboyant characters. We don't really know what he's up to when we first see him in the van, and, as his rip'n'run plan unfolds, we're left wondering where his position is on the streets. Of course, even at the end of the entire show we're not sure what his position is, but on his debut there appears little evidence of any code as we watch him blow off a hopper's kneecap during the raid on the stash. He also appears somewhat sinister when stroking his boyfriend's hair and caressing a baby's face back on his turf; we don't really know what to make of him, but I think this mirrors the attitude of people in the game – they don't know what to make of him either.

Omar's appearance seems cleverly manipulated on this revisit; it doesn't seem as if we're supposed to see him any differently from any others on the street. Perhaps our growing acceptance and adoration of him as time goes by is directly linked to our acceptance of this violent and amoral world as we watch it unfold before our eyes.

RUNNING TOTALS:

McNulty giving a fuck when it's not his turn: up one to three: refusing to help "gut the case" by joining the raid. But it seems a bit of a tantrum in contrast to Herc's team ethic.

Nights on the tiles: steady at two; his beeper/booty call to Ronnie is done in sobriety.

COMMENTS

FrankyFlynn Parallels between the Omar raid and the police's. Omar watches his prey for a while, learns how they work and identifies the stash house before striking. the police go steaming in, with no real evidence or preparation and get the wrong door. Shows how the bureaucracy of institutions hampers the efforts of those within them. the detail knows they need to watch and learn about how the Barksdale crew works before taking any sort of action but their seniors demand almost instant results. Whereas the individual (Omar) is empowered by not being hindered by such needless interference and gets the job done properly.

whatisthere2 my heart goes out for D'Angelo every time he is on screen, his preaching to the crew about removing violence from the game falls on deaf ears but it highlights the parallels between him and McNulty: both are trying to better the institutions they are stuck in, trying to make a difference but getting ignored. D'Angelo shows more flexibility and willingness to listen to reason as his no violence / respect for the client speech came straight out of McNulty in ep2. Chess speech is a classic no doubt about that, btw its the first time I noticed that Wallace rightly pointed out Stringer as a Queen to Barksdale King.

carloscontrole From the chess speech, Bodie asks what are "those little bald-headed bitches" – absolutely cracks me up. The battle in the Pit between two sets of pawns was utterly pointless for the street police and the hoppers but protected the kings and queens of both.

At the end, a cut away to McNulty from the fruitless assault on the Pit finds him listening to "Dirty Old Town" on the radio. Polk. Mahon. A song made famous by The Pogues. I'm beginning to get it.

unstuck I think one of the hooks for newbies is D'Angelo. He has a couple of great scenes (the chess, the McNuggets), he dresses different, he stands out, and right away you see that he is conflicted about his place in the word. On the one hand he is made to feel terrible about Gant's death during Bunk's and McNulty's interrogation, he is actually in tears. Yet with his boys he tries to play it so tough, claiming to have killed someone he didn't. Yet we see him being sensitive towards Wallace.

A telling scene is when he going to an upscale downtown restaurant with his Baby Mama. He wants to fit in with "legit" society, yet he feels out of place. He was born into drug-dealing but he never felt it, much like Namond won't in S4. "Do you think these people know what I'm about?" He says. He's like Stringer with a conscience!

EPISODE 4 – One-word investigation

STEVE BUSFIELD

Has so much ever been conveyed with so few words? Or indeed one word? Or should I say several derivatives of one word? Over four minutes and 40 seconds Bunk and McNulty use 31 fucks, four motherfuckers and one fucking-A to solve the mystery of how Avon Barksdale's ex-girlfriend was killed. Has there ever been anything comparable?

What did we learn this week? That Burrell's golf goes awry when he gets bad news (a joke which returns in season five); that the ruling West Side drug lord wants Omar's head as a trophy (again, a theme revisited in season five); and that Prezbo likes puzzles (although at this stage we think he is a timewaster rather than an inquiring mind).

RUNNING TOTALS:

Herc fuck-ups: up to three with the classic desk-through-a-doorway scene.

Nights on the tiles for McNulty: up to three following his session with Lester, where, too late, he is given advice on how to avoid transfer to his nightmare posting.

COMMENTS

Ell0 I love the 'CSI' scene (Baltimore PD style)… it's analogue detective work in a digital age.

spoiltvictorian The 'Fuck' crime scene really highlights the shrewdness and affirms (in great style) the POlice credentials of Bunk and McNulty, and how easily basic things get overlooked by the other apathetic sods of the BPD.

carloscontrole It's also the first time we meet McNulty's ex-wife, Callie Thorne, initially seen in Homicide. She's superbly cast 'cos you can just imagine them as dynamic, bickering youngsters getting married on a wild, exciting high then throwing pots 'n' pans at each other during marriage as McN continually fucks up.

SaptarshiRay On J-Bird, i think he's the closest thing to a chorus in the whole wire-as-Greek-tragedy debate. We the audience are the only all-seeing ones, the oracle.

Which is why we tend to feel irked that someone in one section doesn't know someone in another – like Omar being unknown to the newspaper, or bunny not really knowing who stringer is, even though he becomes his ci.

But landsman pulls the strings at homicide and knows the dirt on everyone – he's the one that tells Rawls about Jimmy's hatred of boats. But his supervision, sometimes being a good guy, other times being an obstructive bureaucrat, his phonecalls (he breaks the news when detectives die), his classical references (my fave being when he describes Lester as "a vandal at the gates of Rome" after he gets all the vacants opened to the tune of 22 bodies) and of course his heartfelt, morbidly beautiful eulogies – Cole's especially, but as i guess the actor died maybe a lot of the tears were real from the cast.

"He was called. And he served. On a dark corner of the American experiment."

He's our narrator in homicide and the BPD in general, just as Bubbles is our spotlight on the streets and Norman is our deep throat at city hall.

carloscontrole Anyway, I was thinking about Omar and drugs like you do, and had a similar thought about his "generosity" with the vial of smack he allowed that mother to have until her welfare cheque turned up (yeah, right). The child obviously has very little hope of escape and the cycle of despair goes on. What also must be pointed out is the hideous abuse of booze on the other side of the fence. The BPD is portrayed as being awash with the stuff and some employees were barely functional most of the time. Let's face it, grog is a bigger killer of humans than smack. It, too, destroys careers and families and in larger quantities.

I would certainly not have the bare-faced cheek to damn-to-the-very-bowels-of-hell the partaking of a snifter and have sure taken enough of a "taste" to keep the vodka industry safe from this economic downturn and, indeed, the next one. Neither am I a flag waver for smack. But when I worked in the record industry and surveyed the carnage of yer average morning the "Horse Heads" were more able for something approaching "work" than the drunks! Ok, you had to watch where you left your wallet, travel pass, work boots, clothes in general, etc., but the destruction caused by drunkenness was far more obvious and far more common. It's legal, taxed, cheap and available absolutely everywhere. It's criminal.

I thought the idea of Hamsterdam was sensible and obvious and doomed. I loved the story line and think of Bunny more as the Robin Hood character than Omar. Of course, all over the world there are unofficial areas like Hamsterdam. There are only two reasons for going there: selling or buying. You know the rules. On a Friday and Saturday I don't even bother going out in the city centre anymore. Why risk getting my skull split open by folks who can't handle their alcohol? In some pubs you can get seriously fucked up for £15 in two hours whereas a wrap of caffeine, ant killer and a speck of heroin will cost you 20 and probably a blowjob. It's such a dumb state of affairs that I sometimes I think I'm being a simpleton, 'cos I must have missed something along the way.

When it all shakes out I've never taken smack and never will because I saw the damaged junkies at King's Cross rail station before I recognised the damaged drunks all around me. The media told me the former were Bad People but the latter should enjoy this cheeky little red from the New World. Respect is due to David Simon and Ed Burns who never judge. There are scenes in 'The Corner' that showed the cathartic use of smack and coke and there are scenes in "The Wire" that show the cathartic use of whiskey and... damn! (No mixers ever used, that's killed my pun stone dead. Bugger).

We're all owned by big business and we're poisoned either way.

SpoddyFundunglus Carloscontrole – Nice observations re: use of drugs/alcohol in the series. One thing I have been wondering – Avon, Marlo et al seem in the series to deal exclusively in heroin. Is this realistic? Don't most dealers diversify and deal in coke, crack, etc, as well?

Also, I wonder whether the series didn't miss some potentially interesting asides about more quotidian, socially accepted use of illegal drugs among some of the more white and/or middle-class characters. I'm quite sure that at least a few of the characters from the media/political worlds shown in the programme would dabble in weed or coke from time to time, and as for that shitbag cop, Officer Colicchio, that guy is definitely off his head on something. Anyone have any theories on why only alcohol and heroin seem to be the only drugs that exist in The Wire's version of Baltimore?

Stockholmer Steve – Have you seen BASEketball? The scene where Trey and Matt use "Dude" and only "Dude" to convey an entire scene in a fantastic satire on the airheadedness of modern screenwriting.

SpoddyFundunglus Busfield – I'm pretty sure I heard McNulty give a "fuckity" in that scene but it may have been my overactive imagination.

Giving a fuckity when it ain't his turn to give a fuckity...

EPISODE 5 – The Shakespeare theories

STEVE BUSFIELD

Which other TV cop show would see its biggest plot developments played off-screen (the slayings of Omar's sidekicks) or over the course of the whole episode (cracking the pager code)?

But, for me, the significant theme of the week was the development of Avon's character as the leader of a family and a regime: his paranoia as he leaves his girlfriend's house and his "family and blood" speech over the comatose body of D's uncle ("…a little slow, a little late").

And on this theme I thought we could further expound something that has been discussed in recent weeks: the similarities between The Wire and Shakespeare.

starkimarki argued that D'Angelo is Hamlet: "From visual 'clues' such as the introverted demeanour and the black rolltop pullover (instead of the spectacular oversize hoodies and tees), to the realisation of the unsavoury practices of "my uncle the king"). And further developed a cast list:

Avon – Claudius

The murdered security guard – Hamlet Sr

The ghost (I know) – Bunk + McNulty (spirit level – see Jameson's)

Ophelia – Shardene

Gertrude – his mum (obviously)

Polonius – Stringer

Fortinbras – Prop Joe

Norway – east side

Rosencrantz and Guildenstern – Poot and Bodie

Terrible things the ghost encounters while away from Hamlet – Rawls, Burrell et al.

In fine Hamlet style, it is all so good that the structure may be doubled:

McNulty – Hamlet

Bunk – Horatio

Claudius/Polonius – Burrell /Rawls

Fortinbras – The mayor

Ghost – Jameson's

Pirates – Crew of BPD patrol boat

Laertes – Daniels

Regular commenter AxxB (aka Alex Boothroyd) had previously developed a theory that the Barksdale gang were in fact mirroring Richard III:

"Inspired in no small part by Marlo's obsession with wearing the crown, it occurred to me that there were certain strong parallels with a much-discussed period in English history: the War of the Roses.

"Avon Barksdale is, like Edward IV, a great warrior who won the throne after a lengthy war.

"Stringer Bell, like Richard, Duke of Gloucester (Later Richard III), was a loyal supporter of Edward who then betrayed his family and seized power for himself. Although Richard was Edward's actual brother, as opposed to Stringer and Avon's fraternal friendship.

"D'Angelo Barksdale, similar to the princes in the Tower, was the late king's heir, killed while imprisoned – although we know for a fact that Stringer ordered D'Angelo's death, and Richard's involvement in the death/disappearance of the princes is not certain and vehemently debated. Because he didn't do it.

"Marlo Stanfield could be seen as a Henry Tudor figure. Tudor took the throne from Richard in battle, then ruled with an iron fist because all of his subjects knew he had no real (blood) claim to kingship – although Marlo never married Avon's daughter to legitimise himself. And although he, like Henry, relied on others to do his fighting for him, Marlo actually could fight if he had to. Henry VII couldn't beat up a cat.

"Brother Mouzone serves the same purpose as the Earl of Stanley, a warrior long on the Yorkist side, but more loyal to Edward, who eventually turned on Richard III and killed him.

"You could compare Proposition Joe to Richard Neville (the Earl of Warwick), who was known as the Kingmaker and played both sides against each other effectively during the first War of the Roses."

Series five of The Wire is crowded with references and debate about Charles Dickens, but is Shakespeare, in fact, more of an inspiration? Or is it more Greek tragedy? Or is it just that art mirrors real life and The Wire is a dramatised documentary of Baltimore in the 21st Century?

RUNNING TOTALS:

Murders: up two to five with the slayings of Omar's fellow gangsters.

McNulty drunk: up to four. An evening failing to assemble Ikea bedroom furniture. This scene is echoed much later by Kima when she finally realises the importance of family that her devotion to the force has cost her.

COMMENTS

whatisthere2 How about The Wire as Romeo and Juliet? I always saw the series as a love tragedy – McNulty's unrequited love for West Baltimore.

Lucyt How is Shardene anything like Ophelia? She's one of the few Wire characters with both remarkable strength and unambiguous goodness. You could say she is Desdemona (heavenly), Stringer is Iago (devilish, Machiavellian) and D'Angelo is Othello (humanity) but that analogy can only be taken so far, especially as Des was pretty dull.

SaptarshiRay Always thought there was something of Lear about Frank Sobotka trying to hold his kingdom together.

A lot of Julius Caesar too, particularly as AxxB points out about Marlo's obsession with the crown.

Always thought the Greek represented the gods too, the unseen power over everything (Greek gods i guess?), who supplies Baltimore with its hookers, drugs, guns, and just about anything else.

CodProfundity Avon's story is so strong in season one and I sometimes forget that because of Stringer's arc. The dichotomy between the two is possibly my favourite part of the early seasons. Stringer's rationalised, dare I say, neo-liberal attitude and Avon's instinctive, traditional view of The Game are so very different, sure they are both predators but the perspectives they have and the dialogue between them illuminates the argument about the War On Drugs and reformation.

Stockholmer Although Avon is the head honcho, and to an extent, Kima is a narco (and it's Narcotics through Daniels, by proxy that are running the case) it is actually Stringer in the Barksdale clan, and

McNulty for the Company that are the real driving forces behind the two organisations. Both often at odds with leadership on management style, direction and even methodology. This is best summed up in one of the publicity stills for Season 3 – McNulty and Kima driving past Avon and Stringer, with the reflections of McNulty and Kima in the metallic sheen of the car's paintwork. Avon and Kima are oblivious to the others passing; Stringer and Jimmy are eyefucking each other. We know who really runs the show on both sides.

DrinkSoddenMancunian With regard to the Barksdale and Stanfield crews dealing only in heroin, a few ideas. Firstly, I presume that, as in this country, crack and smack are considered to be at the very apex of the drug food chain, that is to say that, whereas if someone deals in coke in this country it is fair to assume that they wouldn't have too much of difficulty procuring any other drugs up to and below that level of heaviness…for example, he who deals in speed will very likely have no issues getting hold of ketamine/mdma/pills/downers/ trips etc whereas it is very rare for anyone who is a member of the starving classes depicted in the Baltimore tower blocks and high rises to have access to anyone selling heroin and crack (the a league of narcotics in terms of sheer risk in taking the stuff) that isn't in some way connected to some sort of gang or organised crime unit. Heroin is, quite simply, the easiest drug to make constant cash out of because of, as Stringer outlined in the previous episode, its obscenely addictive nature. Quite simply, one can take ecstasy at the weekend, acid on a Tuesday night, get stoned the next night then be clean for an entire month without becoming physically addicted to the drug. Although, of course, it is pretty easy to pick up a drug habit from these lesser narcotics, its is much harder to become addicted to them simply because of the fact that, after your trip/pill is finished, you feel pretty wiped out and tired…when your smack is finished you need more smack.

Now the crucial part of all this, and the most heartbreaking one, is that this drive to score more dope is multiplied a hundred fold when you consider the grinding poverty of the junkies depicted in the wire…they facilitate and escalate each others habits and provide a constant stream of revenue for people like Barksdale/ Stanfield etc. Also, there is the emphasis on product. Its within the best interests of a dealer to make sure that he can cut his dope with enough extra bits and pieces to increase its volume, and consequently, his profit, whilst ensuring at least an artificially high standard of purity. Which is why Prop Joe holds all the aces when he hooks up with the Greek and manages to get a hold of the best gear in town later on in the show.

As regards crack, it would seem likely to me that Barksdale and Stanfield probably do sell a little, but its irrelevant to the plot because the characters that are being focused on are all working in a particular spot that is notorious for its heroin and attracts users to that location specifically because of this.

R.e: Shakespearean overtones. I think its overreaching somewhat to directly match up specific characters from the wire and the bards plays, a la D as Hamlet, Frank as Lear etc. While there are undoubtedly similarities in many cases, as has previously been mentioned, this is down to the fact that Shakespeare's plays are heavily indebted to the Greek tragedies of which David Simon is so enthralled…and as they, and subsequently Shakespeare, along with biblical allegory, pretty much shape the entire reading of narrative tropes and universality of themes within literature, at least in this country, we are bound to make the comparison.

CodProfundity – You should indeed say it! Stringer as the metaphor for neo-liberalism is one of the most interesting strands of the show's first three series. He does, after all, count Adam Smiths Wealth of Nations among his influences. Interesting to note the scene in which D and his girl are dining out in this episode, and he says something along the lines of "some things just stay with you". For me this, as well as Bunny's attempts to treat the kids to a civilised meal in season 4 are evidence that gentrification is usually incredibly difficult for those schooled in the cut throat world of a street which takes all its cues from the wider, free market as standard world. This is mirrored too by Marlo's rise, he being, for me, the inevitable outcome of unfettered capitalism. Exploit, by any means necessary and at all human cost, for profit and power.

Now excuse me while I have a cold shower and march on Manchester city centre with my red flag and beret.

Stockholmer On a separate note I would like to ask if any other OG's (Organ Grinders) suffer from Wire-isms. I work in a semi-open plan office as a typical office droid, amongst about 100 others. My boss is a huge Wire fan, as is the guy who sits directly in front of me, along with the guy who sits a couple of desks away behind me. My issue is this: Since the four of us realised we are such huge fans, our lingua franca has adapted thus:

At anytime during the working day, one of us will head to the kitchen to re-up on a coffee from the connect (the little old Swedish lady that drops off the coffee and tea bags). The CEO and GM and any other empty suits are now collectively referred to as the bosses; the operations Director is obviously the Deputy Ops; the younger or newer members of the office are seen as hoppers, shitbirds or mopes; the accounts department over across the way is now the Eastern, whilst our department is the Western; when the phone begins to ring we debate who's up?; the courtyard we share with the other firms that work in our inner-city office is the projects (we have seriously debated moving a battered, orange couch in there); a trip to buy lunch from the Deli is called a rip and run; and when an item of stationary is misplaced it, predictably becomes a stone fuckin' whodunnit. I perpetually annoy the non-Wire watchers in my department by asking you happy now, bitch?

carloscontrole "The Corner" was more specific about the drugs used by smack addicts. It's not as important in "The Wire". A "one and one" would be one vial of heroin and one of coke which, I gather, is THE way to get fucked up good and proper. A Speedball.

I'm surprised too that there weren't any scenes or even references to the monied classes messing with coke or a sneaky spliff. That would have opened up a whole new series and would have been fascinating. Mind you, enough has been crammed in already so…

A few things that occurred to me in this episode. The swearing is, by and large, excellent although the American accent doesn't lend itself to the "c" word or "wanker". Just like the English accent has no chance with "motherfucker".

How come it's only Omar that spots the unmarked cop cars? I mean, those brand new gleaming vehicles might as well have flashing lights and the Keystone Cops draped over the bonnet (sorry, the hood).

And, did anyone else weep like a child during the scene between Bubs and Johnny? It was beautifully played. So touching and so human and so loving. Probably the most affecting scene so far. I'm welling up now, actually…

Stockholmer – the connect and the stone fuckin' whodunnit cracked me up. Thank you!

CodProfundity Carlos, there's one tiny little scene in season 3 in Hamsterdam where a middle/upper-class guy and girl buy a speedball from Bodie, he tries to initiate a little conversation and the girl just blanks him and they drive off. Ok not much of anything in itself but then, in season 4 the girl is seen as a prostitute buying cigarettes from her pimp in Old Face Andre's store and she's then the woman in the NA meeting with her raw and totally heartbreaking speech about being a junkie. It's not much but there's a little nod to the fact that rich kids are using and fucking up on this stuff too – it's not just ghetto kids as some would like to believe.

Carloscontrole *doffs hat to CodProfundity* I would just imagine someone like, say, Carcetti hoovering up a line or two in some posh lav during a charity event or something similar. So-called recreational drug use. There could have been a nice story line woven into the tapestry.

Bard Ass! I haven't got involved with the Shakespeare theory, simply 'cos I don't know enough about the work (he says with shame in his heart). My mum says every story you could ever want is written in the bible, but I wouldn't know anything about that either.

thegirlfrommarz Co-creator Ed Burns explains it this way. "We can do things no other show can do. It's wonderful, because you can plan something in episode nine that doesn't blossom until 35. I remember in the second season we had this woman in the background just scrubbing her steps. And you see her in the background, just scrubbing every episode, and the drug dealers are moving closer and closer, until the final episode – they're sitting on her steps and she has a little "for sale" sign in the window."

SpoddyFundunglus The only drug that hasn't been mentioned so far is perhaps the most ubiquitous in the whole series. Caffeine is exalted almost to the point of religiosity by the BPD and particularly by the permanently sleep-deprived Homicide Unit – this point is underlined when Landsman makes the sign of the cross in front of the coffee machine when presenting it to Kima in Season 4.

DrinkSoddenMancunian – doesn't Avon's business model – family- and honour-oriented, concerned with rules and boundaries as much as with profit – have something in common with 'mercantilist' theories of capitalism?

Stringer's story arc has him unlearning this way of thinking, studying Adam Smith and attempting to put into practice a more ruthless, free-market system. Marlo, on the other hand, doesn't even have to unlearn anything – he is innately profit-driven and non-rule-bound, imbued with free-market logic seemingly without anyone having had to teach it to him. This seems to mirror the way in which (until recently), free-market dogma became the accepted, "natural" norm in the way Western capitalist systems were run. So perhaps we have a version of the story of capitalism over the last 150 or so years, played out between these three men.

DrinkSoddenMancunian Stringer appears to associate gentrification with legitimacy. Is his attempt to reform the drug trade deluded from the start or a small gesture of nobility in an otherwise hideous situation? Whereas Avon is seemingly at peace with the person he is ("just a gangsta' ah'spose") Stringer is always at risk of being plunged back into the murky depths by his inner demons, most tellingly when he attempts to order a hit on Clay Davies, which both Avon and Slim Charles view as suicidal.

EPISODE 6 – Avon calling

PAUL OWEN

Episode six opens with the horrific image of Omar's boyfriend Brandon, his face and body sickeningly mutilated, stretched out across the bonnet of a car, to Wallace and – to a lesser extent – D'Angelo's evident discomfort. This is a very brutal deed to set against everything Stringer and Avon do to impress us throughout the series.

D tries half-heartedly to defend the killing to Wallace – "Sometimes you got to send a message" – and over the course of this episode we see his relationship with the youngster become more and more avuncular (he's much the same with the two dealers whose petty thieving he hides from Stringer).

But the presentation of D'Angelo is far from straightforward here; early on in this episode he explains, in a self-satisfied and dislikable manner, his cynical attitude to women, while the portrait is rounded off with a nicely nervous performance from Larry Gilliard Jr when Uncle Avon comes calling.

Bodie is back on the street – just in time to get beaten up again by Herc and Carv. But afterwards the two give him a lift to his grandma's; what with this and their pool game last week, we can see a nuanced, somewhat symbiotic relationship growing up between Bodie and the two cops, leading up to that great scene in the foyer of the cinema in series three – "See you tomorrow!"

Also back on the street is Johnny Weeks – always a much less sympathetic character than his mentor, Bubbles, who seems to have gone semi-straight here and started working on an EastEnders-style market stall – until Johnny persuades him to take part in a typically wild copper-stealing caper. The image of Bubbles leaning back with a comb in his hair, dribbling as he stares out of the window at Johnny's arrest ("A white man can't walk down the street?"), is an unglamorous depiction of heroin addiction to be sure.

Having cast off his "cuddly housecat" persona, Freamon is now easing into the much more winning role of wise elder statesman. His drawled explanation of his modus operandi – "alllll the pieces matter" – is obviously meant to double as a description of show's jigsaw-puzzle writing style.

It's worth noting too the weird slo-mo scene of Avon and Stringer arriving in the pit, overlaid with a Badlands-style instrumental piece in a rare breach of the show's usual music policy by director Ed Bianchi.

RUNNING TOTALS:

Herc fuck-ups: up one to four: duffing up Bodie again when the poor guy thought he was free and clear.

McNulty giving a fuck when it's not his turn: up one to four: telling Daniels to go over Rawls's head to keep the case alive.

Drunken McNulty: still on four. He even mocked Polk for coming in to work drunk – which seems a bit rich.

COMMENTS

Rofko This is the first real look into the "private lives" of the hoppers

– what they do when they aren't hustling in the pit with the fronting, and occasional insight that you get from that. Wallace is set up to be a tragic case, which obviously he ends up being later in the series, when he is shown waking up all the kids (identities unclear), giving them crisps and juice for their lunch, and sending them off to school.

D'Angelo comes across as more of an tough motherf*cker in this show. What with his "even p*ssy don't come for free", and "all part of the game" talk with Wallace – in stark contrast to his earlier Gandhi-like stance on violence. I don't really think D's views expressed on women are so offensive, taken in context, by the way. He just sees everyone as hustling, just like him. His girlfriend is the hottest woman in the whole five seasons though, I have to say.

I like the "awe" that is put across by putting the music over Avon's slow motion walk in the pit – it really jars with the rest of the musical policy though, even if you are oblivious to its precise nature. The slow motion trick is repeated at least twice with Avon later in the show (although without music – once when he waggles his finger at Daniels when he clocks on to their tail after the east v West BBall game, and then again after D's court case when he turns around. I like the idea that the slo-mo gives – that Avon is somehow operating in a slower reality, giving him more time to react, putting him one-step ahead.

McNulty comes across as an ever more dysfunctional human being – a hopeless father at least. He is a classic "noir" detective. Brilliant.

PaulOwen Watching a second time, I find myself sympathising more with Avon than with Stringer, whereas the first time it was vice versa. Perhaps it's because I now know that Avon's deterministic view of the world is proved right – and proves to be David Simon's/the show's too.

Rofko I have had this Avon or Stringer conversation a few times, and it's definitely an interesting one, even when it was "which one's hotter?" with my girlfriend. The temptation is to go for Stringer because he seems cooler and goes to college. It is true that the second, or third, viewing allows you to see the more applied knowledge and practical reasoning of Avon, and just his greater ability to understand the game's overall nature. The "the street's the street" skit between them is obviously the point where their differences are made most explicit. It's Avon all the way for me anyway. He dresses cooler for one thing. Stringer, however much suaver, darker, taller or whatever, has a little bit of a geography teacher thing going on.

CodProfundity There's a short scene in season 3 with Avon and String taking a meeting with Krawcyk and the planning officers where Avon just can't be bothered with all the bullshit and he makes a sharp turn and walks off, (his mannerisms are incredibly big cat-like in that moment and when I rewatch the series I always think of him like he's a Tiger or Lion, lord of the jungle by virtue of his bloodline and instincts) being the King is a natural state for Barksdale and his intuitive grasp of the Game serves him far better than Stringer's will to reform serves Stringer. However I love Stringer precisely because he was the reformer who wanted to become legitimate, if drugs were legal then Stringer Bell would be on the cover of Fortune 500, you know?

He's the one who gets the best dope from Prop Joe where Avon wouldn't have seen any value in compromise, again in season 3 it's Avon's irrational "I want my corners" belligerency that causes war with Marlo and the business suffers as a result... He's doomed in the end and Avon is proved correct but Stringer's approach would have worked if he hadn't set up Omar and betrayed Mouzone.

Lipshitzs The difference between Avon Barksdale and Stringer Bell is the fact that when Stringer stabbed Avon in the back, Avon ended up in jail. When Avon stabbed Stringer in the back, Stringer was murdered. Avon Barksdale was ruthless to the extreme and I think would have continued to dominate if his main enforcers were not jailed. The way he set up the prison guard and killed inmates with "hot shots" reminded me of The Godfather and the horse's head in terms of conflict resolution.

mcnutty1 Stringer has a naive inherent belief in the system and institutions of society that his cynicism really should conquer. His is a belief in the legitimate American Dream and the natural order as presented by the institutions he knows are corrupt. Like an abused lover he goes back for more punishment, perhaps one of the underlying conceits of the overall 5-series narrative.

Lucyt "all the pieces matter" doesn't just reflect the complexity of writing of this show. It reflects Simon's belief that to understand America properly you have to examine all its components – the intricacies of the institutions that make the country and its citizens as they are. It takes a stance against the easy, ultimately meaningless analysis and solutions that the press, Hollywood and unfortunately politicians all too often offer up as an explanation for what's wrong with society. I'm glad this isn't just a great show that's not really bothered about changing the world.

Watching this episode for the umpteenth time I'm still sickened at the torture inflicted on Brandon. Weird to think that it was perpetuated by Wee-Bey, ultimately one of the most likeable of the gangsters, and one of the better parents in s4.

Lipshitzs Two things sum up Stringer for me, Lester Freamon's reaction when he hears he has become a property developer and Bunk's reaction when visits Bell's apartment and realises he has underestimated who he's been investigating.

PaulOwen Hi Lucyt, you're right, and David Simon's right, and Freamon's right too. But I see Freamon as sometimes taking the role of the voice of David Simon, and at those times he can be as smug and patronising as the man himself, as evidenced by this pretty outrageous quote:

"The first season of The Wire was a training exercise. We were training you to watch television differently."

All the pieces do matter – to tremendously satisfying effect. And maybe he was training us a little bit, although it's galling to admit it. So maybe he's earned the right to be a bit smug.

mcnutty1 The claustrophobia of all the worlds that entrap dealers, junkies, cops etc is the key to Stringer's character.

He's trying to act as a "bidness man" but he'll still "punk your ass" himself. Look at his reaction to leaving Omar alone and then sanctioning the hit on Brandon. Look at his reaction to Davis-gate in Series 3.

He can't get out in the same way as Bubs' suffers a seemingly eternal struggle with getting out. Geographically and psychologically the game dominates every echelon of their lives, it constrains and brutalises them and the institutions of society compound this.

suziebee I've completely changed my views on Avon and String; first time I was all about String, second time I think Avon is smarter. At first we admire String for wanting to get out of the game and think of Avon as his boorish side-kick, holding him back, but Avon is right all along. You cant come up from west Side Bmore and expect to be able to play with the likes of Clay Davis, as Avon tells String so clearly in series 3. He saw yo ghetto ass comin! Really its that Avon has a heart for the game and a real love for the streets (a contradiction of course when its his trade which is ruining them but lets ignore that for now..!); the only time I can think of String showing heart was when he finally confesses he had had D killed. He orders Brandon to be tortured to death (the most brutal slaying in the whole of The Wire in terms of how its carried out), puts Bodie on Wallace, has D killed, and is arrogant and stupid enough to think he can pull one over Brother Mouzone, Omar & Clay! Its more complex than just knowing what String is capable of, and of course its with the benefit of hindsight, but its like different directors/actors can do Hamlet in different ways (that fella Shakespeare again…!).

However, as some of you have pointed out Avon's trick with the hot-shots in Jessop was despicable. BUT it was done for his nephew, he wanted D to tell the wardens and get early parole for good behaviour (guilty conscience there from Avon). Also, the reason String ended up dead when Avon stabs him in the back is because, as Avon saw it, Stringer had gone behind his back by trying to set up Bro Mouzone and get in on Prop Joe's connect, going against the rules of the street. Remember Avon is upset when he finds out String set some of his lackeys on Omar during the Sun morning truce. It demonstrates the great writing and complex characters inhabiting the West Side. Just look at D (the most intriguing character for my money).

There's no doubt that String dresses poorly in series 1, but he is a better dresser than Avon, whose white get-up at the end of series 1 is a shocker!

SpoddyFundunglus String the Panther. Thanks to Paul Owen for reminding me of the "black power" line. Stringer is intellectually curious, as shown by his willingness to immerse himself in economic theory, and driven to change his world for the better, as shown by his attempted reform of his drugs crew into a partially legitimate business enterprise. Both these hungers could have been fed by the black power movement in the 80s, when Stringer was a young man.

The fact that he eventually chooses to pursue these ends in a much more individualistic manner, is perhaps symbolic of the wider failure of the black power groups to cohere into a lasting and effective movement, and the subsequent rise of a depoliticised, me-first, money-loving attitude throughout much of black street culture (as well as many other parts of society).

This is part of Stringer's tragedy, as Paul says, and the fact that it's flipped off in one line is another example of The Wire's effortless cleverness (see also the revelation about Rawls's sexuality).

Rofko Sorry, but Avon's all-white getting arrested get-up is bad-ass. Ghetto fabulous all the way.

EPISODE 7 – Batman and Robin

SAPTARSHI RAY

For a slow-burning drama, this episode packs plenty of action. The detail gets its first concrete piece of probable cause from the wire – a re-up to be carried out by Stinkum. They cannot arrest Stinkum without revealing the wire so the idea is just to snatch the drugs. After a Keystone Cops-style chase through the pit, the Barksdale organisation is bewildered and wary. This in turn leads to Stringer telling the hoppers to rip out the terrace phones, which leads to the wire going down – comprende? No, me neither. But perhaps this is the learning experience the squad needs.

Meanwhile, Judge Phelan is in sleaze overdrive in a meeting with Ronnie and Jimmy. Not content with belittling McNulty's grammar to impress Ronnie, he then draws her into his vortex of slimy sweet nothings. You feel you need to walk naked through a car wash to rinse away the molten feelings of revulsion. And for his *piece de resistance*?

"Jeeeesuuuuusss ... I would love to throw a fuck into her."

Charmed, your honour.

The other major development is the arrest of Bird, another charmer: a toxic specimen of humanity who insults every cop in the room and takes a sound thrashing at the hands of an unlikely set of thrashers – Daniels, Landsman and Greggs.

However, the most powerful scene is the narcotics anonymous meeting that Johnny and Bubs attend, where we meet Walon for the first time, delivering an eloquent and pitiable tale of destitution and addiction. Bubbles is so moved he makes a commitment to get clean, to Johnny's mocking smiles. Andre Royo is commanding as a man struggling with his demons, while Steve Earle is equally superb, drawing on his own drug experiences to add weight and realism to a depressing story.

"If God hadn't wanted for me to get high, he wouldn't have made getting high so much like perfect. I know I have one more high left in me but I doubt I have one more recovery."

Perhaps for the first time we see the naked destruction wrought by drugs on Baltimore's forgotten habitants. White, black, young, old – all addicts, all ravaged by their "disease" and all overflowing with self-loathing and shame. A far cry from our gentle mirth at fisticuffs and McDonald's analogies about the game so far. These are the game's losers.

But not to leave us on too much of a downer, some great comic moments abound. There's McNulty and Bunk's legendary "when it came time to fuck me, you were gentle" scene; Santangelo's trip to a psychic; Omar recognising Bunk as "the first brother I ever seen to play that game with the stick" and Herc and Carver overjoyed at being labelled Batman and Robin on the wire, then proceeding to argue about who is who like schoolboys.

Herc: "Hey, boy wonder, why don't you suck my bat dick?"

RUNNING TOTALS:

McNulty giving a fuck when it's not his turn: up one to five: laying out the internal workings of the BPD to Phelan – thereby gaining a rabbi and a liability.

COMMENTS

whatisthere2 The episode was called "One Arrest" but actually there were two arrests; bird and the Kid with eye-patch that Prez gunned.

D'Angelo has been on a mean streak since last episode as it is Bodie who notices Wallace's absence and asks Poot. Its makes sense that Bodie and Poot his (Wallace's) eventual terminators do nothin to help their friend but its just that even at that early stage you want Bodie to do more.

I do wonder why Santangelo didn't snitch on McNulty? Is it the brotherhood of BPD? but then as we later discover that Carver is Burrell's ear in the squad so thus its not an ethics issue. Santangelo is perhaps just old school and like McNulty is resisting chain of command! Interesting that at end of Series 3 McNulty follows Santangelo's example and joins the foot soldiers of the Western District.

SaptarshiRay I think String sees D as promoted beyond his means and intelligence purely cos he is Avon's nephew, he certainly doesn't respect him as a player or as a person come to that.

As for Santangelo, however much he dislikes McNulty he knows that to snitch on another cop would make him a rat in the dept, plus he simply doesn't want to and is uncomfortable playing politics – when he says "It's not my job to fuck another cop". What Rawls needs is someone like Ed Exley from LA Confidential to do his dirty work.

suziebee The heart of D is best revealed in the attitude of those around him towards him. Wallace refuses to snitch on him but is happy to flip on others, Shardene sees through the act and is horrified to later find out she may have been duped, McNulty is touched enough by him to try and find out the truth about his death, and Bunk & McNulty go to see him and appeal to the better nature they know he has. But look at his uncle and mother and see any other way D could have gone in life. Cognitive dissonance inDEED. And so he is really the heart of the show. Still the best scene is, IMHO, at the end of this series where he is confronted with all the bodies etc, and he tries to explain to a disgusted Bunk & McNulty how he never had any choice in his life. Is there really anything sadder than that? A bright, charismatic black guy in Baltimore could achieve so many things, make the world – or the locale – a better place, or at least be given the opportunity to try. He represents those who are lost before they even begin. God I went off on one a bit there didn't I??! But, y'know, shit goes DEEP.

DrinkSoddenMancunian I think that perhaps, with the music used in and around the pit and the beats heard pumping out of the cars on the street in The Wire, the creators have been a little too eager to display their rapophile credentials, slightly too hip hop literate. At the same time, the abundance of local awareness and familiarity with Bmore culture is missing somewhat from the musical selection. As you correctly point out, the absence of any real Bmore artists in the early series does jar somewhat with Snoop and Chris's coldly hilarious and streetwise knowledge of club music.

It seems to me that the majority of the music in these earlier episodes is drawn from the incredibly fertile crossroads in 90s/early 00's hip hop culture when sophisticated yet edgy producers and mc's either progressed into more hardcore or gangster (an important distinction, juxtapose G-funk and Death Row Records sound on the west coast with the sparseness of Wu Tang and Mobb Deep on the east) musical pastures, leaving those disillusioned with such developments to embrace more abstract and alternative strands of the genre. Still, the most interesting music of this period was created when both these diverging facets bled into each other. I think that's what the Sharpshooters track is very representative of, and if it floats anyone's boat I would highly recommend Darc Mind whose magnum opus Symptomatic of a Greater Ill has recently been re-released by the ever excellent Anticon records. While I don't necessarily think that the likes of Bird, Stinkum etc would be overly averse to this type of music, they don't appear to display any particular desire for anything culturally challenging in the same way that the likes of D or Stringer do, nor do they display the levels of maturity or fatherly nous personified by Avon or Wee Bey.

When Stringer is seen driving around listening to Mos Def in a later scene, I think this is spot on. The increasingly sophisticated and potentially nouveau riche kingpin attempting to legitimise the gloom and fear around him through intellectually profound music. There are also numerous references to the black power movement on Mos's record Black on Both Sides, and a spiritual undercurrent which would no doubt appeal to the side of Stringer's personality which he seems desperate to portray to the outside world: urbane, educated, upwardly mobile and cultured.

EPISODE 8 – "Come at the king, you best not miss"

MARK SMITH

The hour opens with what can only be described as a horrifically cavalier episode of parenting from McNulty. Giving your your kids an insight into your job is one thing, getting them to front-and-follow one of the city's drugs kingpins – even if they did get a licence plate – is entirely, well, McNulty.

I felt a definite Macbethian twitch in the scene between Daniels and Marla, as the pragmatic soon-to-be-councilwoman imbues her husband with ambition ("When you durst do it, then you were a man"). Another of D's Road to Damascus moments arrives with Wee-Bey's treatment (and possibly negligent murder) of the hired party entertainment – but just how many will he need?

Poot's sheer delight at being crowned king for an hour in D's absence – demonstrated by his catwalk-style strut on the orange sofa. "Sheeeet, look at me."

Freamon shows signs of the genius to come with his first Obi-Wan moment, telling Kima: "Interrogation is more art than science. You gotta feel your way through on instinct, mostly."

RUNNING TOTALS:

Murders: up one to six, with Omar's slaying of Stinkum.

McNulty school of parenting: two: the front-and-follow and last week's trip to the morgue with Omar ("It's my night with the kids").

COMMENTS

HenryBrown I know most people think Omar is referring to himself as the king but I love how this ties back into the chess scene. When Omar does come for the Avon, the king, he misses and doesn't get another chance to take him out.

Busfield While Burrell snaps Daniels into line, Avon kicks Orlando into submission. Neat or too neat the comparison between Stringer improving himself at community college, while Herc and Carver learn little from pOlice exams?

Rofko Busfield has hit the nail on the head with two things: the parallelism in the narrative regarding chain of command, and the broad "learning" theme on the one hand (don't forget also Wallace's convo with the kid who wakes him up asking him for help with the simple sums, which he can't do, concluding with the powerful maxim: 'IF YOU MESS UP THE COUNT THEY F*CK YOU UP', alongside the Stringer and Herc/Carv parallel) and, on the other, the continued superiority in every respect of Omar – he outdoes the police and the Barksdales while playing them all.

Some great dialogue in this episode too: McNulty's exchange with the woman whose bathroom Bunk has burned his clothes in to destroy trace evidence:

– He set off the smoke alarm. Twice

– That good, huh?

EPISODE 9 – "Projects got a ball team?"

PAUL OWEN

The heart of this episode is the surprising east side–west side basketball game presided over by Avon Barksdale and his rival from across the expressway, Proposition Joe, who we meet here for the first time.

The game shows that some form of civil society exists even in these ruined, drug-ravaged estates, and Herc and Carv are as taken aback as we are: "Projects got a ball team?" asks Carv. As the two callow officers watch the game through the fence, they enjoy a friendly chat with drug dealers Poot and Bodie, again presented more like competing colleagues than enemies.

But earlier, as they surveyed the empty streets, wondering where everyone had got to, Herc had mused: "Maybe we won." It was a telling comment, reflecting the idea that winning the war on drugs would mean the population of the Baltimore projects disappearing completely, the idea that the police were at war not with specific criminal gangs but with whole areas of the city.

The interaction between Prop Joe and Avon strikes some similarly unexpected notes. The two drug lords engage in a lot of aggressive banter, Avon mocking Joe's suit and clipboard ("Look the part, be the part, motherfucker," replies Joe), and threatening to "light Joe's ass up" if he ever comes west "without a ball". But Barksdale calls him "baby" throughout, his enemy seems unruffled, and later Joe paints a picture suggestive of mutual respect between professional rivals: "We talk now and then. I page his ass." Yet he seems happy to give up Avon's pager number to Omar, surely knowing what Omar plans to do with it.

Instead of "giving a fuck when it's not his turn", McNulty actually seems reluctant to give a fuck at all this episode, refusing to go out with Lieutenant Daniels to get a first look at Avon. He seems ridiculous and overly didactic as he intones: "We get him by voice alone or we don't get him." The script (by David H Melnick and Shamit Choksey) tries hard to prove him right – Sydnor accompanies Daniels and is therefore absent from his post at a key moment.

Still on Avon, in this episode Freamon estimates his income at $20–25m a year. "Where does it all go?" asks Daniels. In light of our previous conversations about the relative merits of Avon and his lieutenant, Stringer Bell, Freamon's answer is illuminating, and surely suggests that the secret of Barksdale and Bell's success lies partly in a mixture of Avon's natural caution with Stringer's business acumen: "He [Avon] shows no flash. He's got no house, no car in his name, no jewellery, no clothes. Just front companies and the property – and political contributions, $75,000 in the last month alone."

It's an incredible – even shocking – amount of money, and probably worth remembering in series 3 when Stringer is arguing that he and Avon ought to leave the drugs game behind and turn all their attention to legitimate property speculation. Avon, of course, is uninterested. Did he foresee the credit crunch?

RUNNING TOTALS:

Omar stick-ups: four. Up one – a very easy one. Omar walks into the low-rises, minor dealers scattering before him in all directions, stands outside a flat with his back to it, and tells the occupants: "You all need to open this door now before I huff and puff." Out of pure fear, they throw down a massive package to the big bad wolf without anyone firing a shot.

Herc fuck-ups: up by half a point to four-and-a-half. It's unclear whether it was him or Carver who lost $7,000 of seized drug money and led Daniels to believe they had stolen it. They both look like numbskulls.

COMMENTS

RezStevens Avon shouting down the ref, then getting even angrier when he goes back on his decision – even Avon Barksdale wouldn't kill someone over something as trivial as a basketball game. Marlo Stanfield on the other hand… compare this scene to his dialogue with the security guard in season four.

Echoes of the last episode as Omar comes at the king.

thegirlfrommarz Although it's kind of out of character for the show (the slo-mo), I still love Avon wagging his finger at Daniels. Ah, Avon. Just a gangsta, I suppose, but so cool. (I too am finding myself thinking more of Avon and less of Stringer this go-around, although that could be because String has spent most of season 1 wearing terrible tracksuit bottoms. When Idris Elba gets back into suits, I may change my mind.)

MarkASmith The scene in which Wallace pleads with d about getting out of the game is just heartbreaking. D obviously seems to spot more than a little of himself in the young hopper and knows he could maybe have the future he himself never had, "at Harvard or some shit". Slightly overreaching, maybe, but the sentiment of opportunity and a life outside of B'more is there.

DesignerBaby I love the camaraderie between Carv/Herc and Poot/Bodie, they both come across as jaded foot-soldiers of corrupt institutions that seem to have a grudging respect for each other.

This exchange precedes Herc and Carver's observation in the last episode when Bodie and his team beat a rival gang selling in the pit – "that's the difference between us and them; we fuck-up and we get state-pension, they fuck-up and they get beat."

EPISODE 10 – From script to screen

STEVE BUSFIELD

Regular contributor Ello has brought David Simon's 2000 proposal for The Wire to our attention (http://leethomson.myzen.co.uk/The_Wire /The_Wire_-_Bible.pdf). Interestingly, Simon pitches the show as a "police procedural".

However, he then goes on to destroy that idea by stating that "the grand theme here is nothing less than a national existentialism" and that the first series is "not so much the dogged police pursuit of the bad guys, but rather a Greek tragedy".

Perusal of Simon's plan is highly recommended, if only to discover that Stringer Bell was originally going to be called "Stringy" and McNulty was almost called McArdle.

Rewatching the first season I have been struck by the fact that series one is, by necessity, a much simpler story than the later series. While nuanced and layered unlike most cops and crooks shows, it is also essentially about the pOlice and their attempts to catch criminals. And this episode is, in some ways, like a more traditional TV show, given the cliffhanger finale.

On the other hand, the preceding hour had included so much more than a "police procedural" would have offered. The episode is entitled The Cost, and in an unobtrusive manner we are shown the human cost of the game: Bubbles struggling to conquer his addiction, revealing that he lost his son, Walon's HIV status, Wallace's developing drug habit brought on by exposure to brutality at such a young age, McNulty's broken marriage, before we even get to the shooting of Kima and Orlando.

The new viewer will also be unaware that the short clip of a politician on a TV screen will turn out to be a key player and one of the largest characters in the show, Clay Davis.

RUNNING TOTALS:

Murders: up one to seven, as Orlando's desire to take a larger cut from the drugs business is cut short. Kima's life is hanging in the balance.

Bubbles attempting to get clean: two. Unlike The Corner, which focuses on the drug takers and the destitution it leaves them in, Bubbles carries most of this role alone in The Wire. (Although Wallace's use is a feature of series one, it is mostly within the context of interfering with his role as a dealer.) His first attempt to clean up after momentary inspiration at the NA meeting with Johnny was short-lived. But in his sister's basement and surrounded by a better life in the park during the sunshine hours and by temptation during the hours of darkness, we can see him struggling with the demons.

COMMENTS

Ello This episode serves as a catalyst for the final act of the season. It is in subsequent episodes that the futures/fates of McNulty ("…anywhere but the river"), Daniel (lost/confiscated property – I think), Freamon (homicide), Carver, Herc, D'Angelo, Avon, Wallace and Stringer are decided. Subsequent episodes reveal the politics of a police officer getting shot and the severity of the consequences for the Barksdale crew. Season 1 ties up nicely, as though David Simon was expecting only one season to get commissioned. Contrarily, season 1 is also the hook. Once viewers entered the game; they didn't leave. Season 2 is probably a better demonstration of the writers' craft. It has a better narrative that demonstrates the scale of David Simon's ambition: the plight of the working man; trafficking drugs/women; the game, with the rise of Proposition Joe and the decline of the Barksdale crew; and penitentiary life. And it's all kicked-off with an irked copper in a church.

RezStevens Reading through that proposal is like peering into an alternate Wire universe: McArdle and Stringy don't really have the same punch, nor does Aaron Barksdale. – Kima dead by episode six? Herc busted for being a 'roid head? Bubbles dying of AIDS? Santangelo an out-and-out traitor? D'Angelo getting out of the game and right back in again? Bodie becoming the new Avon? What is this fresh madness? – Characters from later seasons cropping up so early (Day-Day), under different names (Clay Davis/Dawkins, Judge Phelan/Watkins), or completely unrecognisable (Slim Charles). Such a strange read after seeing how developed the characters were in the series proper, makes you appreciate what some of the actors brought to the table (i.e. Omar on paper versus Michael K. Williams' performance).

Ello I agree that each season can stand on its own, but as David Simon said: "F*#k the casual viewer." The Wire has to be considered a series of five novels. And to fully appreciate it, you have to watch all five seasons. Or else... the deaths of D'Angelo, Prop Joe and Omar wouldn't resonate as they did.

DesignerBaby Think it was said in one of the DVD commentaries that David Simon really didn't think 'The Wire' would go beyond 3 series', and with that in mind tried to tie up each thread and storyline within each series as best he could. I think that adds something to each series, like you're watching a different perspective of Baltimore depending on what season you're at... Not one of my fave episodes – but sets up the aftermath of Kima's shooting nicely. The next 2 episodes are outstanding – probably the only cases where if you were watching 'The Wire' for the first time, you'd be hooked on the evidence of each hour-long show alone.

JayBay footnote to the "Bible". The useless cops (Polk & Mahon) appear as Shea & Varitek. As Simon is obviously a big Orioles fan (the script is peppered with baseball references) I presume these are digs at the Boston Red Sox (whom the Orioles are described as having "held off", I think in the Daniels/Day-Day exchange.) At that time, the Red Sox had a third baseman called Shea Hillenbrand who was noted for his arrogance and petulance. Jason Varitek is the long serving captain of the Red Sox, revered by (we) Red Sox fans as a square-jawed, win at all costs hero – and therefore inevitably reviled by fans of other teams.

EPISODE 11 – The true McNulty

PAUL OWEN

David Simon, the creator of The Wire, has said that his programme set out to inform, not entertain, but that is a little disingenuous – and this week's episode provides a good illustration of the showmanship that always sits comfortably alongside the scenes of social realism, as Simon keeps us guessing about whether Detective Kima Greggs is going to survive being shot last week.

Kima's shooting seems to be the moment most viewers realise they are irreversibly hooked on The Wire and there is a comparable cliffhanger involving union boss Frank Sobotka in series two, and a fairly similar one with drug kingpin Stringer Bell in series three. Of course The Wire informs – we wouldn't be able to write this blog if it didn't – but it's great drama, too, which is probably the key difference from its more dour predecessor, The Corner. Kima pulls through, but, thanks to Simon's original plan for the programme, we now know she could easily have been bumped off as unsentimentally as other key characters are throughout the run – notably D'Angelo.

The shooting brings out an interesting aspect of Detective Jimmy McNulty's character, moving him further away from the TV show type – the hard-drinking Irish cop – that he initially appeared to be, into more unusual psychological territory. He seems mired in guilt about Kima – understandable, except that what happened wasn't actually his fault. He wants to take the blame, to make the shooting be about him instead of about Kima, about his flaws and – by implication – his strengths, too. He sits staring into space melodramatically covered in blood, is loudly sick into a bin, swigs from a little bottle of whiskey in the office; he does everything he can to make himself the centre of attention instead of the woman lying in the hospital bed.

Dominic West heads the programme's cast list and his character was obviously designed as an easily recognisable way in for the viewer in a show with more than its fair share of unfamiliar elements, but it is in this episode that we first realise that McNulty has some pretty unsympathetic characteristics, that the show is not actually meant to centre on him and the action is not meant to be seen through his eyes. He's not the hero of The Wire; he's a character who, like many in the show, has some fairly serious flaws. His sanctimonious and arrogant pronouncements may usually be proved right, but that never makes you warm to him.

This episode also includes the confusing segment where D'Angelo, the inexperienced and conflicted young dealer, thinks Stringer has ordered his enforcer Wee-Bey to murder him. I assumed D was wrong; surely what was actually happening was that D'Angelo was being forced to help Bey shoot another gangster, Little Man, whom Stringer had ruthlessly ordered killed in an earlier scene. But no; instead Wee Bey's ominous mumblings on the journey with D down the dark alleyway to his flat were all leading up to a request for D'Angelo to feed his fish while he went away.

RUNNING TOTALS:

McNulty giving a fuck when it's not his turn: up one to seven. When the detail are asked to jeopardise their case in order to put "dope on the table" for the media, he goes to Judge Phelan for help as usual, but this time Phelan – up for re-election and playing safe – turns him down.

Drunk: up one to six, boozing on the job in the wake of Kima's shooting (sober **Bunk** still on two).

COMMENTS

SaptarshiRay It's true that first time round you think it's quite normal(ish) that jimmy sits around brooding while everyone else runs around trying to help. weirdly it's Rawls who comes out with the most cred in this ep, after telling half the people there getting in the way to get lost and shaking McNulty out of his self-indulgent stupor. he's not an easy man to like but there are times when his brutish, officious manner come in handy – a police getting shot being one of them.

Lingli I'm not sure that McNulty "unwittingly" sends Bubbles back to the low-rises – I thought it fit with the scene where Ronnie says to McNulty, "You'll just use anyone", and I read it as McNulty deliberately ignoring Bubbles' remarks about keeping away, because what he really needed was info.

I think maybe it also says something about how we're sort of conditioned to watch law and order shows that the first time I watched this, a lot of McNulty's more odious character flaws kind of passed me by. It's such a cliche, after all; the hard-drinking, authority-bucking, maverick cop with the disastrous personal life ... it's something that is easily recognised from countless other TV shows. And on a first viewing, I was so caught up in the pace of the story and being desperate to find out what happened next that I kind of gave Jimmy a bye for most of what he did. Well, at least until season 5 – but looking at season one again it seems to me that what would've come off as just completely ridiculous in another show (the whole "serial killer" thing) is totally just an extension of Jimmy's belief that the ends always justify the means, because he is always right.

The other funny thing about this episode is the scene with Rawls – again, a subversion of the cop-show staple scene, where the superior officer eases the guilt of the injured cop's partner. The first time I watched it I remember being really shocked by how incredibly cold Rawls was to McNulty – particularly as I was expecting him to be just a wee bit warm and fuzzy in the wake of Kima's shooting. But when you look at it through the perspective discussed above, that this is Jimmy trying to make it all about him, it makes you think that maybe Rawls, despite all his other faults, really does have McNulty's number.

junkdeluxe I liked the Wee-Bey / D'Angelo scene because, like D, you genuinely don't know what's going to happen, D may get shot, they may have to shoot someone else... anything. The actual result is so innocuous it reinforces just what a fragile existence it is to live in the "game". At any moment your best friend could turn round and shoot you (as happens throughout the Wire – Wallace, Cheese...) or you get called upon to shoot them.

SaptarshiRay i think it's easy to be too hard on McNulty too but it's a tribute to the show that one of our favourite characters can be such a total bastard at times. after all, Omar the fan's fave is a murderer and a thief so our moral compass is all over the place. the clever spin on McNulty is that despite him being one of the best detectives in the city, he never seems to grasp the bigger picture cos of his obsession with each case. but TV is TV, if he were a real cop we'd be asking for him to be imprisoned and so on. but despite all his ridiculous antics, we appreciate jimmy's qualities. that he's a damn good detective.

Lingli I think the tragedy – or almost-tragedy – for McNulty is that he knows his failings; Rawls says as much to him, and even Bunk, who's his buddy, tells him straight up that he's "no good for people". I'm sure that's an element of his drinking and shagging – a sort of self-fulfilling prophecy.

EPISODE 12 – Where's Wallace?

SAPTARSHI RAY

This episode dwells on the fate of Wallace, a boy in a man's world, a figurative pawn in the chess game of the Baltimore projects, whose tale hurtles toward its inevitable and tragic conclusion. The lethal denouement unfolds before our eyes, as the police, D'Angelo and we, the audience, stand by like onlookers at a crucifixion, helpless and hopeless, willing what we know will happen not to happen, hoping beyond hope that Wallace (Michael B Jordan) will escape the fate meted out to him by the gods of the game. But it is not to be, and in a gut-wrenching, heartbreaking scene, it is his two best friends, Bodie (JD Williams) and Poot (Tray Chaney), that dispatch him into the next life on the orders of Stringer Bell.

Wallace's fate dominates not only this episode but has ramifications far and beyond for several characters. For D, it is the last straw as he can no longer resolve the conflict between serving his uncle and the cold, remorseless fatality of survival for Avon; for Daniels, who spends the episode running around with Jimmy trying to track Wallace down, a genuine sense of failure at protecting a child; for Bodie and Poot, their promotion from hoppers to murderers, gazing into the unwavering eye of the game, knowing what they are capable of, and what could easily happen to them. It is the tipping point for the two young 'uns, witnessing the harsh reality of even being thought of as a snitch – something that will eventually return to haunt Bodie.

This underlines just how little else is on offer to these youngsters: why would you stay in the game after seeing that? Knowing you could be killed on the whims of your bosses, or end your days in prison? Because there is no other choice. They both know that to refuse would probably sign their own death warrants.

D repeatedly tries to protect Wallace ("Leave the boy be, Avon. Just leave him be"), trying at first to hide his whereabouts, then attempting to persuade the young hopper to go back to school, and finally, when the truth dawns on him, shouting "Where's Wallace?" at Stringer from behind the jailhouse glass. His repeated, anguished cries echo as a clarion call for his defection from his uncle's affections. D goes his own way, and that way only tragedy lies.

As has been noted many times here, D is a far more influential character in this season on second viewing. He is pivotal to the fortunes of Avon and his clan, and Wallace is pivotal to his own fate. Two essentially decent boys thrust into a malicious, chaotic world that neither fully comprehends or enjoys. And for all Bodie's protestations that Wallace is just a boy, and should act like a man, acting like a father figure and looking after the kids in the house proves him to be twice the man of most of the players in the game.

As for Bodie, he appears all too willing to take out his friend and prove his mettle to his bosses. As with so many characters in The Wire, somehow we end up not only forgiving him, but liking him as the seasons unfold – but in this episode he represents the worst kind of snake, an amoral chancer who is only too happy to do Stringer's bidding. Ultimately it may be Poot who delivers the final shots, but he is the one who sheds the tears too.

RUNNING TOTALS:

Murders: up two to nine: as well as Wallace, the female security guard who identified D is killed, as Avon cleans up every possible lead to his organisation – partially on Levy's advice.

COMMENTS

ella79 I've seen the scene where they shoot Wallace about three or four times now, and I swear every time I watch it I'm desperate for that storyline to end a different way. You've been made to feel so strongly for Wallace, to so hope he might get away and that D might have convinced him to save himself and go back to school, and... God. Watching Wallace in those final episodes makes me feel almost as distraught as watching Dukie in series 4.

The thing about Wallace's death, coming so soon after Kima is shot, was that it drastically changed my appreciation of the Wire. I spent the first 10 episodes or so waiting for something shocking to happen a la The Sopranos, waiting to be startled, but had finally come to understand and appreciate that the Wire wasn't that kind of show. And then it seemed the very next minute the show pulled the rug from under my feet and proved that it *was* that kind of show, if it wanted to be.

Tombo How cold and obsessive McNulty can be. When he and Daniels hear about Wallace Daniels' reaction is grief for Wallace, the first think McNulty says is "that puts Stringer out of the box". Maybe the first time that it becomes clear that, for him, getting Stringer is the only thing that matters?

Paul3294 The fates of Wallace and Bodie are heartbreaking. But I was almost as sad when I saw Poot ending up working at a Foot Locker-type store. Obviously I'm exaggerating, but it underlines the point about not having many options. Dukie also represents this.

SaptarshiRay Did you really react like that when you saw Poot in the store? I was so happy that one, just one hopper managed to escape the game and become a citizen. I guess he & Namond are the only ones that manage it – both through some luck, Poot in that everyone he used to work with was dead or in prison and Namond cos of bunny's intervention. Its part of the show's genius in series 5, when you hope that Dukie goes to Prezbo for help after Poot tells him to keep slinging, but actually scams Prezbo for cash – and Prezbo's look of sadness reflects ours. if only he could have had someone to show him a way out. As he asks Cutty, "how do you get from here to the rest of the world?" and Cutty has no answer.

EPISODE 13 – Naturalism and The Wire

PAUL OWEN

The first series of The Wire ends by placing the programme firmly in a tradition of deterministic naturalism that stretches back to late-19th-century American authors such as Stephen Crane, Theodore Dreiser and Frank Norris. It's a theme that found its purest expression four series later when the show closed by smoothly replacing each of the main characters with a younger, fresher version of him or herself.

The naturalistic authors described a world "in which the individual is an exclusive creation of heredity and environment and consequently by turn either victor or victim of chance – mainly victim, of course," as Jerome Loving of Texas A&M University puts it in his introduction to Norris's 1899 novel McTeague. Like Simon, these authors focused on the urban poor, helping make that a fit subject for literary scrutiny just as Simon has established it as a fit topic for TV drama.

Compare Loving's description of McTeague with conscience-stricken drug dealer D'Angelo's attempt in this episode to explain to detectives Bunk and McNulty how it is that he has got to a point where he is indirectly or directly implicated in half a dozen gruesome murders, almost all of them ordered by his uncle, drugs kingpin Avon Barksdale.

"Y'all don't understand … You grow up in this shit. My grandfather was Butch Stamford. You know who Butch Stamford was in this town? [Bunk and McNulty nod.] All my people, man – my father, my uncles, my cousins – it's just what we do … I was courtside for eight months, and I was freer in jail than I was at home."

The script for this episode is by Simon and his main co-writer, Ed Burns, and this speech by D'Angelo seems to me one of their clearest attempts to present the idea that a person's life is shaped and controlled by the social structures and "institutions" – for Simon, a word that describes the police, the drug "game", the docks, politics, or the media equally well – around them.

The final scenes of the series are a rehearsal for the final scenes of the show as a whole: despite the convictions of key figures (here Avon and D'Angelo), life goes on exactly as it ever did on the drug corners of the projects. Stringer Bell, Barksdale's number two, has taken over at the head of the business, two younger dealers, Poot and Bodie, are beginning to step into the role left vacant by D'Angelo, and the luckless heroin addicts Bubbles and Johnny Weeks are back to pulling their usual "capers" and scams in order to scratch together enough money for a hit.

This cyclicality is also emphasised through key moments of mirroring in the script. Harking back to the first episode, McNulty and Stringer find themselves once again sitting in the public gallery of a courtroom watching a trial, but this time it is Stringer who concedes grudgingly that the other man's victory has been "nicely done".

This naturalistic theme – the idea that the game continues even if the players change, the idea that life in the projects will struggle on to its ultimately awful conclusion no matter how hard anyone tries to alter its course – makes for powerful storytelling, and is probably one of the reasons The Wire is credited with so much intellectual heft.

But isn't it also a somewhat hopeless, even defeatist, attitude? Elijah Anderson, whose A Place on the Corner was in some ways a forerunner of Simon and Burns's brilliant non-fiction book The Corner, has complained that The Wire "left out … the decent people. Even in the worst drug-infested projects, there are many, many God-fearing, churchgoing, brave people who set themselves against the gangs and the addicts, often with remarkable heroism."

I would say that the programme's commitment to a cyclical bleakness where small victories are ultimately subsumed into enormous defeats largely precludes the possibility of change, hope or redemption, and runs the risk of suggesting that nothing can be done to solve the immense problems of inner cities such as Baltimore's.

This may well be true; Simon's attitude certainly seems to be that he is presenting reality as he sees it. When Mark Bowden of the Atlantic Monthly criticised The Wire's bleakness, Simon responded: "This premise that The Wire wasn't real because it didn't show people having good outcomes in west Baltimore ... I don't know what to tell him ... If he's telling me it's not happening, I want to take his fucking entitled ass and drive him to west Baltimore and shove him out of the car, at Monroe and Fayette, and say: 'Find your way back, fucker, because you've got your head up your ass at the Atlantic.'"

It's not the bleakness I mind, but the cyclicality. If it is simply realism for the end of the series to press the reset button, for it to present the drug trade as continuing exactly as it did when the series started, for it to suggest that "Bell is now Barksdale" (as Simon put it in his proposal for the show), that the residents of west Baltimore's fates are fixed before they're born by the grand forces arrayed around them and against them, doesn't that encourage a certain attitude of inertia towards the problem in the viewer? And surely one of Simon's motivations in writing this programme was to provoke the opposite response, to help prod people towards solving the problem?

RUNNING TOTALS:

Murders: nine – most of them claimed by Wee-Bey. And for "another pit sandwich and some potato salad", he'll gladly confess to a few more.

McNulty giving a fuck when it's not his turn: up two to nine. First he goes over Deputy Commissioner Burrell's head to bring the FBI in on the Barksdale case, and then he throws the whole thing back in the feds' faces when they won't do things his way.

Bunk drunk: unbelievably, still two; Bunk has been a paragon of sobriety this series. Who'd have thought it?

COMMENTS

sarahjoanbradley The cyclical and bleak structure of corner life as portrayed by Simon in The Wire doesn't inevitably move the viewer to a "certain attitude of inertia", or a helpless apathy that nothing can be done.

As I read it, the point is that small-scale firefighting, damage limitation and band-aids from the establishment – trying to maintain order, monitoring progress through meaningless stats – don't work and usually serve to alienate. Instead, something more radical, fundamental and inclusive is required if change is to be effected, and the cycle broken.

Simon offers hope through figures such as Bunny Colvin – who, despite his hangdog frustration at getting nowhere, could have changed a lot with his educational schemes in series 3. That is, if the decision makers had backed him up and believed it was worth trying.

Lingli Simon repeatedly does make the point that it's only by making fundamental changes that whole cities like Baltimore can be improved – and this is something that I think he got more and more interested in exploring, as evidenced by season 4, when he looked at the public school system, and series 3, with the Hamsterdam experiment. It feeds into the cyclicality (hm – not sure if that's a real word) of the show as a whole: that people try to change things, whether on a personal, social or professional level, and all it does is muddy the water. The small change you want to make only uncovers the fact that for you to succeed, other changes are going to have to be made by other people.

You can see that on the personal level with D' – for him to change and get out of the game, his family have to let him do it. And first Brianna comes in and leans on him, so he takes the jail sentence; and then even in jail, he's not free of Avon and the pressure that he can exert on his nephew – in person, and through Bri and Donette. The same thing occurs on a social level with Hamsterdam; Bunny starts off thinking he can just punt all the dealers and fiends into a quarantined area – and then he realises they need healthcare, social welfare systems, which are impossible to keep under the radar. Which in turn is mirrored back to us at the end of that season when the mayor is trying so desperately to find a way to make the idea work for him politically – which of course he can't.

And on a political level, of course, this is apparent in every single episode, whether it's party politics at City Hall or personal/professional politics amongst the cops.

Any kind of "happy ending" would have been seen as fake, I think, but there are some small triumphs, aren't there? Shardene, for example: she stays with Lester and becomes a nurse. Namond. Poot. Bubbles, of course. And I think, to back up what Busfield said earlier, we never stop rooting for the characters. It's the personal overlaid with the political; we want these guys to do good. It's one of the reasons why I found season 4 such a hard watch; I so badly wanted all of those lads to do good in the end … and most of them didn't.

Oh, and re: Carv's remark to Herc – another mirror, this time of the comment that one of Wallace's wee siblings (were they siblings?) makes to him when Wallace is trying to help with her maths homework.

He makes her do the problem that's troubling her as if she were out on the street and of course, she does it perfectly, and so he says something like, how can you work out all that but you can't do the question in the book? And she points out that if "you fuck-up the count, y'all get fucked up". Or something along those lines.

I have no idea where those kids went! Who were they all, anyway? Were there any adults in that house? I have to admit that, Doritos and Kool-Aid for breakfast aside, it looked preferable to the group home that poor Randy was put in in season 4. And actually, I thought it also showed a side of Wallace and, in particular, Poot that was utterly quashed out in the Pit.

notyourusual In this episode Brianna pimps her son for the family cause. I've watched this three times now and each time I desperately hope that D will stand up to her, stand his ground and insist on a different path for himself but D's capitulation seals his fate. There's a brief, little vignette towards the end where we see D' Angelo with his head bowed and his mother looming over him looking out at the triumphant Levy. There's such a sense of oppression in this scene. It's too late for D' Angelo now: he already took a wrong step, he really needed to be a few steps ahead of the game. However hard he later tries to distance himself from the Barksdale crew he will never escape Stringer's machinations.

After his cruel murder what came back to haunt me are those eloquent words of Avon to his nephew back in episode 5 at the uncle's hospital bedside:

"...be a little slow...a little late – just once. And how you ain't gonna never be slow, never be late?"

Interview: Dominic West

ANDREW ANTHONY

Until quite recently Dominic West was a stranger to the general public. Since leaving drama school in 1996 he had appeared in several notable plays, worked on a couple of Shakespeare films and made himself something of a go-to guy when it came to casting the obnoxious British boyfriend in American romantic comedies. But, in spite of some excellent reviews, he was essentially the kind of actor who would leave audiences as he found them, none the wiser as to who he was.

Seven years ago, West left England and went to work in the American backwater of Baltimore on a TV cop series being put together by the writer David Simon with no recognisable stars or famous names. In Britain it was screened on the obscure FX channel and registered viewing figures of around 30,000. Nor was it a great deal more popular in America. Among the tiny audience, however, was a small army of adoring critics, several of whom went so far as to proclaim the series the best TV drama in history. Word of mouth spread, a DVD audience grew, and it became a cult phenomenon on both sides of the Atlantic. The show was called The Wire and it has made West if not quite a name, then known.

The Wire told the story of a group of detectives locked in a doomed battle with inner-city drug warlords. The narrative was multilayered, featuring scores of characters, and it eschewed easy resolutions. But nothing in the plot could rival the amazing knowledge that Detective McNulty, the hard-drinking, bed-hopping, working-class Irish-American and star of the ensemble, was in fact played by an Englishman, and not just any Englishman, but that most curious and mythologised of creatures: an Old Etonian. West inhabited the part of Jimmy McNulty so fully and convincingly that it seemed as if he'd been rehearsing for it his whole life. In fact, he sent in a self-made audition tape – "a Robert De Niro impression, really" – on spec at the last minute. Within a few days he was flown to America, where he spent a couple of weeks trailing Baltimore cops. Then he shot the pilot.

As the de facto lead, West in effect had to carry the first season. If he hadn't seemed authentic, the whole show would have failed.

"Originally they wanted Ray Winstone," says West. "But I think he turned them down because he didn't want to live in Baltimore for five years. Maybe they were desperate or maybe I did a great tape. I don't know."

Now back in London, West lives with Catherine FitzGerald and their two-year-old daughter and baby boy in Shepherd's Bush. FitzGerald is the former Countess Durham, and daughter of Desmond FitzGerald, the Knight of Glin. West had a previous relationship with Polly Astor, granddaughter of Lord Astor, with whom he has a nine-year-old daughter.

All the aristocratic connections might suggest the Old Etonian really is a member of some gilded elite. And as previous interviewers have tended to make much of his upper-class tones, I was prepared to meet a man who sounded like a mixture of Donald Sinden and Henry Blofeld. But, in fact, his voice is not really posh at all. It's his language, not his accent, that's fruity. He swears with the same boundless ease that McNulty – catchphrase: "What the fuck did I do?" – brought to the business of casual profanity.

I asked him why he thought no terrestrial channel had picked up The Wire in Britain. "I don't know," he mused. "I always blamed it on there being far too many black people. We should have had more white people and we would have been a glorious success and won loads of Emmys."

The point, which shouldn't require explaining, is that he thinks no such thing. On the contrary, he had felt self-conscious when he joined up with the show, not so much because he was an Englishman playing a guy from Baltimore but because he was a white man playing what was in effect the lead in a largely black show.

"It was always accepted that you had to have a white lead," he says, "otherwise no one would watch it. I felt a bit uncomfortable about that, or more uncomfortable than I did being a Brit stealing an American job. But it was always a great atmosphere among the actors. Among the principals, we all had the same trailer. We all got treated like shit. We were all subordinate to the writing."

He speaks about his years on The Wire with obvious affection, like someone recalling a beautiful land to which they know they'll never return. There has been some talk about making a feature film but David Simon has said that if it were ever made, it would have to be a prequel. "That's OK for the black characters," says West, "but I'd have to have a facelift."

At the same time, he's relieved that the marathon is over. He had to spend half of each year in Baltimore and, though he liked the city, it left him a long way from his daughter with the London-based Astor. At the end of every season he'd tell Simon he didn't think he could do another. "David would have to try to persuade me, you know, offer me loads more sex scenes. Half those sex scenes were to try and keep me quiet."

West grew up in a wealthy Catholic family in a village on the outskirts of Sheffield. His father, who owned a plastics factory, decided to send his youngest son to Eton. He was terrified, he says, of returning to Sheffield during the holidays and being asked where he went to school. "It used to be excruciating."

After Eton, he went to Trinity College in Dublin, where he studied English. Dublin was a liberation, he says, because it was so far removed from Eton. "The Irish were fascinated by the idea [of the public school]. 'What goes on there? Do yous fock each other?' They rather liked it. And the girls loved it."

He appeared in a short film, while at university, and got paid for the first time. Almost without thinking, he knew that this was the life he wanted to lead. He also met FitzGerald at Trinity. As he told an American interviewer last year: "[She's] my girlfriend from university days. She dumped me back then and she married someone else, and now we're on the rebound and we're back together."

From Trinity he went to the Guildhall to study drama, and he hasn't been out of work since graduating. "I remember being mystified whenever people said, 'What are you going to do?' and I said, 'Be an actor,' and they'd say [deep theatrical voice], 'Oh, it's very hard.' Seems like a piece of piss to me," he laughs. "Hard's going to the fucking office. But no, I've been fairly lucky. Unfortunately it's been a tale of intense luck and privilege. But there you go."

He joined the Peter Hall Company and within a few years he landed his first Hollywood rom-com, alongside Sandra Bullock in 28 Days. One successful actor who met West during this early period of his career recalls there being quite a buzz about him in the profession.

Yet at the turn of the millennium, with stardom apparently within his grasp, West made an odd decision. He joined the circus. Not just any circus, it's true, but the acrobatic, avant-garde Argentinean circus De La Guarda. Still, it was a circus, and though Cary Grant and Burt Lancaster paid their dues under a big top, that was before they started acting. Elsewhere, West has spoken of his attraction to the physical discipline – he had to perform dance routines while suspended in the air by wire – but with me he spoke wistfully of the "beautiful Argentinean dancers".

I assumed that he would have been bombarded with offers after The Wire, but he says that the best offers have come from American TV and he's not prepared to commit himself again for a long period. "So I'm quite happy to play [disfigured villain] Jigsaw in Punisher for four really fun weeks in Montreal, rather than a really great part for six years in Baltimore."

In any case, he says he doesn't much like acting on TV. "Telly is a director's or writer's medium, but acting in telly is really boring because it's so repetitive and goes on for so long." What he'd prefer to do is direct. He went behind the camera for episode seven of the final season of The Wire and relished the experience. He directed a scene which called for stunt cars, stunt police, stunt motorcyclists and a stunt helicopter. "I thought I was Michael Bay [the blockbuster action director] for a bit. Oh, it was fantastic. I'm desperate, desperate to do more."

He's trying to get into directing American TV shows like Heroes, and is hopeful David Simon may give him a slot on his new series set in New Orleans, Treme. For those of us still struggling with withdrawal symptoms from The Wire, the good news is that, while we're unlikely to see Jimmy McNulty again, there's a lot more to come from Dominic West.

In praise of ... The Bunk

SAPTARSHI RAY

William "Bunk" Moreland, played by Wendell Pierce, is the rock upon which the church of Baltimore's murder police is built. Freamons and McNultys come and go, journeying from the plateaus of narcotics and major crimes to the nadirs of marine patrol and pawn shop detail, but the Bunk remains strictly homicide throughout all five seasons of The Wire.

Based on the real-life detective Oscar "Rick" Requer, a pioneering black Baltimore cop in the 1960s (who was paid the compliment of having the character of the veteran cop who trained Lester named after him in the show), Bunk plays the straight man to McNulty's wayward maverick and Lester Freamon's cerebral obsessive. But this is the Wire, and straight men come replete with "pinstripe lawyerly affectations", drink problems and a penchant for puss-i.

Bunk is my favourite character, one I was easily drawn to, which was pretty predictable really as I too am a man of heft who enjoys a taste as much as the next barfly and aspires to gilt-edged repartee.

Bunk: Boy, them Greeks and those twisted-ass names.

McNulty: Man, lay off the Greeks. They invented civilisation.

Bunk: Yeah? Ass-fucking, too.

But it is not Bunk's sling-blade wit alone that engages us, it is his understanding of the community he patrols, his ability to discriminate between career criminals and those who did what they had to do, and above all else, the detective's unwavering, unquestionable dedication to police work.

Among the cops in the show, Bunk consistently proves himself natural police. He combines McNulty's bravado, Lester's clarity of thought and Kima's street smarts with a profound knowledge of human nature to follow each case from several different angles.

Even from the first episode, Bunk is the primary in the murder of the state's witness, William Gant, who testified against D'Angelo Barksdale – the first act that ultimately leads to revealing the extent of Avon's organisation and the squad we come to know and love as they track him with the titular phone tap. But it is Bunk that ultimately solves the case by procuring none other than Omar Little as a witness, fingering Avon's hitman Bird for the crime.

In season two, Bunk, along with Lester, catches the call on 14 dead prostitutes in a "can" at the port, and, while the guilty sailor gets away, it is this pair that eventually figure out what happened on that ship before it docked in Baltimore.

In season three, while the result only leads to a charge of failing to dispose of a dead animal, it is Bunk who cracks Cheese in the interrogation room, when the detail thinks they record him discussing a murder.

Bunk [pretending to weep]: Boo hoo hoo ... He was my dawg, man. I ain't sleep since I capped his ass. Lookin' up, he be all bloody and shit. He had much love for me, even then. I ain't never gonna find another dawg like him ... boo hoo hoo.

Cheese [genuinely weeping]: Y'all some cold-ass motherfuckers, man.

In season four, who else but the Bunk cracks the case of the murder of corner boy Lex, in retaliation for shooting dead Marlo's lieutenant Fruit over a girl, after appealing to his parents to speak out? The case spirals, however, when Cool Lester Smooth finally figures out what Chris and Snoop have been doing with their victims.

And, in the last season, while McNulty veers off into a vortex of self-loathing and abject ridiculousness with his serial killer deception, it is Bunk who ultimately gets Chris locked up for the murder of Michael's stepfather – thereby at least seeing some result from the case of the 22 bodies in the vacants, a case that plagues both the major crimes squad and homicide for practically all of season five. And he manages this in spite of a department that refuses to touch his case as it focuses its efforts on McNulty's phantom menace.

But perhaps what marks Bunk apart as a true police is his relationship with Omar: like everything else in this eloquent programme, a complex interaction between two men and their codes of honour.

As Omar's gang carry out another rip 'n' run at a Barksdale stash house in season three, one of the crew, Tosha, gets shot. Bunk arrives at the scene and instantly recognises Omar's MO, but wrongly believes the dead girl to be a civilian. As he sees kids pretending to be Omar and replaying the shoot-out on the street outside, the Bunk's righteous fury is ignited and he seeks out Omar.

After tracking him down, Bunk not only squares up to the fearsome shotgun-wielding dervish, but pinches him in the one place he knows it will hurt – his honour. The two went to the same school and grew up in the same neighbourhood and, while Omar made the best of what he could, Bunk knows he still takes some pride in being a son of the west side. Bunk claims it was Omar's fault the girl died and that his flamboyant violence see kids emulate him, only they have no call for his precious code.

"As rough as that neighbourhood could be, we had us a community. Nobody, no victim, who didn't matter. And now all we got is bodies, and predatory motherfuckers like you. And out where that girl fell, I saw kids acting like Omar, calling you by name, glorifying your ass. Makes me sick, motherfucker, how far we done fell."

As Omar tells Butchie later: "The fat man's given me an itch I can't scratch." Omar helps Bunk and recovers the gun used to shoot Officer Dozerman to allay some of his guilt. And the favour is returned after Omar is framed by Chris and Snoop over the shooting of a delivery woman – Bunk is one of the only ones who believes him when he says he would never put his gun on a civilian. Eventually, Bunk finds out the truth and gets Omar released from prison, but in return extracts a promise that he will kill no more people, in a powerful scene laced with one's morality and another's regret. A promise Omar fully intends to keep – until he hears of Butchie's death.

But when he's not being a police, Bunk is a drunk, a raucous, hilarious drunk. Unleashing easygoing banter, befogged in blue cigar smoke, perched on a bar stool screaming Jimmy's name, his crass yet sometimes effective charm with the ladies, his "nights out" with McNulty at the railway cutting throwing back whiskey, voiding his guts outside Kavanaugh's... If being elected means being the guy people most want to have a beer with, President Bunk should surely only be a tipple away.

And though he does have his darker moments, particularly his harshness on Jimmy when he tries to clean his act up, we can mostly forgive him as we wanted the old Jimmy back too.

Bunk: Feel like a taste?

McNulty: Not tonight, but you should come over for dinner sometime.

Bunk: [looks aghast] Dinner?!

And in only the way a best friend can, he then chastises Jimmy when he does go back to his boozing and philandering ways. This, despite Jimmy's help over the years – such as extricating him from a woman's house after a one-night stand; and the pair of them solving a case with the use of an expletive.

"You've lost your fuckin' mind Jimmy, look at you! Half late every third night, dead drunk every second. Nut deep in random pussy. What little time you do spend sober and limp-dick, you're working murders that don't even exist!"

But perhaps McNulty himself sums up their friendship best when in a tender, inebriated moment at the bar, he tells the Bunk just why he loves him.

McNulty: It's 'cause when it came time for you to fuck me, you were very gentle.

Bunk: You damn right.

McNulty: See, 'cause you could have hauled me out of the garage and just bent me over the hood of a radio car, and – no, you were, you were very gentle.

Bunk: I knew it was your first time. I wanted to make that shit special.

McNulty: It was, man. It fucking was.

Whether it's his adherence to police work or his pithy one-liners you like, the Bunk is a grand element in a grand show and as with all its aspects you have to embrace his contradictions. As the man himself says: "The job isn't about picking the stories we like best."

Series Two

On the Waterfront

EPISODE 1 – The credit crunch Wire

JUDITH SOAL

Straight to the business of the season in the opening scene. McNulty, recently demoted to the harbour police, is on marine patrol with his new partner Diggins. Amid sweeping views of the sea and the sky there are lingering shots of burnt-out buildings, rusted metal work, broken bridges and general decay on the shore as McNulty and Diggins make their way to answer a distress call. "My father used to work there", says McNulty, gesturing to the shipyards. Apparently Diggins's uncle did too. But we discover that both men were laid off in the 70s. And just in case it's not yet clear, the ship they've been called to is not carrying cargo to be offloaded in the port, but is rather a "party boat" for the great and good. Its name: Capitol Gains.

As David Simon told the Guardian's Guide: "[Series two is a] meditation on the death of work and the betrayal of the American working class, it is a deliberate argument that unencumbered capitalism is not a substitute for social policy; that on its own, without a social compact, raw capitalism is destined to serve the few at the expense of the many."

It's as if Simon knew that when our coverage got back to series two, the world would be suffering an economic crisis brought on by unfettered capitalism, and that Capitol Gains would have come to signify another of The Wire's main treatises: the abuse of the system by those elected to serve us – in this case MPs making hay with our money.

After finally tuning in to the lingo and getting your head round the cast of characters in the first season, it's somewhat disconcerting to be confronted with a whole new set of personalities (Frank Sobotka, Nick, Ziggy, the Greek, Beadie, etc), a new (Polish) dialect, and a different social milieu (the docks). And after the emotional high of last week's finale, the pace can seem a bit slow. It's half an hour before we get our first body, more than 20 minutes before we see Stringer Bell (still a highlight for me I'm afraid), and a full 55 minutes before the spine really tingles (when Beadie opens the hidden compartment in the container and a woman's arm falls out). In some ways it shows the confidence (some might say arrogance) of the Wiremakers – it's not enough for us to have stayed with them through the trials of the first series, we have to start the work all over again this time. They even boast about it in the opening quote: "Ain't never gonna be what it was" – a clear reference to the decline of the docks but I think there's a message in there for us too.

Yet, despite the muted tone, the episode does a lot of work. It sets out some central conflicts of the season – Stan Valchek and the police versus Frank and the dockers; Stringer v Avon: Ziggy v Sergei/"Boris" and the drug hierarchy; McNulty v homicide (as ever) etc.

And there are some great scenes – like when Bodie and Dragon are on the way to Philadelphia for a major re-up and Bodie discovers that radio stations change when you leave your hometown.

Bodie: Why would anyone want to leave Baltimore man?

Why indeed.

FAVOURITE QUOTE:

"The Bunk can't swim, and I ain't too good at floatin' neithers."

RUNNING TOTALS:

Murders: 14 (although I don't think we know exactly how many dead women are in the container yet), which makes 23 for both series together.

McNulty giving a fuck when it's not his turn: the demotivated McNulty, who seems determined not to rock the boat (ha ha) early on, is soon back in business when he points out to Rawls that the body found floating in the harbour had defensive wounds on her hands and arms so is unlikely to have jumped. But when Rawls hands the case over to Baltimore County, McNulty goes into overdrive and calculates the prevailing tides to prove that the woman must have died on the other side of the bridge – in Rawls's domain. (Not missing a beat, Landsman declares McNulty the "Prince of Tides".) I make that two "giving a fucks", adding up to 11 overall.

COMMENTS

CodProfundity Apart from possibly season 4, the second has always seemed the most fulfilling as a single story. I grew to appreciate the camaraderie amongst the dockers and their (drinking) culture, so much so me and some friends tried a raw egg dropped into pints on a stag weekend once, it's not to be recommended. I find all three Sobotka men to be compelling characters, sure I like Frank more than I like Nick or Ziggy but those two still have great arcs that speak to just how the drug trade and the death of industry has trapped people in those communities. They have little chance of escaping it and in Ziggy's case escaping the shadow of his Father and the legends of the dock.

judithsoal i agree about frank, he's great and probably the star of this episode – which again shows the confidence (arrogance) of simon and co, making him the main player when we don't know him at all. and it shows their brilliance at sketching character without having to go through lengthy introductions and spelling it out – like when frank goes on about waking up every morning with "an angry blue-veined diamond cutter", only to twist it and add: "three-and-a-half inches of hard blue steel". it tells you a lot about him. also the look on his face at the end when he hears about the dead women – you know that's genuine concern, not worry about whether it will affect his lucrative sidelines.

SaptarshiRay I think the weirdest sensation is you almost think, "hang on, in most shows McNulty would have gone on the boat and come back by now. it will get referenced once or twice in the first episode and then it'll never get mentioned again. You're telling me they're actually going to show his exile?"

And from the off, we're dealing with such a different B-more. The whites are the underclass and many blacks are the man – I know it hasn't happened yet but especially when bunk & Lester walk into the docker's bar as positions of authority, being pOlice, and most of the white stevedores eyeing them suspiciously. It's clear this show is different to others and i think why season 2 gets such a bad rep is it's such a break in the story arc, we're almost left feeling cheated.

Lipshitzs Season 2 makes no distinction between struggling white working class people and their black counterparts. Although maybe this is no surprise as historically Poles have had as hard a time as the Irish in the Anglo-Saxon dominated world.

Perhaps the most interesting additions to the show are The Greeks. They display an unscrupulous ruthless way of doing business. And a pointer to all the Avons, Stringers and Marlos – if you want to avoid prosecution infiltrate the FBI.

Busfield This is the point that The Wire moves from being a very good show about cops and drug dealers into being the sprawling, "Dickensian" epic that we come to know and love. Although new and challenging and different, season one is essentially a show about the pOlice and their battle with organised crime (even Bubbles mostly fits into this narrow picture first time around). As Judith says, season two immediately plunges us into a wider world, without warning, taking in the docks and the Greeks and the church. And yet we are also immediately updated on most of the major players from season one too. How much is that for the viewer to take in? Because we are watching second time around we know what role Frank and Beadie and Valchek and the Greeks will play, but were we not very disorientated and confused first time around? It's hard to tell with hindsight.

Again, as Judith says, the producers have the confidence to leave us without a crime to focus on for half the episode, and instead we are thrown into the Baltimore Polack community, on the docks, in the police, and in the Catholic Church. Indeed, what this episode (and series) gives us is a longing for a sense of belonging. The need for a community. The Polish, the Greeks, the church, the dockers. Even (or perhaps especially) the band in the bar playing one of my all-time favourite songs, a song about working class struggle and belonging – sadly belonging in the sense of "I owe my soul to the company store".

Lingli There are some fabulous moments in this first episode – from Herc's crowing over the ignorance of the white drug dealers ("dumb as a box of rocks") and his advocation of affirmative action "if white guys are gonna sell drugs in Baltimore", to the marvellous coiffure of Wanda, one of the Homicide admin staff, to McNulty's screwing with Rawls ... and overall, of course, the elegant set-up of several seemingly disparate storylines which will coalesce as the season progresses. Looking back, it really does seem that Simon and co. hit their stride with this season.

Busfield Lipshitzs/Suzie – Just as important as the Greek's mole is, surely, the fact that they are importers/traffickers, no hanging around the corners and towers for them, and they are too far up the food chain for an under-resourced, overworked pOlice department to reach.

"You must be The Greek."

"Well, I am Greek."

joedoone Re The Greek's FBI insider, I don't think he is a mole; he hasn't been corrupted by the Greek. He has enlisted the Greek as an intelligence asset, post-9/11, and that is why he protects the Greek. This is why the Greek repays him for his valuable information (and, at the same time, takes revenge on the Colombians after they have refused to pay the agreed price for the stolen chemicals). It's not exactly heartwarming to think that the FBI would facilitate the drug industry in the name of "a greater good", i.e. counter-terrorism, but stranger things have happened in real life.

RedThreat What a crappy window Valchek offered compared to the Stevedores! Don't know if it's another sly allusion to the decline of US manufacturing/craftsmanship but Sobotka's is made in Germany, Valchek's is US made.

EPISODE 2 – Black and white

PAUL OWEN

In series two, The Wire widens its scope to examine the lives of the longshoremen – mostly white – who struggle to make a living on the decaying Baltimore docks. In doing so, it reveals its primary theme to be not race – as might have been surmised from the last series – but class, that most unfashionable subject in American art, and specifically the decline of the working class.

Nicky Sobotka – the competent young dockworker with a girlfriend, a young child and not enough work – is the character that most clearly embodies this. In David Simon and Ed Burns's previous TV series, The Corner, we saw how the black working and middle class of the 1970s and 80s was gradually worn down in places such as West Baltimore to reach the state of dependence on the drug economy we see in The Wire. In series two, Nicky personifies a similar fall for the whites of the inner city.

In this episode, his younger cousin, the volatile and unpredictable Ziggy, offers him a cut of a drug deal. "Fuck that shit, Zig," Nicky replies firmly. "I got work today." But gradually, as his hours get cut back even further and the amount of money to be made from dealing becomes more and more tempting, Nicky will slip seamlessly into the world of drug packages and dangerous street-corner "beefs" familiar to us from series one. The last series showed the police as something close to an occupying army in black estates; here we see that the white working class too views them as something close to an instinctive enemy.

This series can be seen as Simon and Burns's elegy to the working class, and this particular episode (directed by Ed Bianchi) and last week's contain some lovingly shot images of industrial decline, long roads curving away from factories fallen silent, Nicky trying hopelessly to start his car as the camera pulls back to reveal an enormous, decaying landscape of smashed windows and dirty walls, all as broken and useless as Nicky's vehicle.

The racial politics of this series are also interesting. Last week, Saptarshi Ray mentioned the scene where Bunk Moreland and Lester Freamon, two impressive, well-dressed black detectives, walk into the white, working-class bar as clear representatives of power and authority. In this episode, we meet White Mike, a Caucasian drug dealer, stamping his feet in the cold of a street corner, huddled inside an enormous blue fur-lined parka; this scene is followed immediately by one showing Stringer Bell, the black drugs kingpin, going to visit his boss, Avon Barksdale, in prison. Like Avon, he's treated like royalty by the prison staff. He wears a long, expensive-looking black coat accessorised tastefully with a grey and black scarf; even Avon wears a Department of Correction denim jacket that seems a cut above other prisonwear.

We have discussed the lack of racist banter among the white police officers, and how realistic or unrealistic that is. I argued that Baltimore's being majority black creates a different dynamic between the two races than that in the US as a whole, and the police force, as a racially mixed profession, reflects this. Series two does not shy away from showing us racism on the white-dominated docks, and even the celebrated "You happen to be white" scene where Nicky upbraids a white dealer for talking as if he's black (so successful, perhaps, because it speaks to a guilty conscience in the white viewer who ends each episode by happily murmuring the black slang to him or herself) definitely reveals an attitude of racial superiority and even contempt in Nicky.

RUNNING TOTALS:

Murders: up one to 24, with the murder of the sailor responsible for the deaths of 14 prostitutes. Here we see for the first time what the Greeks are capable of – a torture and murder almost as brutal as that of Brandon by the Barksdales last series – and also which one of them is really in charge.

McNulty giving a fuck when it's not his turn: up one to 12, as he presumptuously takes over Beadie Russell's case. "What does the marine unit have to do with 13 dead girls in a can?" she asks. "Not a thing," he replies.

Drunk: up one to eight, as Jimmy celebrates landing his old boss with responsibility for solving the murders. Nobody wants them, it seems, not even Freamon – and he's practically a saint.

COMMENTS

CodProfundity I was thinking about Nicky the other day and it's after he goes to see his Aunt's old house (remodelled and with McNulty's ex showing people round) that he decides to take his payment from Double G and Eton in Heroin. Seeing his old neighbourhood undergoing gentrification and realising just how physically near and yet so far he and his peers are from that world is what drives him to become a dealer – it's not just the decline of industry and the working class it's the "other America's" insatiable desire to forget the huge swathes of people and culture and then to move in on that territory, price the poorer people out and paint over them ever existing.

whatisthere2 Stringer really coming into his own and ditching the track suits for tailored trousers and long black overcoats which make him look like the banker/economist he has always desired to be. Avon's politeness is impressive as well, he can't really believe that the Prison officer is not prepared to listen to him and goes "Pardon Me" – that was a good moment.

The abuse of power continues, this time its Valchek, Rawls has a fair go it as well trying to dump the 13 Jane Does on marine unit but they have Jimmy McNulty fighting for them in the shadows and Rawls has to take them on – and never ending hatred for Jimmy.

D'Angelo, the gangster with a heart from series one is toppling under drug addiction, carrying the weight for the family! its sad to see D go down and the signs are high posted for his decline. In the season one he is so desperately trying to escape the inherited fate of his family but he never could and it was listening to his mother that becomes his Achilles heel. Nicky follows his uncle and brother into smuggling and drugs – its the same human story / tragedy just different sectors of the economy.

JayBay Paul – do you really think Nicky is betraying an attitude of "racial superiority"? It seemed to be more (well merited) contempt (agree with you there) for the street dealer so lacking confidence in his own identity that he affects a cod black accent. Surely all he is doing is representing everyman's desire to slap down idiots like that (all too prevalent in England as well).

er...for the avoidance of doubt this stricture does not apply to me when I use words or phrases picked up from The Wire, obviously!

PaulOwen I think what you're saying is right, but his insistence that "I'm also white" so can't be treated like this goes beyond that.

What is so wrong with what Frog does anyway? Isn't he just adapting his speech, mannerisms and dress to those around him, his workmates and contemporaries? Don't we all do that to a greater or lesser extent? Is it because he crosses a racial line that he seems so laughable? If it is about pride in his cultural identity, rather than racial identity, then he clearly identifies more clearly with the cultural identity of the black street dealers than the white working class. Is that not allowed? Do you have to stick to the cultural identity of your own race? Is Stringer betraying his own cultural identity when he puts on a business suit and travels to New York with a briefcase to have a meeting with a lawyer in a skyscraper?

CodProfundity I think (and it's definitely only a guess because I don't have much of a problem with the way Frog or White Mike speak and dress) people find a white guy with those mannerism to be an affectation whereas perhaps they don't see it that way for black people behaving in the same style. Nicky's reaction to it comes from a few different places, firstly his low level racism against "project niggers" so even though Nicky doesn't think less of Ott and the other black stevedores and workers, drug dealers of any colour are worthy of his contempt – that he uses racist language to describe them is weirdly but fittingly a much more of a class thing than a race thing. The second place it comes from is Nick's own guilty feeling about dealing drugs, he doesn't want to admit that he's feeling bad about it so takes on a holier than thou attitude to his business – it's undercut brilliantly when he glances up to a window and sees an old woman looking at him on her stoop as if he is every other dealer in the world.

Oh, and Frog and White Mike are drug dealers in a de-industrialised soon to be forgotten wasteland, really the only pop-cultural phenomena that's popular and speaks to their situation is rap/hip-hop, not just (or even mostly in some cases) the music but everything that goes with it.

Lingli First time around I just found the conversation funny. There certainly is an attitude of racial superiority demonstrated by Nicky and Ziggy – as CodProfundity says, it's not aimed at all black people, but they definitely look down on the dealers, despite, really, not being any better themselves. The respect Nicky shows to the Greeks is interesting too, from that perspective: makes you wonder how he would've behaved if he was dealing with, I don't know, Colombians or Moroccans or something. And yet Polish–Americans certainly had their share of prejudice against them (in the Stephen King books – okay, not exactly sociological treatises but bear with me – that deal with the era of his childhood, the '50s and '60s, the characters invariably tell Polish jokes the way we used to tell Irish ones), and I don't suppose Nicky is unaware of this.

I think Stringer's desire for social mobility is shown in a similar light in season three, where Avon makes it quite clear that, firstly, he just doesn't see the point of moving into the property business (not least because it's not fun to him), and secondly, when it becomes clear how Stringer's been taken for a ride, where Avon bluntly tells Stringer what a fool he's been. From my recollection, it's not couched entirely in racial terms, but they're in there.

Perhaps the difference is that these are people moving in opposite directions: String is coming from the projects, trying to move into legitimate business, and Nicky is coming from a legitimate (but ultimately failing) line of work to an illegal but much more lucrative one. I guess we see one as moving up and the other as moving down. But the whole issue of race in America is so fraught and open to argument – and we aren't just talking about race, of course, this is really about class, as we understand it over here. And you can't have class unless someone thinks they're above someone else.

PaulOwen Lingli, I think Avon tells Stringer, "They saw your ghetto ass coming," so it seems to me a combined racial/class aspect.

CodProfundity I'm not sure I understand how changing your voice can be a betrayal of your own essence. I speak differently in many different situations, from how I converse with my boss to hanging out with mates and having a laugh, to dealing with police, or with my elderly grandmother, none of that betrays my essence it just means I recognise that other people respond in a more positive manner depending on how the conversation goes. Yes Frog has taken on "gangster" style and it's very very similar to how Bodie or Poot et al speak – but they are acting in this affected manner as well – you think some of the black kids weren't whiny and getting dragged to Sunday school by their mother? This sort of slang isn't specifically a black thing, that's what I don't think some people realise. It's a cultural thing and Frog's culture is corner dealing heroin in a rundown part of Baltimore, it's appropriate for him to speak in the way he does.

Lingli in a couple of episodes when Carv and Kima are on a stakeout and overhear Frog speaking, Carv does say, in a disgusted tone, "They steal everything," so maybe Frog wouldn't be received that well by Bodie and co…

EPISODE 3 – Parents

MARK SMITH

My heart aches for Frank Sobotka. The man is single-handedly trying to preserve an entire way of life – a working-class ideal and ideology that is crumbling before his eyes. Does anyone really believe that if Baltimore's shipping could provide the dockers with a regular, full working week that he would even contemplate siphoning off his contraband?

His union slush fund, which he uses variously to supplement the fading income of desperate union members (see the unnamed guy's "change, from Frank Sobotka" at the bar) and to try to influence Baltimore's corrupt decision-making class, is Frank's impotent attempt to do something – anything – to help his workers.

The scene where a dapper Frank is told to "make nice" with the slippery eel himself, Clay Davis, just epitomises the series' juxtaposition of "need" and "greed". You can see the look of disgust and anger in Frank's eyes.

Virtually all the dockers seem to be involved in criminality in some way, but they are still merely pawns for the greater, and more immoral, pursuit of wealth by the Greek and his cartel on one side, and the politicians on the other. And so it goes.

Some lovely comic touches this week. Freamon's xenophobic outburst after the montage of clueless, non-anglophone ship workers chief among them. "English, motherfuckers!" Also loved Landsman's description of Freamon as displaying "tweedy impertinence".

RUNNING TOTALS:

McNulty giving a fuck when it's not his turn: up one to 13, after his guilt-trip on finding out that Bunk and Beadie had swallowed the dead girls. "Officer McNulty could have paid no mind; when friends are suffering he bleeds too." Or maybe he's just trying to get close to Beadie, eh?

Drunk: up one to nine, when McNulty, Bunk and Beadie are sharing a beverage. "Is daddy working late too?" our favourite Catholic womaniser asks on hearing Beadie has two kids.

COMMENTS

MikeLymane he may have been an accessory to 14 murders, but one look at his face at the end of the first episode tells you what you need to know in my opinion. With a man in his position, so many things are decided on such fine margins. Maintaining that balance clearly proved impossible, and while he has obviously facilitated terrible events he wears his intentions on his sleeve and it is clear what kind of man he wants to be, and what he wants to do for the people around him.

Second time round seeing the meeting with Clay Davis (*spit*) made my skin crawl too, the contrast between the two men could not be more stark.

PaulOwen Frank's a very sympathetic character despite dipping his toe into crime – which it is always clear he does to help his colleagues and the principle or idea of a union and of dock work.

I love that scene where he confronts Vondas about the dead girls, asking Vondas why he didn't tell him what was in there? Vondas starts listing: "Guns, chemicals, bombs, nuclear bombs," or something, and Frank looks progressively more horrified. But he ends up making it clear that Vondas has to tell him if "something's breathing in them cans".

He's a good guy, a struggler, a tragic figure. I was very sad at what happened as the series closed.

midatlantic I agree that Frank is a tragic figure, but his tragic flaw, in the Shakespearean sense, is his obsession with saving the traditional work at the docks. He has no Plan B, and therefore he invests everything, including his integrity, to the docks. Let's say that I see him as corrupted rather than corrupt. He wants to be Prospero but he is in the end Canute. This does not, however, absolve him of responsibility. He is smart and strong enough to be held responsible for his choices.

Also, Frank does enjoy the power he has, which is an almost paternal authority and loyalty over the checkers. As a consequence, he becomes a bad father to his real son. He seems oblivious to Ziggy's behaviour until it erupts into violence. He has corrupted his nephew, who is a surrogate-son figure. Interestingly, Ziggy refers to a brother, presumably older, who has gone to community college. This brother is never mentioned again, and is therefore arguably estranged from his family to some extent. Frank's obsession with saving jobs on the docks would leave little room for a son who had moved on from that. My instinct that this is the case is reinforced by Frank's hostility to the lobbyist who relates how his family has moved up in the world over three generations through education. The hostility can partly be explained by his sense that the lobbyist is bragging and claiming to be better than Frank, but I think there is also an attitude in Frank that rejecting the docks is somehow a moral failing. As a result, I can see Frank becoming distant from a son who has decided to do something else, even if he rationally thinks that it was a good choice for the son.

In fact, it occurred to me that there is something of a theme of bad fathers in this series. In addition to Frank, there is the Prez–Valchek conflict. If you want to put a charitable interpretation on Valchek's acts, and I offer this solely in the spirit of a devil's advocate, he is actually being a good father to his daughter. Having failed to convince the daughter not to marry Prez, he is determined to ensure that Prez is successful within the BPD and is not punished for his misconduct. However, I think the better interpretation is that Valchek is a controlling so-and-so who probably terrorises his daughter as much as his son in law. And of course, we have McNulty, who wants to be a good father and reconcile with his ex-wife, but handles it incredibly badly. Nick also wants to be a good father, to provide for his child, but this desire is subverted into further criminality.

CodProfundity I think people are taking a bit too much of an insular view in their criticisms of Frank and Ziggy. It's The Wire after all, everyone is trapped and forced into compromise. Yes Frank thinks he's the only one capable of saving the docks…because he is, without his slush fund there'd be no money for lobbyists or greasing Davis and the likes already greasy palms. Sure he's a bit big headed but I don't think he's as myopic or self serving as some people do. His relationship with Ziggy isn't just about the two of them either, it's about an entire culture coming to an end. I never got the impression Frank forced Ziggy into working on the dock, I'd say there being a brother at community college is evidence that Frank is OK with education and bettering yourself but that the sheer history and camaraderie of the stevedores is hugely appealing to Ziggy. As for the scene with Frank and the lawyer, Frank's anger comes from the fact much of the social mobility afforded to some has come at the huge expense of other people's prospects – that is the main treatise of The Wire after all.

cinephiliac Bad fathers, or the sins of the father being visited on the son, does seem to be a theme, perhaps more so because there are more male than female characters given the the milieu – though D'Angelo's mother probably wouldn't win a mother-of-the-year award, even though she's portrayed as doing what she thinks is best for the family, albeit from a skewered perspective. As we know, one of the greatest strengths of The Wire is that characters are neither all good or all bad but a mass of contradictions and complexities.

notyourusual I've been thinking about what it might have been like for Ziggy growing up and how did he get to be such a mess. A telltale scene, well it's a fleeting moment really – is in the bar where the checker has been sent by Frank to have a drink on him and is handed that wad of money by Doris (is that her name)? Ziggy is also at the bar watching this transaction closely but saying nothing. The checker says to Ziggy what a great man his dad is but Ziggy's face is registering an entirely different emotion. It's a poignant moment that seems to say yes Frank is there for everybody but there's something missing for Zig. I've said in a previous blog how childlike I find Ziggy, in his impulsive behaviour and craving for attention. He seems always to be trying to fill a void with one ill-thought out scheme after another. Something didn't quite come together for Ziggy and he latches onto Nicky and elicits from his cousin a protective almost paternal role. But Nicky can't of course protect him from himself and frustration has been building inside Ziggy until it explodes in that dreadful moment of pure rage.

Episode 3 is full of great one-on-ones: Avon in one of his most eloquent scenes, visiting D'Angelo in the prison library to try and repair their relationship. Did it ever cross his mind that D might ignore his plea to lay off the drugs? or was he just so confident of his "paternal" authority and of D's loyalty having once given his word? Certainly he brings all his powers of persuasion into play and when he says at the end that it's all about the love it's a powerful and emotional statement. Which makes the ending of the episode all the more chilling; this splitting off of emotion when it suits: this curtain that comes down indiscriminately on anyone outside of family.

Love the intimacy of the scene between Omar and the sulking Dante! We'd seen Dante's eyes positively smouldering with jealousy every time the two women are on the scene.

Other great one-on-ones: Stringer and Donette, Valchek and Burrell.

Lingli I definitely read the relationship between Ziggy and Frank as one where Ziggy feels that the union and the stevedores always came first. Isn't there a conversation later in the series where Ziggy says to his father something about, when he was a kid, he thought Frank was always working and then when he got older he realised he was actually often as not in the bar? I guess you could look at Ziggy's choice to become a docker as a way to get attention from his dad – not even that, but just to be part of this family, this brotherhood. The very first scene with Ziggy shows him having lost a can and Frank firing him; and then one of the other dockers tells the irate driver who's been yelling at Zig that actually, there's no way Zig would get fired: because "that's his old man", (or words to that effect).

The odd thing about that later conversation between Frank and Ziggy is that Ziggy seems to be saying to Frank that it's okay; he accepts that this is the way things were and there's nothing Frank can do about it. And yet only a short time later Ziggy's in jail and Frank's rushing to be by his side: just to be told, again, that there's nothing he can do. notyourusual is right: Ziggy really is like a child and never does he seem more so than when he gets up to go back into the cells. However infuriated you've been by him through the season, I defy anyone not to have their heart break a little for him at that moment. And Frank, too, of course: this is a man who prides himself – who bases his self-worth – on being able to fix things.

I also loved the scene with Dante pouting; although Omar's reaction to watching the girls take off the dealers he's been so carefully scoping is great, too. Compare the way he treats them with the way Stringer talks to Donette: you never, ever get the feeling String sees Donette as an equal; in fact, as I've said before, I don't get the feeling he even sees her as much of a person.

He and Avon do both see others as pieces on a chessboard; they're alike in that. But where we see Avon's connections to his family – not just in the way he holds D'Angelo's son, or visits D's other uncle, but also in the way he's shamed (or at least made uncomfortable) by Brianna, and troubled by the way D's cold to him – who do we see Stringer actually acting warmly towards? In the whole three series he's in, I can't identify anyone who seems to mean something to him, other than Avon. Donette, I think – for all that she's gorgeous – is mostly desirable to him because she was D'Angelo's girl. I can't think of any camaraderie or even a lot of respect between him and the guys he works with; not compared, say, to the way Avon and Slim Charles are. The man is cold. Or maybe not just cold; maybe just super-self-contained. Just like McNulty discovers when they finally go to String's apartment, we never get to know him, and neither does anyone else.

Lingli I feel kind of sorry for Donette – she gets some stick from Brianna and String (and yeah, she's is the mother of D'Angelo's son), but D was shacking up with Shardene in the first series, so it's not like he was an angel...

notyourusual Lingli – I agree about String seizing the opportunity with Donette because she is D's girl but I don't feel sorry for her. In a way I think she and String are quite well suited. She doesn't visit D until String reminds her of what is at stake should D decide to go state-side, namely the very nice apartment and the money. I don't feel there was much love lost between her and D. Back in series 1 the restaurant scene was quite a telling one. Donette clearly had no sympathy with D'Angelo's unease: she was dismissive and gave him very short shrift. I did think back then that she was in it just for the good things in life and she'd go along with whoever would provide it.

Lingli notyourusual, no, I agree with you about Donette – I think she's interested in D' only as long as he can keep on with the nice things; and she makes a play for Stringer, or at least makes it quite clear that she's interested in him, with the whole "it's a shame to let a new shirt go to waste" schtick.

But I do still kind of feel sorry for her ... because I think in a way she's just as trapped as Ziggy and Nicky are. What are her alternatives? In a way, she's just maximising her economic potential; using her youth and her looks to provide a decent (by the standards of most of the Wire's people, way above decent) lifestyle, not just for herself but for her wee boy.

Not to try and reignite the issue of misogyny again, but the women in the Wire are possibly in an even worse place than the men. Not to excuse their behaviour, but perhaps to explain it – Donette goes with D and then with String as a means to an end (although he's probably not that much of a chore, if you get my drift...) Brianna keeps the Barksdale empire rolling as much because she has a nice home and fancy car through it as to give Avon something to come back to. And Namond's gorgon of a mother puts him out on the corner because, let's face it, where else is she going to get the money to fund the lifestyle she and her son are accustomed to, once Bri cuts her off? (The fact that Bri and Namond's mother seem willing to sacrifice their sons for their lifestyle kind of stretches credibility for me, but that's another issue.)

There are women who make something different of their lives and aren't dependent: Tonya and whassername, who run with Omar; the woman Cutty carries a torch for, who gets out of the neighbourhood and becomes a teacher; and there's Snoop, of course. Although I have to confess, it took me several episodes to be really sure Snoop was a girl. I'm not saying that these women necessarily make major successes of their lives – two of them are shot dead, after all – but they do manage a level of autonomy, at least.

I guess I feel for Donette because she has a hostage to fortune in her son, and that resonates with me because I've two wee ones myself. But I agree she should've taken the baby to see D, for all sorts of reasons.

EPISODE 4 – Plight of the stevedores

SAPTARSHI RAY

This series is a testament to Frank Sobotka's struggle. The stevedore boss is tragedy writ large and his story has always reminded me of a real life one, the act of another frustrated man, left with little option but to dabble in crime to try and save his business and employees.

John DeLorean was a carmaker and entrepreneur who embodied the 80s ethos of "greed is good" and illustrated perfectly the decade's obsession with style over substance. And the DeLorean DMC-12 sports car, which will forever be associated with the Back to the Future films, oozed that oft-derided decade's opulence.

Badged as an example of the enterprising spirit so admired by Reagan and Thatcher, DeLorean left a successful career at General Motors in 1972 to form his own company and located his plant in Dunmurry, Northern Ireland, after financial incentives from the British government. The plant made over 9,000 cars from 1981 to 1982, but soon entered receivership as the sleek, gull-winged cars were just too expensive for a mass market and were not yet the movie icon they would come to be, flux capacitor and all.

In the summer of 1982, John DeLorean was arrested by the FBI for cocaine smuggling. A former drug smuggler named James Hoffman, who was now an FBI informant, approached DeLorean with "a way to save his company". The auto company boss went along with the scheme, which involved cocaine being hidden in auto parts and shipped into ports across the world, but left a letter with his lawyer before he went to a meeting with "investors", to be opened if he did not return. Which he didn't, as he was arrested.

The trial was a circus and DeLorean was cleared of all charges after the FBI was found to have (quite blatantly) entrapped the businessman. The judge described it as "the last act of a desperate man trying to save his company". DeLorean always claimed he only agreed to meet such shady figures as he had nowhere else to turn, and that once he knew drugs were involved he tried to back out but then his children were threatened (by undercover FBI agents, believe it or not).

The parallels with Frank are everywhere: desperation, attempting to save his fellow workers, police attention, nefarious characters … Christ, even FBI informants. And while Valchek would probably love nothing more than to entrap Frank, at least the detail watching him is made up of good pOlice.

DeLorean was no angel; the Guardian's obituary even described him as "engineer, car maker and conman" and his critics thought he was more amenable to the drug-smuggling plan than suggested, but it is hard to see how anyone would not at least have heard out a possible solution to their problems. Why the FBI specifically targeted him is less clear. Perhaps DeLorean too beat a police chief to donating a stained glass window to a church's nave.

RUNNING TOTALS:

Murders: up by five to 29, as the hot shot bodies are counted

McNulty dubious parenting: up one to three, after signing off alimony forms he has no intention of paying merely to try and get back with his ex.

Bubbles attempting to get clean: not just yet; more phones to steal and radiators to carry so still on two.

COMMENTS

RedThreat I don't think the DeLorean analogy holds. DeLorean seems to have been a bit of a playboy chancer, all Dream Cars and Dream Girls and hanging out with Raquel Welch. I doubt Neon Neon will be making a concept album about Frank!!!!

I've been racking my brains for a better real life equivalent to Frank – maybe Arthur Scargill? Another Union man with the best of intentions but a big ego and fighting in vain against the winds of change.

whatisthere2 Ditto DeLorean acted out of personal interest whereas Frank is in shady waters because he wants to save the community and docks. I can see Sap's underlying relevance for a desperate man to turn to drugs/ dodgy dealings as a last resort.

Coming back to the Shakespearean narrative and Merchant of Venice came to mind: Greeks as Shylock, no one can cross the Greeks with out paying their pound of flesh.

Janne When I first saw season 2 it struck me as quite strange they were Greek. Why Greek ethnicity for this criminal gang? Russian, Albanian, Armenian, Yugoslavian all seem like more obvious/ stereotypical/boring choices to portray the "European crime syndicate". Is there any real story behind Greeks? Is there maybe a large Greek minority in Baltimore that actually makes this choice the realistic one?

suziebee Janne they aren't Greek are they? Remember near the end of the series when the Greek and Vondas are in the hotel? "And of course...I'm not even Greek!"

whatisthere2 Introducing the Greeks was possibly David Simon's idea, he has always carried the torch for The Wire being a Greek tragedy, so a bit of role reversal and make them the oppressor in typical DS fashion.

thegg I think it's clear from the script that he is using the Greek nationality as a cover to mask his true identity. In addition he uses worry beads which can be typical affectation of middle-aged Greek men as part of his cover.

In terms of his true nationality, I always thought of the framing of the shot for this scene was the big clue. In the background you can see the gilted "onion domes" of, presumably, a Russian orthodox church. I think the effect is designed to be ambiguous but the intent is clear..

EPISODE 5 – Parallel lives

JUDITH SOAL

Frank Sobotka looks ready to snap as the realisation of his dependence on the Greek's money sinks in. He hates himself for being part of an operation that led to the Jane Does' death in the container but is powerless to escape it. (The episode's title, Undertow, refers to currents that trap swimmers in the way he is trapped here.)

Stringer is feeling the heat over having an "inferior product in an aggressive marketplace", as he puts it. Ziggy has a few days to avoid death by Cheese (Method Man). Bunk, Freamon and Beadie need to make some progress in the Jane Does' inquiry to get Rawls off their backs, and Valchek is desperate to find his surveillance vehicle.

These parallels offer a great way of highlighting the characters' contrasting responses: Frank shouts (a lot) but ultimately acquiesces; Stringer adopts the WorldCom business model by renaming the product; Nick turns to negotiation to get Ziggy off the hook; Beadie responds to implicit criticism from Bunk by calling on an ex-boyfriend to find out more about the docks (it's a significant moment in her character development – she's one of the few rising to the challenge), and Valchek gets vindictive.

FAVOURITE QUOTE:

"The same fuck-ups in the same shit detail working out of the same shithouse kinda office. You people lack for personal growth, you know that?" – Freamon

RUNNING TOTALS:

McNulty giving a fuck when it's not his turn: up one to 15 as McNulty takes a day trip to try to identify his Jane Doe.

Herc fuck-ups: the toothpick may be irritating Carver but you can't call that a fuck-up. Four and a half.

COMMENTS

midatlantic The first time the comparison with Shakespeare occurred to me, it was the use of soliloquy. Frank's defiant response to the subpoenas in the excerpt posted this week is a good example. My sense is that you don't tend to get those type of long speeches that are meditations on the state of the world or the state of the character's soul in other series.

In the first series D'Angelo gets a lot of these type of soliloquy-type speeches, which is when I started to think of him as a Hamlet figure (the image became so potent that when he was killed, his body left in a pose of suicide, my mental soundtrack emoted "Good night, sweet prince, and flights of angels thee to thy rest").

While David Simon himself talks about The Wire being like Greek tragedy, the linguistic style seems more like Shakespearean tragedy. For example, there seems to be nothing in The Wire which could be analogised to the Chorus in Greek tragedies.

notyourusual isn't Ziggy caught up in that unspoken code that dictates offspring should continue the family line. I think that brief mention of the brother we never see or hear of again is highly significant; he's the one that got away, Ziggy remains in a world to which he really isn't suited. Ziggy might have flourished in the nerdy world of computer technology etc. Instead his every enterprise has him as a laughing stock or in serious trouble

midatlantic All very true, although I am a bit sceptical that Ziggy could have been much of a success at anything, as he lacks much, if any self-discipline. He does have some cleverness, but I think he would have had to have been in a very different environment to maximise it. I think that's what I meant about fate being more disembodied than in Greek tragedy. The result is equally inevitable, but it is not usually the result of someone choosing to play with Ziggy's (for example) life.

EPISODE 6 – Levy and Omar: who is the real criminal?

PAUL OWEN

This episode begins with a celebrated courtroom exchange between shotgun-toting robber Omar Little and defence lawyer Maurice Levy.

Levy: You are amoral, are you not? You are feeding off the violence and the despair of the drug trade. You are stealing from those who themselves are stealing the lifeblood from our city. You are a parasite who leaches off the culture of drugs ...

Omar (interrupting): Just like you, man.

Levy: Excuse me?

Omar: I got the shotgun, you got the briefcase. It's all in the game though, right?

(The judge shrugs as if acquiescing to his argument.)

It's a powerful scene, written by David Simon, and it plays a key part in establishing the myth of Omar as a modern-day Robin Hood who "ain't never put my gun on no citizen". But is it really plausible for him to suggest that he and Levy are morally comparable?

In series five, Levy is revealed to be implicated directly in criminal activity, and at the end of series one we see him implicitly encouraging drug kingpins Avon Barksdale and Stringer Bell to murder witnesses who could threaten them. But Omar doesn't know this; he's criticising Levy for doing his job, for making a living representing those accused of some of Baltimore's most destructive, violent crimes. According to Omar, he and Levy are both integral parts of the drug trade that is crushing the poorer areas of the city; they both make their living by "feeding off" the criminal narcotics industry, he argues.

Omar, as he freely admits, "robs drug dealers" for profit. In the pursuit of this aim, we have seen him use brutal violence, up to the point of attempted murder. As he points out, his moral "code" only allows him to attack those in the drug trade. The law doesn't recognise such a distinction as valid (in theory, although the police of The Wire do seem to in practice). Do we?

Levy is a lawyer who represents drug dealers and other more serious violent criminals connected with the trade – all the way up to murderers. Is The Wire suggesting that that is morally wrong? Shouldn't criminals, no matter how dislikeable, no matter how terrible their crimes, be entitled to competent legal representation? I think so.

Since we're talking about Levy, it's probably worth asking here whether the presentation of him as venal, corrupt and parasitical is antisemitic. He is the only prominent character we explicitly know to be Jewish, alluding to his faith himself through cultural references such as the brisket that always seems to be waiting for him at home.

In the final episode, after Herc – once a police officer, now Levy's private investigator – betrays his former colleagues by helping sabotage their case against drug lord Marlo, a delighted Levy rewards him with a dinner invite and the news that he is now "mishpocha" (family); thus a welcome into Jewishness is associated with Herc's personal betrayal and the decline of his professional values. The way Levy conforms to such negative stereotypes is especially notable since most other major figures in the programme are presented in a rounded way that allows them to display both positive and negative characteristics. Does it affect this analysis to know that Simon is himself Jewish? On balance, I think it does, but it is fair to note that most viewers would probably not be aware of this.

Also interesting in this episode is the prison book club scene where D'Angelo Barksdale, Avon's doomed nephew, movingly discusses F Scott Fitzgerald's The Great Gatsby.

Fitzgerald's book celebrates the beauty inherent in Americans' attempts to remake themselves in a new image, even when that doesn't succeed, perhaps especially when it doesn't succeed. "So we beat on, boats against the current … "

But D'Angelo sees in Jay Gatsby's failure to successfully reinvent himself his own failure to transcend his family, his upbringing, and all the other malign forces arrayed against him, a failure that has led him to the prison he finds himself in now. I don't think he sees much beauty in that, and I don't think The Wire does either.

As D'Angelo puts it: "It's like: you can change up, right? You can say you somebody new, you can give yourself a whole new story. But what came first is who you really are."

RUNNING TOTALS:

Murders: up one to 30, with the shocking strangulation of D'Angelo in the prison library.

Bunk drunk: up one to three after his night out with McNulty, a good effort that sees him throwing up into the waste paper basket the next day, to Lieutenant Daniels's disgust.

COMMENTS

UninventiveName Simon himself can't be accused of antisemitism with Levy because of his Jewish background but if you take that out of the equation (and, as you say, most viewers won't know that Simon is Jewish) then all you're left with is an entirely negative portrayal of the only Jewish character in the show that conforms to a lot of stereotypes. Simon often defends this by saying that there are plenty of Jewish lawyers that are genuinely like that in Baltimore – and I don't doubt it – but he could have shown both sides to the coin. It may be that Levy may seem more of a two-dimensional "evil" character than others on the show (with the exception of Marlo) because we never find out about his background or personal life. Characters such as Wee-Bey are morally dark really but we see moments of humanity from him and because of how well the street environment is shown we can at least see how he is a product of his environment. We're never really given that kind of context with Levy.

Anyway, leaving that aside, Omar's comments are half-true I suppose. They are entirely true about Levy (and I wouldn't be so quick to assume Omar doesn't know about Levy's involvement with the Barksdale crew, he's a fairly observant fellow) and lawyers like him, but about criminal lawyers in general less so. While I don't think anyone could disagree that criminal lawyers prosper from the existence of crime, which is partly what Omar is saying, to insinuate that they are as moral as a murderer because of that is taking it a bit far. Many (I would hope most) would argue that it's a moral right for everyone to have a fair trial, I suppose it depends on how you think the "bad guys" should be dealt with which is also a moral problem that the (amazing) series Dexter also raises.

BeaverLasVegas On your point about the prison book club scene; for me this is the single central theme of The Wire, that the premise of the American Dream; of the right of every individual to remake himself, no longer functions. America, the land of opportunity, has become as class-bound and lacking in social mobility as Dickens's London and its no accident that Simon has made these references to Dickens. The characters who thrive are the ones who don't try to go too far against the grain, those who question their role in the game or whatever network they are part of, end up coming to a bad end.

notyourusual But D' goes on to say:

"The only thing that make you different is what you really do. Gatsby, all them books in his library – he frontin with all them books but if you pull one down off the shelf ain't none of the pages ever been turned and he ain't read nay one of them books. Gatsby, he was what he was and he did what he did and 'cos he wasn't ready to get real with the story that shit caught up with him."

As I see it D was well and truly ready to "get real with the story". He had disassociated himself from Avon, disgusted with the hot shot murders: he ignored his uncles advances. He had clearly told Donette and his mother to "leave him be" and importantly, before the book club scene, he flushes his stash down the toilet.

I realise that David Simon seems to agree that there are "no second acts in American lives" but I think it very cruel for the sake of this world view to have D Angelo murdered just as he was about to turn some pages of his own.

RedThreat Who is the real criminal? Depends what you mean by criminal. Omar certainly had a moral code which, despite its flaws, he followed to the end and it's always going to be easy to root for him ahead of the charmless and amoral Levy. We don't get much backstory to Levy, for all we know he could simply be focused on getting as much money as he can to pay for his nephew's Leukaemia treatment, but you've got to doubt this from the little clues you get. As has been noted, he has no qualms about advising Avon to "clean-up loose-ends" in Season 1. You may also remember his treatment of D when Bunk and McNulty lay it on thick about the witness who got shot when D writes a letter of apology to a fictional bereaved family. I think Levy more or less clips him around the head and uses the phrase: "You people". Whatever his backstory, you do get the impression he's not a pleasant person.

I don't think David Simon deserves criticism for not balancing out his portrayal of any particular group, I don't think he's that clumsy or contrived (and isn't Landsman Jewish?). We don't get hung up on his portrayal of Irish–Americans as twinkle-in-the-eye drunks, Polacks as fat-headed labourers, ex-soviets as either ruthless gangsters or as sex industry workers. Levy could have been a Honduran transsexual for all I cared, what made him bad was what he did!

SaptarshiRay I don't think it matters that Levy's Jewish. Isn't Clay Davis's lawyer of Italian origin? And one of the slimiest individuals in the show? He and Colicchio are the only Italian–Americans i can think of in the programme – not a particularly pleasant portrait either. but does it matter? Oh, and Carcetti.

i just think simon doesn't like lawyers – and McNulty's "it's all one big club and everyone goes to the same country clubs" reproachful speech to Ronnie in season one reflect this. even when they screw each other in court, they all go to the same drinks evenings and play squash together. they take it all too impersonally for McNulty – ergo simon/burns etc

All the lawyers, even the good guys, are shown as still having a weakness for flattery and career-driven – always weighing up any case against what it will mean for them personally – even Ronnie and her boss, who are about the most ethical lawyers in the show. as shown by Pearlman's hesitance in issuing the warrants before the election but her new boss saying it showed guts – in which she sighs Lester's name in thanks.

as for Omar, i think he's talking about lawyers in general too. he has Levy down pat, he and his ilk live off the "violence and misery of the drug trade" as much as Omar but it begs the question, what would Omar do if there was no drug trade? can't see him working at a factory somehow but nor mugging old ladies. Levy would be defending celebrities or suing the police dept or the city like any other ambulance chaser.

joedoone No way is Levy just doing his job; that might apply to lawyers on the taxi rank principle, whereby they take whatever case that comes along. Levy is on a retainer. He knows exactly what his clients are, and what they do, and where his salary comes from. He is just as deep in the criminal conspiracy as they are. He is just like the syndicate lawyer in Public Enemies.

dirtycheat On the Levy v Omar point I thought I would throw in a lawyer's perspective (though I am not a criminal lawyer).

It seems to be agreed that a lawyer who is simply defending his client would have the moral high ground over Omar. On the other hand someone in the position of Levy who is up to his neck in the drug trade is worse than Omar. However, if Levy was not actually doing anything criminal himself and was just defending his clients aggressively but knowing that they were involved in the drugs trade, there is more of a grey area. For what it's worth, the law society code of ethics in the UK says a lawyer should defend all clients to the extent permitted by law, but should not run a defence that is contrary to specific facts he is aware of. For example, if Levy knows for a fact that Bird killed Gant he can still challenge the quality of evidence produced by the prosecution, but cannot allow Bird to take the stand and say he did not do it.

I am also interested in the strength of Omar's moral code. He would never pull a gun on a citizen. This allows us to like him because as citizens ourselves we do not have to feel threatened by him. But, the Wire has taught us that not every one in the Game is a bad person and many people – including the corner boys Omar often turns his gun on – have few realistic options in life.

The point about options is another reason why we prefer Omar to Levy. Levy could easily have chosen an honest life and still have been reasonably wealthy. For guys like Omar who are born on the streets what choice is there? The Game or a minimum wage job. Saying that, Omar seems to enjoys what he does – both the money and the rip and run. Given the choice between working in a cafe at the airport and robbing drug dealers, Omar would always chose the latter. On balance though, for me Omar still beats Levy on this point on the grounds that we don't know what Omar would have become if he had the opportunities in life that Levy presumably had.

Wigface In The Wire Levy is perceived as nasty not because of his religion or culture but because of his actions and his job. He exists in the Wire, just as Bill Rawls and Herc do, to show that dishonesty, criminality, lack of clear morals and thirst for power are not behaviours linked only to the poor, and in the case of Baltimore, mainly black, community. Even McNulty and Bunk, the sometime heroes of the show, are entirely questionable in their morality.

What makes the Wire so truly brilliant is the way nobody – no police officer, no representative of any of our celebrated minorities, no drug addict or child – escapes wholly unscathed from Simon and Burns' criticism. It is, in that way, more like real life than anything I've ever seen before, and reducing it to discussions about possible racism and antisemitism entirely misses the point.

Even Lester Freamon succumbs in the end to stereotyping and cons in the name of keeping the wire open…

RexGo I'm from Baltimore and worked for 20 years as a prosecutor there. It is always amusing to recognise people I knew and worked with (or opposed in court) among The Wire's characters. Levy is quite obviously based on a well-known Baltimore defence counsel, now disbarred and last seen driving a taxi cab, who represented the drug kingpin on whom the Avon Barksdale character is based. I'm sure the writers had no antisemitic intentions. The real-life "Levy" was always talking about the brisket waiting at home. They were just having fun creating a character based on a guy they knew – like Judge Phelan and Bunk, both immediately recognisable to anybody who worked in Baltimore's courthouse. (I tried a double murder with the real-life "Bunk" as the lead detective. He was a great one and a delight to work with. In season 5 I got to work as an extra in two episodes – a background homicide detective – and shared some "Bunk" stories with the actor playing him, who had met and gotten acquainted with his character's model.)

EPISODE 7 – The women of The Wire

TOM HOPKINS (AKA TOMBO)

"Do you know what I fell in love with first? Do you? Your ambition. Where did that man go?"

As the detail moves on to tracking cans and D'Angelo is laid to rest, it's a couple of smaller moments that I'd like to focus on.

First, the cracks in Daniels's marriage get a little bit wider as Marla makes clear her disappointment at her husband still being pOlice. Second, Brianna is inconsolable as D's funeral approaches. Is it fanciful to suggest that at least part of that is down to the knowledge that if she'd let him walk away from the game he'd probably still be alive?

For me, these two events highlight a particular aspect of The Wire, an unusually cynical view of its female characters.

In most popular culture, at least culture based on the rough and tumble end of life, women are portrayed either as a civilising influence (Kay Adams's doomed attempts to keep Michael Corleone out of the olive oil business or, if you're taking GCSE English Lit this year, the reason why there are no girls in Lord of the Flies) or as helpless victims waiting to be rescued (most bad action films and a fair number of good ones). The women of The Wire take on different roles.

First up, there are the women who throw themselves so completely into the game that they become, in some senses, indistinguishable from the boys. Snoop is the most obvious example of this, Chris's protégé and every bit as fearsome. But is Kima so very different?

Still, as terrifying and unsettling as Snoop undoubtedly is, there's a sort of honesty to what she does. I'm not sure you can say the same about Brianna. It's a bleak worldview that has the strongest female characters acting as instigators, pushing their husbands, brothers and sons further into the game and making sure they stay in no matter what. Brianna pushed D to toe the line right to the end and it seems she'd been doing so all his life. When it looked like he might inform on the Barksdale crew over Wallace she made it clear that "You ain't got to worry about my child, I raised that boy and I raised him right." Doesn't seem like the lad had much chance from day one.

Still, in Brianna's defence, D is at least third generation Bawlmore drug family so presumably she was born into the game too. As I think has been mentioned on the boards already, maybe she was only passing on her upbringing to him? Unless I'm missing something though, I don't think De'Londa Brice has any such excuse.

De'Londa's obviously got used to the good life with Wee-Bey and it's pretty clear that on her list of priorities Namond's well-being comes some way below the boy keeping her in the manner to which she's become accustomed. Although we maybe should have guessed that her nurturing skills weren't up to much given Bey had to get someone else to look after his fish when he went to Philly.

Again, on the other side of the tracks the story's not so very different. Marla Daniels is in a different game from Brianna and De'Londa, but she pushes Cedric just the same. If we're on the Shakespearean/classical trip then she's probably Lady Macbeth whilst they're Agrippina.

So, who does that leave us with? Theresa uses Jimmy as much as he uses everybody else. Nerese? Sheeeeeeeeeiiiiitttt, I'm not sure she's any straighter than Clay Davis. Smarter maybe, but not straighter.

Of course there are exceptions, but, just like for the boys, it seems that in this world the girls who aren't takers get took. Miss Anna does right by Randy and gets her house firebombed for her troubles, Beadie does right by everyone and gets saddled with McNulty.

So what's The Wire telling us? That women are occasionally good, occasionally bad but mostly flawed and weak. Just like men. That's a sort of equality, right?

QUOTE OF THE WEEK:

"It just couldn't stand up to the modern urban crime environment." Herc bemoans the demise of Mr Fuzzy Dunlop.

COMMENTS

RedThreat I agree there are strong female characters in The Wire (other examples you don't mention are Rhonda and the one who helps Carcetti get elected, who both have complexity and some backstory, particularly Rhonda) but I'd argue they don't get the same bite of the cherry as the men do in terms of developing their stories or presenting inner turmoil. It's rare that you feel a "first person" thing when the women are involved (the soapy stuff around Kima's indifference to becoming a "father", for instance, left me cold). I find myself getting annoyed with any accusations of racism directed at The Wire (as avid comments readers may have noticed from stuff I've written on here before!) but with the women characters I think there's a point here. I wouldn't call it sexism, just a failure to identify.

The writers are men, so maybe they just naturally find it difficult to focus on women and their deeper motives unless they are behaving like men (me too, queue "take my wife, please do" type thoughts!), but we do get snippets of more traditionally feminine traits: Brianna is torn as a mother, someone in a previous comment mentioned McNulty pushing her guilt buttons when explaining why he didn't bring his concerns about D's "suicide" to her first and you can see it rip her up inside, really good acting for me. But there are omissions where you suspect the writers could naturally have given a bigger voice to a female character but were hesitant about exploring things further: you never see Ziggy's mum ("you leave her out of this" as Frank says, and they do), what happened to Bodie's grandma? She had a wonderful little chat with Herc in Season 1 (there's a similar character living bang in the middle of Hamsterdam, Season 3, who just comes across as mad as a bottle of chips). What did Omar end up telling his grandma? Why is Michael's mum such a complete f*ck up? What drives every lonely women in West Baltimore to start baking pies for Cutty??!!

lileskimo I've always had a problem with the Wire's portrayal of women and not because they're shown as flawed but because their flaws are not examined in the same way as the men's are. The writers do an excellent job of showing how the game shapes the people who encounter it, how it's a struggle for Bubbles, Cutty, D'Angelo, Wallace et al to escape it. It does not excuse or justify the behaviour of those who perpetuate it but it at least examines how they grew up in it, are trapped within it and their behaviour is determined by it. This is especially true in season 4 when you see the young 'uns drawn into the game in a heartbreaking and inevitable way. The problem is, this is all looked at from a male perspective. Where the writers give us an understanding of how the men got to be the way they are, they do not do the same for the women. You end up with a raft of "Lady Macbeth" characters (in Shakespeare – great, since then one of the single most over used misogynistic stock characters in film/TV) who are like they way they are because... well, they just are. Bad wives, bad mothers. Fair enough they are defined only by their relationship to the men in their lives, in the world of the game that's pretty much all they can do. But why not look at that? Why not look at D'Angelo's mother and how such a clearly astute, intelligent, business-minded, ruthless woman is limited to the role of "mother". If she was male she'd be running the show! Same applies to De'Londa – yes, she's a nasty piece of work. Yes, she manipulates her son in a sickening way. Yes, she shows nothing but concern for material things. So do most of the men in the game too, but at least they get a certain amount of understanding from the writers as we see them pulled into the game and formed by it. In season 4, where are the 12, 13, 14 year old girls? The ones who start to learn that they're valued only for their bodies, who have babies too young (something looked at in the excellent book The Corner), who have everything needed to become a player but are only permitted to be played? Who are fiercely ambitious for their men as they are not allowed ambition themselves?

It's interesting that Snoop and Kima are the only functioning women in a man's world, they are both gay and so can to a certain extent be themselves without the pressure of their relation to a husband/boyfriend. Even then, the writers deal with Kima by, in effect, giving her the "male" role – she cheats, struggles against domesticity and is distant from her partner and child. So not much more is explored to do with her being specifically female – just the same, traditionally masculine behaviour transposed onto a woman. As for Snoop, well the level of hatred directed towards her on previous wire postings, in my opinion, shows either a one-dimensional portrayal that does not go much past "this person is a bad person" or else a disturbing level of double-standards in posters that relish the amorality of other, male characters.

midatlantic A couple of comments that relate primarily to Rhonda and to Teri, both lawyers in aggressively male environments of politics and criminal prosecution. What I like and admire about The Wire is that, while there may be limitations to the way they portray women, in Rhonda and Teri you them at least avoiding two common traps about the cliched way women are portrayed on TV and in films.

First, they don't turn Rhonda into Ally McBeal, even though we see her through relationship ups and downs. If she does any soul-searching about her dysfunctional relationship with McNulty, we don't see it beyond a few pointed remarks she makes directly to him rather than to (stereotypically female) confidantes. And she does get herself out of that relationship and into a better one with Daniels. She does comparatively little carping about Daniels' continuing support for Marla's political career, and thereby avoids the whiny/clingy cliche too.

Second, Teri doesn't use sex to get power, she uses power to get sex. It is not admirable, and it may mean that she is another "man in disguise" character, but it is refreshing just for a change to see a politically powerful woman, still young enough to be sexually desirable to men, not being portrayed as manipulating her sexuality. You don't have to like or admire Teri, but you have to respect the fact that her success derives from understanding the Game of politics. In fact, I loved that her first encounter with McNulty was a complete role reversal, with her ignoring him after sex in favour of work.

timthemonkey I can't help but think you sold poor Beadie short, as most people do. Whilst she's not "natural pOlice", under Lester's guidance she does show some talent for proper police work after years of being essentially a glorified security guard. Also she is the only character in the wire to successfully balance a career with a stable home life with the kids. She even made to rein in McNulty, a man once dubbed "no good for people" by his best friend, let's not forget, and turn him in to a functioning adult, for a time anyway. That in itself deserves a medal!

PepperT As a female viewer, I never had any problem with the way women were portrayed. The Wire gives us insight into the big Game. To me its portrayal of hierarchies work and the politics involved in the struggle for power were done brilliantly. And let's face it, the Game as it stands today was invented by and is still largely played by men. The amount of influence women have on this was realistically demonstrated in the show. It is a portrayal of urban America, not Scandinavia.

Lingli I'm sure I read on the "What Real Thugs Think of the Wire" blog that the "thugs" in question were also disturbed by the lack of female representation, one of them going as far as to say that it's the women who run things, who make all the decisions. I wonder if it is to do with Simon and Burns just not being that good at writing women – in which case, why not get in a couple of female writers?

mathnawi The women are either angels, fallen or otherwise (Beadie and Freamon's ex-stripper girlfriend), ball busting Lady MacBs (Brianna etc) or basically written as men.

jessicaeccles As a avid female viewer of "The Wire" I have never had a problem with the way the female characters are portrayed. Categorising them as angels or wh*res seems a pretty accurate way as to how they are seen by the male characters.

The scene that always made me wince was when Shardene put D'Angelo on the spot after her friend had been found dead. She asked him if she was trash and all he could says was that she was beautiful. You could see that he had no comprehension that she might identify with the murdered girl – because even as one of the more sensitive characters he could not see the girls as people.

In a world where women are only seen as commodities, it's not surprising that they are only out for what they can get.

And I do love the way the so desperately right-on poster thinks that any women like Kima who is not enthralled with parenthood and likes her job "acts like a man" …

UninventiveName I do think there is a case to be made for the lack of female representation in season 4 and 5, which is fairly inexcusable.

Rhayader Snoop did make at least one reference to her sexuality. When Bunk and Kima stopped Snoop and Chris in season 4 – the same stop during which they discovered the hidden gun compartment in the SUV – Bunk makes a comment about wanting pussy. Snoop responds that she would like the same thing.

jessicaeccles I have a bit of a crush on Rhonda. She's warm, funny, stroppy. She does a difficult job well, and she gets to see Cedric with his shirt off. And AT NO POINT is the phrase "biological clock" mentioned. Nor is it seen as a big deal that she has no husband or kids. I can guarantee you that in 99% of dramas, she would have to be portrayed as conflicted or missing something. Nor is she judged for sleeping with Jimmy and then moving on to a better man when she gets tired of his shit.

And the Wonderful Beadie also points out that no mark husband thought she had her priorities wrong in loving her job. But she doesn't give the job up. Mr Simon, for all his flaws, seems to understand that some women do really love working.

Shamone Firstly, as a feminist academic, I find it rather Macho-Revisionist to even postulate the premise of this article... And secondly, even if we are to countenance the proposition of the "treatment" of women – with all the projected connotations of victimhood that implies – this article should certainly have been commissioned to a female writer, not an agent of the patriarchy (however unwitting). I can't help wondering whether this closet aggression is some manner of dimly shrouded male jealousy at the manifest female power as the source of life?

McNultyWire There you go Shamone, giving a fuck when it aint your turn to give a fuck.

lileskimo Interview with David Simon:

13) Your female characters are very strong people. Are they based on anyone you actually know?

I tend to suspect that my female characters are, to quote a famous criticism of Hemingway, men with tits... I think it is among my weaknesses and I work harder on those scenes, I think, because I feel vulnerable. In the journalism, the answer to your question is obvious: Fran Boyd is most definitely based on Fran Boyd, Tyreeka on Tyreeka. By allowing themselves to be portrayed and letting me get to know them, they allowed me to write women better than I otherwise would. Fictionally, Kima Greggs is based on a couple of lesbian officers I knew, but largely, I write her as a man and then, I confess, its Sonja Sohn who adds all the subtlety in her performance. So, if it's thin ice, I'm still above it, at any rate.

EPISODE 8 – What do you do with the hump?

ROB WILLIS (AKA REDTHREAT)

Humps are everywhere: in your office, driving your bus, on the other end of a "helpline". One reason I was drawn so deeply into The Wire is the show's representation of public sector dysfunction. Where incompetence cannot carry the ultimate penalty, the hump will find a home.

A hump is a badly motivated incompetent, and we're not used to seeing them on TV. Most cop shows are full of highly motivated people with limitless resources tying up all their personal loose ends by the end of each episode. Irredeemable humps may make the occasional cameo from Internal Investigations, but only to throw a few hurdles in the path of the hero.

But we know life isn't like this. In public institutions incapable of recognising and rewarding real achievement, no good deed will go unpunished. As players climb the greasy career pole and real pOlice – or their equivalents – quietly make cases as best they can, the humps wait for the right moment to ask for overtime or retirement.

So what do you do with your hump? Hump management in The Wire consists of shunting them around. Detective Cole is assigned elsewhere when Landsman has to take the 13 Jane Does. The detail that kicks off season one is a collection of BPD cast-offs: Prez, Santangelo, Polk and Mahon (plus Lester – a hump as far as the department is concerned). Polk is so bad he gets passed around twice, returning in the detail of humps Burrell throws together at the start of season two.

You could say there's a culture of humpness at BPD. Despite Lester's brilliance, he spends a lot of time tinkering with his miniature furniture. Bunk undermines a meeting with a ranking officer by retching into a wastepaper bin. Landsman, in between bursts of deceptively effective man-management, will peer at proceedings over a copy of Club International.

Despite this, The Wire shows that a hump can be redeemed. Prez is twice saved from a career of humpdom, first by Lester's paternalism and then by finding his vocation in teaching. Daniels refuses to dump a hump on another team when Polk turns up drunk in season one. Polk is last seen contented in season five, and Daniels is glad things worked out for him.

Humps can help, too. Daniels accepts Prez on his detail but gets the almost invisibly efficient Sydnor in return. The affable but humpish Lieutenant Asher in season four obliviously lets Freamon follow the money trail to Clay while he designs his retirement home. Burrell twice hopes a detail of humps will keep his political allies happy by not doing anything silly like solving crimes.

The show contrasts the lack of similar slack available on the corners. You fall asleep in homicide and some wag cuts off your tie (obviously there's a lot of guys falling asleep on the job); you doze off in the pit and Bodie slings a bottle at you, smashing inches above your head. A Carver quote from the end of season two encapsulates this difference perfectly: "They screw up, they get beaten. We screw up, we get a pension."

And so to Thomas "Herc" Hauk. Is he a hump? I suggest he's not. He's an idiot and we count his fuck-ups on an episode by episode basis, but he lacks one key ingredient: poor motivation. He's ambitious, opportunistic and refuses to be seen as a failure. He exploits his moment with the mayor to get a promotion; he pumps his old colleagues for info when working for Levy; he spins a yarn about being credit-crunched to get Carver to use his card to buy the expensive mic.

Even the bonkers Fuzzy Dunlop scam displays some warped initiative. But he and his sort are more dangerous than humps; ambitious incompetents who refuse to recognise their limitations. No matter how many times he fucks up, he's still back for more. No reflection, no sense of regret or failure, just a conviction that he isn't getting the rewards he deserves.

So let's celebrate a world that looks after its humps. They have a function in the hive and their lack of ambition is a useful safely valve – if we're honest there's probably a bit of hump in all of us.

RUNNING TOTALS:

McNulty drunk: two more. Once when he crashes his car, twice. Once when he's perching on his battered car the next night with Bunko. I'm not allowing his drinks with Beadie – the fact he walks away from her house without trying it on indicates clear sobriety. So the number hits a dozen.

COMMENTS

pompeyplayup I have to disagree with you here. Herc is most definitely a hump. His total inaction when it comes to Randy or to

Bubbles who both suffer life-changing moments as a result is inexcusable.

On the other hand, Prez is no hump. He's natural poh-lice when it comes to following the paper trail. Yes he's not cut out for the street but that does not make him more of a hump than Herc, who does not seem to be cut out for anything much at all.

isotope I don't think Herc is a hump…for all his poor judgment, he's courageous and diligent, which is more than can be said for Polk and Mahon.

sarahjoanbradley I found Herc to be a total and utter irredeemable idiot for all 5 series. I think this is nicely illustrated by the differing fates of Carver and Herc – initially they both seem like a pair of morons, destined to bumble along, cracking heads and filling their pockets until pension years – but Carv develops into a loyal and semi-efficient poh-lice, who at least learns some lessons and becomes something of a leader. Herc remains a self-serving muddled prat throughout.

midatlantic Prez is manifestly in the wrong job, and is incompetent at crucial aspects of it. However, I don't think anyone can accuse him of poor motivation. In series 1, after his assault on a local boy results in his being confined to office duties, he appears to be coasting, but in fact takes the initiative to uncover the code that masks the pager numbers. If I remember correctly, it is only after this revelation of his talents that Lester takes Prez under his wing. Part of the difficulty for Prez is that even his talents aren't much valued by other police. This is evident in Landsman's character assassination following Prez's shooting of Waggoner in series 3.

We often don't get all the background we would like on characters. This is certainly true with Prez. You have to wonder why he entered the BPD in the first place. There's no mention, for example, of a family tradition of being a police officer. He clearly has enough college education to become a trainee teacher in the apparent gap of about a year between series 3 and 4. Did Prez marry Valchek's daughter before or after becoming a police officer? It is impossible to say, but it does seem credible that his career was sponsored (and therefore trapped) by Valchek right from the beginning. Certainly Valchek kills Prez's career with kindness (the most charitable interpretation) by constantly rescuing him from his errors, and worse.

I also don't think you can attribute Lester's furniture-making to aspects of hump-ness. Partly, you could attribute it to his belief that a police officer needs to have a life beyond "the case" (see Ep. 9, Series 3). Partly, I expect it was to keep his mind active, and possibly even to from going insane, on the long years of pawn shop duty.

SaptarshiRay Herc is undoubtedly a moron, with too much bluster, little brain, tact or common sense. And i like how we're often led into believing he's going to change (apologising to one of the hopper's grans – i forget whose, telling 2 young recruits about making a case with your brain, using his initiative) but never really does.

On the other hand, he uses tactics we would say make good, creative officers if it were someone else. Both Fuzzy Dunlop and the camera are not intrinsically bad ideas, they are just poorly executed by idiots. And Herc spends his time trying to make up for his cock-ups, which lead to so many people suffering. I can never forgive him for Randy and Bubs, yet at the same time you can plainly see all the guy wants to be is good police.

I think if he'd been transferred to SWAT or riot patrol, he may have been an asset to the BPD but a detective is not what he was born to be.

EPISODE 9 – Whose war is it anyway?

SAPTARSHI RAY

Baltimore's finest, shrewdest, dumbest, most powerful and most petty make deals in a series of moments that act as touchstones for several storylines that will come to reshape the city and its inhabitants over the next few episodes.

Valchek accuses Burrell of reneging on their deal to somehow implicate Frank Sobotka in some – any – form of crime. Stringer makes a deal with Proposition Joe to take his product after a shootout on a corner leads to a nine-year-old boy being killed and the BPD shutting down the drug trade for a few days. Ziggy makes a deal with Gleckas to offload some cars he's looking to steal. Nick Sobotka makes a deal with Vondas and White Mike to start peddling g-pacs. The Greek exploits the war on terror to exchange tip-offs for information on drugs bound for Colombian "narco-terrorists" with his FBI handler. And, finally, Avon makes a deal to bring some extra muscle to his organisation's ranks – the bow-tied, Atlantic Monthly-reading, Walther PPK-carrying bad motherfucker, Brother Mouzone.

Valchek's petty one-upmanship leads directly to the detail discovering the Greek. The call placed by McNulty's Fed buddy, Fitz, to Agent Ernesto Koutris leads directly to a road that has Frank's murder at the end of it. And Ziggy's attempt to lift himself into higher criminal circles leads ultimately to his own tragic climax.

So while we can be rationally sceptical over whether the players' fates are predestined, we can certainly see that many of them are the victims of their own hubris, parochialism or plain stupidity.

And the results are not necessarily bad for the characters in question. The Greek, as you would expect, uses a piece of bad luck to his advantage. Despite Gleckas popping up on the detail's radar through surveillance of the docks, a deal that has gone awry with the Colombians allows him to horsetrade with Agent Koutris, thereby gaining his favour and favours.

"The world is smaller now" he says, "and the FBI are very interested in this," as the war on terror encroaches on the war on drugs, not for the first time. The deal between the FBI and the Greek takes wider interests of national security as its mantra, with collateral damage, such as local police investigations, perfectly acceptable. Koutris gets info on drug smuggling and volatile chemicals transported through international shipping channels, while the Greek gets info on people snooping into his affairs. A simple illustration of how the abstract has an impact on the specific.

The drugs brought in and sold on by the Greek, repackaged by Bodie and his crew as "Bin Ladens" and "WMDs" ("this shit will mass-destruct your ass"), leading to shootouts on the corner that kill a child getting ready for school … For that boy's mother, and this corner of the Western, the war on terror and the war on drugs are indistinguishable.

QUOTE OF THE WEEK:

"Calm the fuck down! It ain't like they're going to flush a half dozen whores down the toilet!" – Bunk chastises an overzealous officer during the brothel raid.

RUNNING TOTALS:

Murders: up one to 31: the poor kid shot through his window during the gun battle on the corner – leading Bunny Colvin, on his first appearance, to question "just what the hell is it that we're doing?"

McNulty giving a fuck when it's not his turn: in a literal sense Jimmy does this with the two prostitutes while going undercover with a hilariously bad English accent at the brothel (ooh the layers of irony), but it doesn't really count.

Herc fuck-ups: still on six and a half, though he does show some self-awareness this week, as he hilariously says to Carver: "I'm starting to think that as criminal investigators we're not really respected."

COMMENTS

Tombo I think I might have to admit to being something of a hump here. I'd always assumed that Koutris was dirty, rather than this being an accepted FBI trade off.

SaptarshiRay hey Tombo – I think most of us were in the same boat first time round, i thought he was a mole and i think the fact he has a Greek name is a deliberate red herring – but then i put that down to Mr Pelecanos's influence – he loves exploring his Greek roots and community in his books so why shouldn't he here? – Fitz's speech in the last episode clears it all up. Though it stretches credibility a little bit for me that a high-ranking agent would be so overtly complicit in a murder – frank. or does it? the name of the game is terror. btw who is it that Fitz manages to blag surveillance on for jimmy as he enters their name as mohammed abdul ahmed or something, and stick it through as a terror case? was it avon himself?

midatlantic SaptarshiRay, It was Stringer Bell. McNulty mentions that his real first name is Russell, but Fitz says that for the purpose of the wiretap, he name was Ahmed.

McNultyWire Bloody hell this blog makes my brain hurt! I'm not altogether convinced that Agent Koutris is clean. Its not beyond the realms of possibility that he is in the pay of the Greek rather than affording him protection in the interests of 'homeland security'. No one advances in the BPD without making shady deals and getting into bed with the enemy so why would we believe an FBI agent is any different. Surely the advantage to the Greek was in removing the Colombians from the market place and leaving them with a monopoly. A parallel here with Marlo forcing Avon out – same shit, different toilet. Fitz buys into the terror argument because of Koutris's new role in the FBI not because he has any real evidence.

btw brain hurt is infinitely preferable to brain death of most other US TV.

ElDerino I think Koutris is clean, largely because that makes a better fit with the general depiction of the FBI in the series. By and large, the FBI are shown in a fairly negative light – their level of resources makes a painful contrast with those of the city pOlice, but it's clear that their priorities are intensely political: they're only interested in terrorist-related material, union-busting and taking down corrupt Democratic politicians; the only time they're any use in improving real-life matters is when Fitz helps out on the sly. In that context, it makes it all the more galling if Koutris is actually on the straight.

whatisthere2 Koutris is definitely dirty, he is in deep with The Greek, also it is him that gets Frank killed by leaking his evidence on drugs to The Greek.

joedoone Koutris is not dirty, except in the sense of the many "accommodations" which America makes in its "War On Terror". The Greeks are intelligence assets, to be protected against mere law enforcement, and that is what Koutris does. When Daniels, near the end of Season Three, needs to shorten the time in which cellphone companies process wiretap applications, he tells the FBI's Fitzhugh "You still owe me for that docklands thing", and Fitz obliges, temporarily transforming Russell Stringer Bell into an "Ahmed". Incidentally, anyone know why Stringer is called Stringer? Better than Poot or Puddin or Peanut, at least.

What the FBI does to protect its assets in The Wire is small beer to what has gone on in real life, e.g. when Churchill let German attacks go ahead rather than alert them to the fact that the British had cracked the Enigma code. Bletchley Park stayed a secret till the 1970s. During The Troubles, assets were protected and information was sat upon. I'm sure we never hear but a fraction of what goes on.

EPISODE 10 – Going postal

JUDITH SOAL

The moment when Ziggy walks back into the warehouse and shoots Double G dead has to come as one of the show's most shocking.

Not only the fact that a Baltimore nobody could take out one of the Greek's top men, but also Ziggy's personal transformation from an immature object of ridicule to a person of (rather severe) consequence.

And of course the explanation is in the ridicule. For as well as going to a lot of trouble to recreate life in the pOlice and on the streets etc authentically, the Wiremakers have done their homework when it comes to the psychology of their characters. Although Ziggy's behaviour is astounding, it certainly rings true. So much so that I think he could come straight out of the psychiatrists' bible, the Diagnostic and Statistical Manual of Mental Disorders, and be given a clinical diagnosis of narcissistic personality disorder.

Narcissism is characterised by a kind of grandiosity or "bigging yourself up" – as we've seen Ziggy do countless times, probably to hide a low self esteem, as well as a failure to empathise with others (think duck). Although we are all a bit narcissistic, especially as children, it becomes a disorder when you get stuck in fixed patterns of behaviour and are unable to evaluate situations realistically or respond appropriately.

We've spoken quite a lot about how the characters are determined by their social and political milieu, but clearly there's more to Ziggy's problems than that. Psychiatrists don't know what causes personality disorders but suggest (as they always do) it has something to do with internal vulnerability (nature) and early parenting (nurture): in the case of narcissism they stress inconsistent parenting involving excessive praise or criticism that is not balanced by realistic feedback. Frank, anyone?

People with personality disorders tend to function fairly well (as opposed to, say, those with psychotic illnesses) until the pressure really piles on. We can see it building up on Ziggy over the past few weeks: he fails at being a drug dealer, Nick cuts him out of the action with the Greeks, his colleagues push him into a humiliating fight with Maui, the duck dies, etc. It's interesting that the insult that pushes him over the edge – being called a Malaka (wanker) by Double G – is the same one that George mutters quietly when Nick first brings Ziggy to the diner.

The experts tell us that when narcissists are rejected, humiliated or criticised the most common response is one of rage – and again The Wire plays it perfectly.

Other points of interest from this week's episode:

- We've talked quite a bit about the possible stereotyping of Levy as the only recognisable Jew. What about Brother Mouzone as the only known Muslim (as well as the suggested links to the Nation of Islam, he says Allahu Akbar (God is greatest) when Omar shoots him)?

- The scene when Frank accuses Nick of not doing enough to look after his cousin, and Nick hands it straight back: "You're his father."

- That fantastic final scene where McNulty sits painfully typing up the documents necessary for the search warrant with one finger while the Greeks clear out the warehouse and flush the evidence down the drain. Poetry.

FAVOURITE QUOTE:

Omar's T-shirt: "I am the American dream."

RUNNING TOTALS:

Herc fuck-ups: up by a half to seven – he and Carver are too busy chatting to notice when Spiros leaves the diner, but it doesn't really matter because there's a bug in the car.

Bubbles attempting to get clean: still two. Bubs does a lot of staying dirty.

COMMENTS

midatlantic As a "compare and contrast", it's worth remembering that there are two characters who react violently to a humiliation in this episode. We also have the wonderful scene of Prez punching Valchek out. But we don't think of Prez as having had a mental breakdown, at least I don't. It seems almost a rational, although not reasonable, response to a public, partly physical humiliation by his father in law. It is a reminder to him that Valchek does not consider him his own man. Furthermore, Valchek wants to take him out of an environment where he is effective and valued. At the beginning of this episode, we have the montage of Prez assembling the evidence on the case to date, giving the viewer a clear demonstration of his skills. And then this. Simon and co. do the same thing in series 3, where in the two episodes preceding Prez's shooting of Det. Waggoner, there are a number of scenes showing Prez's effectiveness as an investigator.

I think we would regard Prez as having been provoked into violence, however unwise his reaction was – and certainly that is the way that Daniels plays the incident in order to convince Valchek not to pursue it publicly. On the other hand, Ziggy's reaction seems entirely out of proportion to the provocation he receives, irrational and out of control.

McNultyWire I'll leave the psychiatric assessments to those more qualified than me but its my guess Ziggy was one doctor's appointment away from a course of Ritolin.

Family is a recurring theme in the Wire and the general standpoint is that family is "everything". However, throughout the series we see this tested and challenged. The Ziggy storyline explores family within the Polish blue collar culture in failing industry in a failing city. Family cant really help because "family" is too busy surviving. Frank is father to the union more than to his son and Nick is struggling to even be a family. Both get involved in crime to protect their "family". Ziggy (ADHD and all) is searching for some place in all this but never quite finds it. The best he can do is flash his dick in public, draw attention to himself with a duck and fail to get respect when he does pull off a decent scam (the car thefts).

Ziggy rings true to to me, I knew kids like him growing up. We looked up to them and they frightened us right up to the point we realised they were all piss and wind. Trouble is in Baltimore they can get a gun!

Paul3294 Let's not forget before we start waving the DSM around that Ziggy was ripped off and manhandled (again) just before he shot Gleckas, so there was a motive. Candidates who "go postal" usually kill indiscriminately. The surprising thing for me is that he didn't drive away.

For a show with so many gangsters, there wasn't that many sociopathic killings. Forgetting the rights and wrongs there was logic behind most murders. Apart from the manner in which Chris Partlow kills Michael's stepfather, now there's a case for the DSM.

And Kenard.

Baronvonberghausen In regards to your definition of his personality, I'm intrigued to see if his response after the shooting is textbook "narcissistic personality disorder".

He seems genuinely sickened by the sight of his reckless handiwork when talking about it with Frank, does this sense of remorse fit into your diagnosis?

judithsoal good point baron – i think it does in a way. narcissist PDs are not on the psychotic spectrum and so still have some contact with reality, he realises this is not going to end well for him – and i think he's demonstrating more self-pity than remorse here, evidenced by him making Landsman change the statement to say that GG begged him not to shoot. (altho that one detail did strike me as a touch odd). but PDs are capable of remorse, in patches.

you could say that the presence of so much anti-social behaviour on the streets has more to do with the context than any intrinsic mental illness, which is of course true. perhaps it's just that those with anti-social traits thrive in this environment, and rise to the top.

(oh, and just because Zig had a motive doesn't mean his reaction wasn't informed by a psychological problem. nick wouldn't have done that).

alvanoto Ziggy has a big cock, though, so how can he have low self-esteem?

EPISODE 11 – Facing the music

PAUL OWEN

When The Wire breaks its music policy, it does so with a bang. The final seven or eight minutes of this episode – in which the insistent wail of Efige Efige by Stelios Kazantzidis wafts in and out of the Greeks' goodbye dinner, the conversations between Frank and Nicky

Sobotka, and the calls and faxes to and from the FBI, Agent Koutris, and the Greek – are simply stunning, and end in an unbearably tense moment as the union boss marches towards the drug suppliers under the immense concrete pillars of Baltimore's Key Bridge, and the Greek gives his No 2, Vondas, the verdict that seals Frank's fate: "Your way. It won't work."

The fact that the programme rarely uses such incidental music makes moments like these all the more powerful. Another memorable example comes after apprentice hitman Michael's first murder in series four: his mentor, Chris Partlow, murmurs: "You can look him in the eye now. No matter who he is or what he's done, you look him right in the eye," and Paul Weller's steel guitar chimes gradually in over Michael's nodding, half-conscious face, the streetlights playing over the back of the car in a superb, Scorsese-esque fusion of words and music.

But the Frank Sobotka scene here also draws attention to another aspect of the programme: its pacing, which is really quite unusual. The first few episodes of every series as a rule proceed in a rather stately manner, introducing a character here and a character flaw there, drawing attention, often quite subtly, to all the guns that, in Chekhov's metaphor, will presumably go off later on.

Then, about two thirds of the way through, there is usually a huge, dramatic event – Kima's shooting, or Omar and Brother Mouzone's tracking down of Stringer Bell – which suddenly speeds the whole thing up immeasurably and sets the last few episodes rolling along at a great lick as all the loose ends are suddenly gathered together.

This approach has an upside: it means the last third of every series is very exciting. I remember first watching this week's episode late on a work night last year; I think it was past one by the time it finished. But I could not go to bed. I had to put the next episode on and find out what was going to happen to Frank.

But the unusual pacing can also be seen as a flaw, and I think it becomes a problem in two series – this one and series four – when it is combined with the introduction of whole sets of crucial new characters, not as background, as when we first meet politician Tommy Carcetti or the Baltimore Sun journalists, but as the focus of the show. Then the early episodes can drag, and it probably takes too long until the viewer is properly engaged with the series.

We learn a lot about Frank in this episode, written by David Simon and novelist George Pelecanos, or maybe a lot of what we've worked out for ourselves is made explicit for the first time. "I knew I was wrong," he tells policewoman Beadie Russell of his dealings with the Greeks. "But in my head I thought I was wrong for the right reasons." His conversation with his brother exposes the same exculpatory defence: that every time he committed a crime it was to help the union, the dockworkers, and the industry of the docks itself. Yet his lobbyist makes it clear to Frank that his illegal activities have scuppered any prospect of reopening the grain pier, the event he thought would save the shipyard.

Frank's lament that "we used to make shit in this country, build shit. Now we just put our hand in the next guy's pocket", is one of the key messages of the whole show. Looked at more widely, it helps to explain why the working-class culture of the Baltimore housing estates has been replaced by an economy that revolves around illegal drugs.

Yet Frank remains a moral figure. Nicky, his nephew, is as impressed by the Greeks' professionalism and urbanity as the viewer is, as readers have pointed out on this blog and as is amply illustrated here: "Many names, many passports ... " Yet Frank refuses to be impressed, and is in fact disgusted with them and disgusted with Nicky. "I don't fucking want you with me, Nick," he yells. "Go home."

And in prison, as he watches his skinny and battered son Ziggy surrounded and almost effaced by the massive, intimidating prisoners around him, Frank instinctively stands up, needing to help but for once completely powerless. Perhaps he always has been powerless, but we, and he, can only see it clearly now.

A couple more things to note here. David Simon has a quick cameo as an aggressive reporter (what else?) shouting questions at Frank as he is "perp-walked" out in front of the press. And is Vondas's soft spot for Nicky supposed to be romantic? What are we to make of this exchange:

The Greek: You are fond of him, Spiros. You should have had a son.

Vondas: But then I would have had a wife.

FAVOURITE QUOTE:

McNulty: You know what they call a guy who pays that much attention to his clothes, don't you?

Bunk: Um hm. A grown-up.

RUNNING TOTALS:

Omar stick-ups: five. Omar blasts away at Brother Mouzone, before realising his silly mistake and promptly calling an ambulance.

COMMENTS

McNultyWire We don't hear many statements like the one from the Greek about Nick and Vondas. Can anyone think of words such as "fond" being used in any other context? It's often implied through reference to "family" but as I've said before I think this is a falsehood.

It's not said but I suggest Daniels is fond of Carter, Prez is fond of Dukie, Steve Earle (?) is fond of Bubbles and McNulty is fond of Bodie. Others?

Jesulovesbarca The glory of Season 2 is seeing Sobotka trying to hold together a world that is collapsing around him. Sobotka – like all 1940s Hollywood's version of union bosses – is honourably fighting for his crew members. Furthermore, Season 2 might talk of the decay of the Baltimore sea side docks but it could also be talking about the Detroit – places where, once upon a time, a White or Black man could earn a decent wage without having to contend to outsourcing or government imposed terms on industry operations. Contrast Sobotka's actions with The Greek who cannot be bothered with the corpses of dead Russian and other Slavic prostitutes in his possession.

Squinky I think the comment about Nick is made purely in a fatherly way – I can't see anything to suggest otherwise. The follow-up line "Then I would have had a wife" is surely a wry comment on the downside of having children – i.e. being married.

Hairything To those of you who have said you liked *Efige Efige*, you should check out the *rebetika* genre, which is contemporary to blues and uncannily similar in terms of social history and subject matter. It emerged from the slums of Greek cities filled with refugees from Asia Minor after the war with Turkey, and many of the songs are about doing drugs, heartbreak, murdering the person doing the heartbreaking, doing time in prison, generally being quite hard etc. If you are interested in checking it out more, some good starting points are Sotiria Bellou, Markos Vamvakaris, Vassilis Tsitsanis and many others. Stelios Kazantzidis himself is also a great artist, though most of his stuff wouldn't quite be classified as *rebetiko*.

EPISODE 12 – Always business

PAUL OWEN

Series two ends with dockworker and minor criminal Nicky Sobotka crying in the rain for his lost relatives and his lost industry, over the grimly ironic sounds of I Feel Alright by Steve Earle. This final episode, directed by Robert F Colesberry, is full of opposing images: beautiful wide shots of the colourful shipping containers and the dock machinery towering over them, glorious depictions of industrial decay. It opens almost bucolically, with the radio chirping that "it's gonna be partly cloudy, breezy and warm today with highs around 80", and the sun going up over the cranes and the weeds. But it's all suffused with a sense of dread. We see the same shot of the Key Bridge that we saw last week as Frank Sobotka walked towards the Greeks, and we know that the union boss is dead.

At the end of the last series, we discussed the cyclical nature of the programme, and the montage that ends this season establishes that theme once again. Where last time drug lord Avon Barksdale was jailed but his lieutenant Stringer Bell went free, with their operation basically left intact, here the two most senior narcotics traffickers – the Greek and Vondas – both escape to sell drugs another day. And we see a new batch of foreign prostitutes unloaded from a shipping container to replace the ones who were killed at the start of the series.

The programme gradually resumes its focus on the black housing estates and sets the scene for the next series – although I think it's a shame for the show's overall feel that none of the dock characters are ever knitted back into its fabric (Greeks aside), reinforcing the perception of this series as the odd one out. Heroin addict Bubbles reveals to detectives Kima and McNulty that supposed rivals Stringer and Proposition Joe are now sharing territory – "cats and dogs, sleeping together," as Kima puts it. Omar promises "I'm going hard after Stringer". And we see a bad-tempered prison meeting between Stringer and Avon that ends with a somewhat reluctant fist bump that suggests that the old partnership – "us, man" – is entering rocky waters.

Avon concedes that Stringer can temporarily run the business as he sees fit – "at least until I get home you do" – but when Stringer tries to tell him that "every market-based business moves in cycles", he cuts in: "String, this ain't about your motherfucking business class. It ain't that part of it. It's that other thing."

As we have discussed, with hindsight, Avon now seems the more clear-headed in these discussions. I recently read Roberto Saviano's book Gomorrah, in which the author contrasts the Cosa Nostra of Sicily and 'Ndrangheta of Calabria with the Camorra of Naples:

"One of the declarations about the Sicilian Mafiosi that shocked me most was made by the Casalesi pentito Carmine Schiavone, in a 2005 interview. He talked about Cosa Nostra as if it were an organisation enslaved to politicians and, unlike the Caserta Camorristi, incapable of thinking in business terms. According to Schiavone, the Mafia wanted to become a sort of antistate, but this was not a business issue. The state – antistate paradigm doesn't exist. All there is, is a territory where you do business – with, through, or without the state."

There are many differences between the Italian mafias and the Barksdale gang in The Wire – the mafias' widespread involvement in legitimate business, neutralisation of the police, international reach, enormous scale, and intricate political influence (Stringer should have marched the west side to the polls to vote for Clay Davis's opponent when the state senator double-crossed him).

But there are also similarities, not least in the contrasting attitudes to business we see above, which match Avon and Stringer's, but also in the way the gang/mafia is knitted into and drawn from the community, and replenishes itself periodically from that source, as well as the use of violence as punishment, intimidation and to resolve commercial problems.

Napolitans involved with the mafia refer to it as "the system", which has obvious parallels with "the game", the name for the drug economy that might have been a more apposite title for David Simon's programme than The Wire.

"Every arrest and maxi-trial seems more like a way of replacing cops and breaking business cycles than something capable of destroying a system," Saviano writes. We are shown something similar at the end of each series of The Wire.

FAVOURITE QUOTE:

The Greek: "And, of course, I'm not even Greek …"

RUNNING TOTALS:

Murders: up one to 33, with the killing of Frank Sobotka.

Bubbles attempting to get clean: no chance; he's caught stealing medicine from an ambulance. Kima is not impressed. Still two.

COMMENTS

Pompeyplayup Ed Burns has said that modern day policing was inspired by The French Connection whilst drug gangs were inspired by The Godfather:

The Godfather had a similar effect on the other side. It basically taught these emerging heroin gangs how to do business, how you set up your structure, with the code and the organization, the way you should have a boss, under-bosses—you know, capos. It got black, inner-city heroin dealers into the same mind-set

RedThreat The real French connection is mentioned by Prop when discussing a dealer Stringer had never heard of (as has been mentioned on here recently).

The first time I watched Nicky's montage I was sure he was gonna get whacked. It was just how it seemed all set up for tragedy, he left the Motel and got rid of his minder, claimed no one f*cks with us on our territory then leant on a fence by a deserted road, but it was probably the writer/directors just playing with our heads.

There was a direct contrast between differing levels of the criminal food chain when Sergei hunts down Cheese as a favour for Nicky and Cheese find himself quite overwhelmed by what I assume were seriously trained ex-secret-service men from the other side of the iron curtain. The Greeks seem so assuming but they had some serious muscle.

But I thought Sergei rolled over a little too easily in the interview room, I'm pretty sure the chair wouldn't have phased him. And the actor obviously gave up on the gym and the roids for a later cameo – was it when Avon surprises Marlo in the prison visiting room? – looking a bit portly after all that more-ish prison food!

Cheese is often the fall guy isn't he? Loses face to Sergei, loses the dog fight, gets shot by Brother Mouzone and just when he thinks he's on top, Slim takes him out.

Wengerball The end of series montages are always so depressing, we have just spent three months working a case, trying to give a fuck (when it isn't our turn), watch with great care and attention and then really nothing has changed, i guess that's why the game stays the game (nb i am aware that i used "we", but after the focus and attention we put into each episode we deserve some credit for the results of the BPD).

One thing that wasn't totally clear, when the FBI threatened the Union with closure if they didn't change the leadership, they immediately took the picture of black challenger down, leaving Frank unopposed, but obviously Frank was dead by this point, so did the FBI close the Union branch? and were the union just sticking to the FBI by refusing to change leadership? any help would be greatly appreciated.

McNultyWire I'm sure leaving Frank unopposed was sticking one to the FBI and recognition of his leadership. West Wing fans will remember Will Bailey as campaign manager who got a dead politician elected so maybe Union elections in the US can also "raise the dead".

RedThreat It was a "stick it to the man" gesture as well. And as the Feds threatened, the Stevedores were locked out of the Union building pretty shortly afterwards. So heroic in defeat but a pretty futile gesture in the end?

And another message from The Wire about the fate of the working man?

benjip when nick shows up later on to shout at the mayor for building new houses that the average man can't afford instead of saving the docks – shouldn't he be in the witness protection program or something?

ElectricDragon This is from Alan Sepinwall's blog on that episode in S5: For those wondering why Nick — last seen entering Witness Protection after taking his uncle's deal to testify against Vondas and The Greek — is back hanging with his port buddies, I asked David Simon, who said that Nick, like lots of people who go into Witness Protection, eventually left the program because he missed his old life and family. (And since Vondas and The Greek were never caught or brought to trial, I doubt the feds kicked up much fuss at saving that expense.)

Joedoone The Wire is a much better name for the series than The Game. It ties in with Simon's assertion that the viewer should have to lean into the programme in order to make sense of what is going on, and not just on the surface but underneath. Getting the wire is only the start of the process; if those on the listening end don't pay attention, and interpret, and make connections, then the wire isn't of much use. It takes good police to make it work. It takes a little effort on the part of the viewer to really understand what is going on, and then the rewards are huge. Pay attention, and be paid back.

PropFallKindly Surely the point about the East/West Baltimore gangs is summed up by the Russian when Omar robs the shipment: "Fucking amateurs".

With the exception of Prop Joe, and attempts by Stringer, they are just street gangbangers with short-term vision who end up dead or in prison.

They cannot be compared to the mafia. That is the whole thing. They are all just eating themselves.

Interview: Michael K Williams

SAM DELANEY

Barack Obama recently named Omar Little as his favourite character in his favourite show. "That's not an endorsement," the presidential hopeful added carefully. "He's not my favourite person but he's a fascinating character." Barack was right. Of all the brilliantly drawn, authentically complex and relentlessly captivating characters in this show's sprawling cast, he is surely the most engaging.

Devotees of the Baltimore-set urban drama are as passionate and obsessive as the sort of crazies who turn up to Star Trek conventions dressed as Lieutenant Uhura. And once they start setting up conventions in honour of The Wire you can be sure that most fans will turn up dressed in a big long mac, carrying a double-barrelled shotgun just like their hero. He is loved because he is meaner, funnier, cooler and braver than any other character you've ever seen on TV. He is unpredictable, complicated and brilliantly strange. Amid all the the show's vicious drug dealers, corrupt politicians and compromised cops, Omar is the only figure who adheres to a strict, if perverse, moral code. He also has a way-cool facial scar. Put simply, Omar Little is the most unique character in the most unique television show of all time.

Midway through the third episode of The Wire, we catch our first glimpse of him. He sits by the side of the low-rise housing projects in a van – all scarred and scary. He tugs insolently on a cigarette while he scopes out the young drug hoppers going about their business. The camera dwells on his narrowed eyes as he plots his next move with sinister, methodical calm. You're not quite sure who he is or what he's up to, but you're instantly engrossed.

"They originally said seven episodes and you're out of here," says Michael K Williams, the man who plays him, "but after the first few weeks filming, David Simon and Ed Burns [the show's creators] came up to me on set and said they loved the passion I was bringing to it. They said they wanted to expand the role and told me to go and watch The Wild Bunch. They'd based a lot of the character on those old westerns." His croaking drawl is just like Omar's but the stuff he says isn't. It's strange to hear him self-deprecate, guffaw and use phrases like: "Dance was my first passion." Nevertheless, Williams's performances are heavily informed by his own eventful upbringing.

"I grew up in East Flatbush in Brooklyn, which was an intense neighbourhood filled with different West Indian cultures," he says. "I never dealt drugs or went to jail but I was always getting myself in what I call knuckleheaded trouble. Jumping into situations I could have avoided. The gangsters knew who I was and left me alone."

On the night of his 25th birthday he got involved in a bar brawl in which he was slashed across the face with a razor, leaving him with that distinctive scar. "Me and two friends were jumped," he says. "I didn't have time to worry about myself because my friend was cut even worse. He passed out and was losing blood fast so I had to get him to hospital before he died."

But not all of Williams's life played like an episode of The Wire. For much of the 1990s, he worked as a professional dancer with the likes of Crystal Waters, Technotronic and CC Peniston. "I got paid to travel the world doing what I loved for seven years," he says. "But in the end age caught up with me." His striking looks attracted the interest of casting directors and the odd acting job arose. He trained at drama college and was soon cast in Bringing out the Dead, during which Martin Scorsese told him he was a damned fine actor.

Then things slowed down for a few years. He was working at his mother's daycare centre to make ends meet when he received a script from The Wire's producers. "I read the character and thought, This looks like fun," he says. "I quickly decided that I didn't want to play this guy like an alpha male. I wanted to play him with sensitivity and integrity. He wouldn't scream or shout or get respect by intimidating people."

Compared to most of the violent street kids caught up in The Wire's drug game, Omar cuts an almost Wildean figure. He swaggers through the streets of Baltimore like a gun-toting dandy in his long coat and fancy headscarves. He is poetic, lacing his dialogue with old-fashioned, incongruous phrases like "indeed", "do tell" and "I think not". He is a mine of insight and wisdom on the ugly, broken world he lives in. "Out there it's play or get played," he observes. When he robs an illicit card game, psychotic drug lord Marlo Stanfield fixes him with an evil glare and hisses, "That's my money." Omar just smirks and explains, "Money ain't got no owners, only spenders."

"Everyone knows who Omar is," says Williams. "He makes no excuses for what he is. He is not duplicitous in any way. That's not only rare in the show but in real life, too."

Omar's ethical code is endearing, if often eccentric. He robs a shopkeeper of his drug stash – then pays him for a packet of cigarettes, taking care to check he's given the correct change. He rarely loses his temper and never swears. "It was Ed [Burns] who first suggested that Omar should prize his own self-control in a way that so many other characters in The Wire do not," David Simon has said.

Omar's defining scene comes in season two when he appears in court to testify against a gang member accused of murder. He waltzes into the courtroom ostentatiously toying with the tie he has casually looped around his neck for the occasion. "What exactly do you do for a living?" asks the state's attorney once he's taken the stand. "I robs drug dealers," he grins proudly. She asks how someone in his line of work could stay alive for so long. "Day at a time, I suppose," he shrugs. Then comes his cross examination at the hands of corrupt gang-lawyer Maurice Levy.

"You are amoral, are you not? You are feeding off the violence and the despair of the drug trade. You are stealing from those who themselves are stealing the lifeblood from our city. You are a parasite who leeches off the culture of drugs…" Omar interrupts him: "Just like you, man." The lawyer stops in his tracks and splutters, "Excuse me? What?" Omar leans forward. "I got the shotgun, you got the briefcase. Its all in the game though, right?"

It's one of Williams's favourite scenes. "That was the moment I felt I'd finally got the character right," he says. "I'd spent a long time on the streets of Baltimore going deep into that world. I would be out after 2am, seeing fights, hearing shots fired. I needed to learn the details of how they walked, how they spoke. Baltimore is different to Brooklyn."

Williams also got to spend time with Donnie Andrews, a real-life former stick-up man on whom the character was partly based. He appears in season four as one of the henchmen who protect Omar in prison, and again in season five. "I never asked Donnie about his past," says Williams. "But there was a quiet menace to him that I was just able to absorb while he was on set."

Sometimes, aside from all the authentic touches, Omar just does weird shit. Like when he saunters to the cornershop in his silk pyjamas to buy Honey Nut Cheerios. Or the way he whistles that spooky tune everywhere he goes. "It's The Farmer in the Yard," Williams says. "The writers told me to whistle it. It makes me feel like Elmer Fudd. I walk into those scenes thinking to myself: It's wabbit season!"

Brilliantly, Omar's sexuality is neither here nor there to most of the plot lines. But it is relevant to the overall picture. David Simon explains: "I thought Omar, as an unaffiliated character, could be boldly and openly homosexual in a way that a gay man within the organised drug trade or within the police department could not be." Williams saw Omar's sexuality as the thing most likely to make it a stand-out role. "The way I decided to play it was, So what?" he says. "Yeah, he's gay, but that's not the thing you're gonna remember him for if you meet him down an alley. It's that shotgun that will have you worried, not his gayness. I didn't want it to define him." Now, he hopes, the character is helping to change attitudes. "In the hood, especially among the black community, homosexuality is taboo," he says. "But I get real gangsters coming up and saying, 'Omar's my man! I love Omar!' I think it might have made some people think differently about things."

In season five, Omar features in some of the show's most dramatic scenes ever. Those left with a sense of withdrawal once its all over can take some comfort from Michael K Williams's growing presence on our screens. His Hollywood stock is rising, with recent appearances in The Incredible Hulk and Spike Lee's forthcoming war epic, Miracle at St Anna. But he will always be remembered for playing one of TV's greatest ever characters. Lately, he's even won his mother round. "The Wire was never her cup of tea," he says. "But then she read the Barack Obama quote and that changed her mind. I managed to introduce them and he called her mom. She's so thrilled she might even watch an episode some day!"

Great town for a shoot-out: the architecture of The Wire

STEVE ROSE

I've never been to Baltimore, but I have a good idea where to buy heroin, sleep rough, get drunk with policemen, hold a top-secret gang meeting and even dispose of a dead body. I feel I know Baltimore better than my own city, and no doubt other viewers of The Wire feel the same.

It has become a cliche to say "the city is the star", but with The Wire there's no way around it. Most place-specific TV shows do little more than allude to their setting and architecture in the title sequence, then retreat to the safety of the set; The Wire, on the other hand, is shot in unadorned, real-life Baltimore. It shows you the parts of the city you never usually see: the ports, prisons, courthouses, boxing gyms, discount stores and, most of all, the shabby inner-city streets where the war between the police and the drug gangs is endlessly waged.

But Baltimore's architecture is not just there to be looked at – it also helps drive the action along. If there is a generic Baltimore landscape, it is the "rowhouses": small, flat-roofed, two-storey terraced houses. The classier ones have marble front steps and painted brick, but more often they are clad in "formstone", a locally invented fake stone cladding. Hundreds of thousands of rowhouses were built during the 19th and early 20th centuries, when Baltimore was one of the busiest ports in the US. Since the 1950s, Baltimore's population has dropped from 1 million to about two-thirds of that, leaving street after street of empty rowhouses. In 1998, there were an estimated 40,000 vacant homes in the city. Great places for hiding dead bodies.

In The Wire's third season, a rogue policeman turns a whole derelict neighbourhood into an experimental junkie community without anyone noticing. The maze of overgrown alleys behind the rowhouses also facilitates shoot-outs, violent assaults, foot chases and drug deals.

Modern architecture does not fare much better. A key location in the first season is a mid-rise 1960s housing project. The drug dealers operate openly from a sofa in the middle of the development's courtyard, making a mockery of the architects' attempts to foster "community" through openness and visibility. The high-rises are even worse. The police don't dare venture there alone. At one stage, a forest of tower blocks is dynamited by The Wire's publicity-seeking mayor, who announces the dawning of a new era of safe, affordable low-rise homes. As the old buildings crumble, Bodie, one of the local hoodlums, is understandably sceptical: "They gonna tear this building down and they're gonna build some new shit – but people? They don't give a fuck about people."

Leading academics would agree with Bodie's analysis. In his book, Spaces of Hope, the Marxist geographer David Harvey details how Baltimore's much-vaunted "urban renewal" became just another facet of the problem. Baltimore, "for the most part, [is] a mess," says Harvey. "Not the kind of enchanting mess that makes cities such interesting places to explore, but an awful mess." Inner-city decay has infected it like a virus. Those who can afford to do so have moved far out into rural gated communities; the urban poor have been moved to less visible areas in the suburbs; powerful local institutions, such as Johns Hopkins University, have snapped up the cheap city-centre real estate and redeveloped it.

If there were to be a sixth season of The Wire, you'd want it to focus on the planners, developers and architects who made the city the way it is. Over the course of the show, many of the chief gangsters seek to get out of "the game" by going into property development, which involves a certain amount of financial lubrication at City Hall. The real-estate sharks prove to be more than a match for the drug gangs, however. The port workers also see their working-class landscape being turned into yuppie flats. The Wire reminds us that there are no simple solutions to urban problems, at a time when societies all over the world are deliberating over architectural cures and fixes. In the words of Lester Freamon, the show's most meticulous and articulate detective: "All the pieces matter."

Series Three

Just a gangster

EPISODE 1 – String theory

SAPTARSHI RAY

Season three opens with the demolition of the infamous towers, home and greenhouse to many of our favourite dealers and hoppers. As the buildings fall, many are closing a chapter in their past and looking into an uncertain future. Avon is in jail, along with most of his crew; Marlo comes into our lives; the detail turns its attentions to the east side by trying to get the loose-lipped buffoon Drac promoted to lieutenant (the post goes to Cheese); Bodie and Poot are on their own, and Stringer Bell is looking to revolutionise the game.

If Avon treads like a cat around the pits and the streets he runs, Stringer prowls like a wolf, taking everything in as he surveys his landscape. Idris Elba's extraordinary performance grows with each episode and, as he matures into the role, Stringer becomes simultaneously more menacing and more helpless. No mean feat.

As his desire to go straight and become accepted into the social elite of Baltimore grows, his credibility among his own troops begins to wane. He starts seeing Avon as an impediment to his own success, while his brother in arms begins viewing him with suspicion – one of the most gripping, tortuous and ultimately tragic storylines of all the five series.

Nowhere is this illustrated better than in the "boardroom" scene when Stringer tries to school what's left of his crew in the ways of high finance with his oft-repeated mission statement: "Product, motherfuckers, product." His argument that there is no need for beefs, territory or attitude on the streets is met with scepticism; his insistence on hoppers raising their hands and the "chair recognising your ass" meets with bemusement; and finally his claim that all the crews will be one big happy family on the corners meets with outright disbelief, as Poot asks: "Do the chair know we gonna look like punk-ass bitches out there?"

And, for all his affectations, his polo-necks and blazers, his Adam Smith books and economics classes, his commercial acumen and his thirst for social standing, it is not reasoned argument but ghetto attitude that he turns to when cornered, as he explodes in a fury at Poot. Even when Shamrock reminds him that Poot followed the rules and had the floor, Stringer's boardroom persona gets lost in a fog of frustrated rage. "This nigger's too fucking ignorant to have the floor," he spits.

This cycle repeats itself later in the season, as String gets led on a merry dance by Clay Davis and his uptown cohorts, culminating in String demanding Slim Charles shoot the senator. Yet again, he turns to what he knows, making a mockery of all his "it's all just business" speeches. As Avon and Charles point out, the heat from killing Davis could shut them down forever.

FAVOURITE QUOTE:

"Gentlemen, scuff yourselves up a little and learn the stare."
Bunny Colvin schools two new recruits to the western district.

RUNNING TOTALS:

Murders: up five to 38, as homicide gets five bodies in one night.

McNulty giving a fuck when it's not his turn: up one to 18, as he continues his quest to bring in Stringer and goes back through the files on Wallace's death.

Dubious parenting: Up one to four after his jealousy over his ex's new boyfriend sees him wrench his boys from their front-row seats at the baseball to accompany him in the cheap seats.

Herc fuck-ups: up by a half to seven and a half, as it's he who spots what he thinks is the stash, which turns out to be a dummy package. Though I am tempted to knock it off again for his cranking up the Shaft theme tune in his car while in pursuit of the hoppers.

EPISODE 2 – Twin towers

JUDITH SOAL

The Wire is very much a post-9/11 show, with significant references to America's fight against terrorism. But never is this more obvious than in season three, which begins with the destruction of the Baltimore towers as a direct allusion to the collapse of the twin towers in New York. And just as the fall of the twin towers led to the wars in Afghanistan and Iraq, so the end of the towers in Baltimore leads to a violent turf war between the Barksdale and Stanfield crews.

Clearly, the war on drugs and the inevitability of its failure is also being used as a metaphor for the war on terror. Street drugs are branded WMDs and more than once Baltimore is likened to Fallujah or Baghdad. For every drug dealer arrested on the corner or every Taliban fighter killed in Afghanistan, 20 more will step up to take their place unless the root causes of the problems are addressed. As much as the show is a call for the authorities to revolutionise their approach to tackling the drug trade, it is also a plea for a radical rethink of American foreign policy.

The theme of season three is reform, and a clear line is drawn between band-aid attempts to make it look like something is being done about the problem (for example demolishing the housing projects) and radical policies that might actually make a difference (such as Hamsterdam).

The inherent self-interest in most attempts at "reform" and the suggestion that the war in Iraq had more to do with America's thirst for oil than 9/11 is raised later in the series when Avon bemoans the cost of his own battles with Marlo, to which Slim Charles replies: "It don't matter who did what to whom. Fact is, we went to war and now there ain't no going back … If it's a lie, then we fight on the lie. But we gotta fight."

FAVOURITE QUOTE:

"All good things come to those who wait." Freamon explaining why Cheese is talking about a murder on the phone – just before the case collapses and they lose the wiretap because the "murder" victim happens to be a dog.

RUNNING TOTALS:

Murders: up four to 42, if you don't count the dog.

McNulty giving a fuck when it's not his turn: up one to 19 as he investigates D's death, speaking to that lovely but strange pathologist and visiting Donette.

EPISODE 3 – Drug use and dead soldiers

MARK SMITH

Series three starts its assault on city government and bureaucracy with two "dead soldiers" from opposing sides of the law, who meet their ends in contrasting ways, yet are both used to illuminate the amoral futility of the city's drugs policing.

Tosha's death, catching a stray one smack in the head from Dante after Omar orders his crew to "bang out" yet another Barksdale stash-house, is the second tragedy to befall our favourite B'more mercenary. Of greater significance is the fact that homicide treat her as a "real" victim – a citizen. Any death that encroaches on the world outside the corners and the game merits a different response. So surely Colvin's Hamsterdam, which we see being chosen here, is merely an extension of this ad hoc policy? Don't encroach on their world, and they won't encroach on ours – the equilibrium is maintained.

Colvin calls the brown paper bag law "a great moment of civic compromise". With Hamsterdam, he (and, of course, David Simon) is questioning why another great compromise cannot be reached with drug laws and policing in America after a century of manifest failure.

America's zero-tolerance approach to illegal drug-taking and addiction is responsible for the highest rate of imprisonment in the world, eroding civil rights, and placing one out of four young black men under some form of state control. The Wire's Baltimore is a paradigm of the 21st century American city. Linguistically, for example, the American National Institute on Drug Abuse will not issue official documents that even contain the phrase "drug use". Most European governments and bodies will use the term "drug misuse", but in the US it is always "drug abuse", underlining the ideological perspective that non-abusive use of illicit drugs is not possible.

The Economist magazine has called for legalisation as the "least bad policy", noting that all creditable recent studies showed "no correlation between the harshness of drug laws and the incidence of drug-taking". The Wire is fundamentally a manifestation of this truth, and in large part a moral case for action to remedy it – as well as a rollicking drama.

So we see Colvin taking his first baby steps to creating Hamsterdam, making sure it's more than eight blocks away from Stewart Hill elementary school. Later, when he wins back his howling district officers with a promise that the drug-free zone is merely a ruse, I'm not sure he believes it himself.

The second "dead soldier" in the episode is Cole, whose booze-soaked wake at Kavanaugh's prompts one of Landsman's few sympathetic scenes. "We are pOlice," he says, in a toast that deals with the futility of BPD's ongoing struggle. McNulty seems convinced that the fact that Cole solved a few cases should have given him some kind of immunity to an ignoble death at the hands of a StairMaster. Likewise, Kima, taking the Bunk role again in this episode, romanticises McNulty's tales of working cases so late that he wasn't home for the missus with almost whimsical longing. She needs to stop hanging round with him.

QUOTE OF THE WEEK:

Omar: "How do," as he pops up to surprise the stash guard.

RUNNING TOTALS:

Murders: up two to 44 in Omar's ill-fated raid on another Barksdale stash.

McNulty giving a fuck when it wasn't his turn: up one to 20, as he turns Columbo in the prison to confirm his suspicions about D's "suicide".

Drunk: up one to 13, with Kima as his partner-in-crime, as their characters seemingly converge.

Omar stick-ups: up one to seven.

EPISODE 4 – Cutting loose

PAUL OWEN

This episode starts with a small scene that echoes a larger theme that runs throughout this series. Detectives Greggs and McNulty are arranging how much they are going to pay heroin addict Bubbles for information about drug corners in west Baltimore. "Let's treat it like a real job," says Kima. "Say five an hour, 30 on the day, max."

Bubs recalls the last time he "punched a clock": "Had one of those stock-boy jobs, one of those cheapest-guys-in-town stores. Unloading appliances, taking air conditioners and shit out to the customers." He lost the job, though, because "I put a clock radio in a trash can one day trying to be cute, got caught. I ain't even need a clock radio."

The scene shifts to Dennis "Cutty" Wise, the former inmate attempting to go straight, riding along in the back of a battered truck with his Hispanic workmates, while well-off, self-satisfied gangsters idle at the lights in brand-new SUVs. Cutty's role here is to illustrate the difficulties of switching to the straight life amid the many and obvious temptations of "the game". His labouring supervisor tells him: "Yeah, it's hot. Every day. And you gonna be riding in the back of that hard truck, bouncin' around, every day … I'm just sayin': You wanna stay on the straight, ain't gonna be no big reward to it. This is it right here."

Cutty finds the grind and low pay of a labouring job hard to take after the respect and money that comes easily in the drug world. And, as drug kingpin Avon Barksdale points out later: "You ain't done shit else. Know what I'm saying? So what you gonna do?" Walter Thabit fleshes out a similar case in his book How East New York Became a Ghetto:

"Consider a typical young man in his late teens. He didn't have a high school diploma; he had dropped out years ago. He had applied for jobs and found that people didn't understand what he was saying. He had a tough time filling out an application, and nobody offered him any kind of job. He looked into his future and saw nothing out there. He got the message: he stopped looking."

In a bitter, sarcastic passage in their book about west Baltimore, The Corner, David Simon and Ed Burns make the same point: "If we were the damned of the American cities, we would not fail. We would rise above the corner. And when we tell ourselves such things, we unthinkingly assume that we would be consigned to places like Fayette Street fully equipped, with all the graces and disciplines, talents and training that we now possess ... Amid the stench of so much defeat and despair, we would kick fate in the teeth and claim our deserved victory. We would escape to live the life we were supposed to live, the life we are living now ... Why? The truth is plain: we were not born to be niggers."

The programme shows straight life to be difficult, crime to be easy. The official world shuts the door on Cutty again and again when he tries to set up his gym, yet when he asks for funding from Avon (here at his most Godfather-like, generous and responsible) it is immediately forthcoming, in spades.

Yet Cutty does escape, does "rise above the corner", does succeed, and in doing so he takes on another role in the programme. George Pelecanos – the novelist who co-wrote this week's episode with Simon – has spoken about why he felt Cutty was important:

"There were times I wanted to maybe give a little bit more of a moral centre to some of the characters. I championed Cutty, the guy who comes out of prison and opens a boxing gym. You look at that storyline and it's got my stamp on it. David and I argued in a good way about these things."

Pelecanos has written two novels about characters attempting to reform: Drama City (2006) and The Way Home (2009). Blogger Andy Sywak recalls him talking about Cutty at a book signing:

"Pelecanos spoke about how he was instrumental in introducing a character on the show who would win. The character of Cutty was his idea. Much like his novels, where the hard-working man usually emerges triumphant, so too does Cutty navigate the drug world to come out on top with his boxing gym."

Does Cutty come out on top? More or less, although it's touch and go when novice thug Michael takes against him, paranoid about his fatherly attention. He never gets his ex-girlfriend back; she has made the transition from the world of the corner and "ain't for you no more. She ain't for none of our kind." It is shocking when, in the pay of Barksdale, he slaps a woman hard in the street, and he certainly has his sleazy side – although the programme is careful to show how this loses him the respect of the boys whose mothers he sleeps with.

But in sum Cutty stands out in the projects as a force for good and even for hope, and he makes a good partner for policeman Carver as the latter's outreach work in the community improves. Avon seems to recognise this, or something like it, in the tense scene when Cutty resigns from "the game". "He was a man in his time," says Slim Charles, and Avon corrects him: "He a man today."

QUOTE OF THE WEEK:

Bunk's shameless chat-up line: "My mom died about a week ago ... "

RUNNING TOTALS:

McNulty giving a fuck when it's not his turn: up one to 21, still working on Stringer Bell when he should be on Kintel.

Drunk: up one to 14.

Dubious parenting: up one to five for not paying his alimony.

EPISODE 5 – Dressed to kill

SIMON JEFFERY

Avon's time in the Maryland state prison is bookended by two impressive outfits. Arrested at the end of series one, he is led away from Orlando's in a cream Kangol short-sleeved track top and matching baggy three-quarter-length trousers, like some sort of drug-dealing Edwardian golfer with a penchant for neutrals.

On his release, in this episode, he climbs into Stringer's SUV clutching a box of freshly packed and pressed clothes to replace his prison-issue denims. "Ah yeah, you got my shit," he grins. Next scene the car cruises down a country road back to Baltimore as Avon tosses his jail clothing out the window.

Clothes, for those high enough up the ranks, are important to the Barksdale crew. You see this in the first season when D'Angelo spends an age colour-coordinating his essentially similar clothes from a well-stocked closet before a date with Shardene.

Notably, and despite initial appearances, this fits in with Freamon's earlier assessment that Avon (and by extension his crew) shows "no flash ... no jewellery, no clothes". It's streetwear – albeit in abundance

– not "flash". Compare this to the ostentatious leather coat with the fur trim Ziggy splashes out on in season two, the one that leads Nick Sobotka to chastise him for flaunting his ill-gotten wealth.

So far, so gangster. But who knew before The Wire that plainclothes Baltimore pOlice gave such high regard to their attire? In season two, Landsman directs port police liaison Beadie Russell to step out of uniform: "We work plainclothes in homicide, which is not to say the clothes need be plain." He points out Freamon's "brash, tweedy impertinence" and Bunk's "pinstriped, lawyerly affections". He suggests she wear a pantsuit in "earth tones".

Beadie aside (maybe adding more ammunition to the argument that The Wire's female characters are less interestingly portrayed than its men), character-through-dress extends throughout the police department. Look at the peacockish braids and buttons of the senior officers. On the non-unformed side, Carver's clothes become sharper, more fitted, more metrosexual as he moves up the ranks. His signature look is his police badge worn as a medallion.

But not McNulty, defiantly in the uniform of the regular guy. Square-jawed Dominic West is possibly too much the Hollywood leading man, so that anything other than casual-fit jeans and T-shirts with the occasional suit could strain credibility. Still, this leads to comedy. From the end of season two, as Bunk talks McNulty through the buttons on a suspect's Perry Ellis blazer, comes the following quote:

McNulty: You know what they call a guy who pays that much attention to his clothes, don't you?

Bunk: Um hm. A grown-up.

There's plenty more: McNulty's awkward pre-court shopping trip with Omar (he buys a tie but wears it flamboyantly, ie not with a suit), Bunk in a pink shirt on his clothes-burning night of marital infidelity and, only marginally less slapstick, Omar's efforts to carry a gun in his silk dressing gown.

But back to Avon's real post-incarceration outfit, the one that complements the golfer-attire of his arrest. The crux of this episode is the change in the relationship between Avon and Stringer. Early on Stringer has assembled the Baltimore gangs in order to hammer out the deal that sets up the cooperative. "No beef, no drama, just business."

At Avon's homecoming party a few days after, the two are both dressed, ostensibly, in evening wear – each is wearing a dress shirt with wing-tipped collars. But where Avon (and I wish I could get away with this) wears his shirt open-necked with a lightly-pinstriped grey single-breasted suit and white sneakers, Stringer is in full black tie. Avon: dressed successful but with a nod to the street; Stringer: bow tie and tuxedo, the uniform of an American CEO at a function. If there is a single moment that visually encapsulates the tensions that will lead the two to betray each other, this is it. Stringer, tragically naive, believes he can leverage criminal wealth into legitimacy. Avon will never leave the security of what he knows, the game.

FAVOURITE QUOTE:

Stringer when he spots minute-taker Shamrock at the co-op meeting: "Are you taking notes on a criminal fucking conspiracy?"

RUNNING TOTALS:

Murders: up one to 45. Sapper and Gerard beat an errant dealer to death. Not to make this summary of the episode too neat, but he and his shopping bag-laden girlfriend had been seen spending too much on clothes and jewellery.

McNulty drunk: bored by serious talk at an open evening for a school his ex-wife wants to send their sons to, he moves to the bar and flirts with Terri D'Agostino. She sleeps with him. Up one to 15.

Dubious parenting: see above. Up one to six.

EPISODE 6 – "Just a gangster, I suppose ..."

PAUL OWEN

This is the episode – written by David Simon and Rafael Alvarez, and packed with memorable scenes – where the contrast between Stringer Bell's approach to the drug business and Avon Barksdale's begins to come to a head. While kingpin Avon was in prison, Stringer, his second in command, gradually reorganised their business along free-market lines, attempting to abandon the traditional model of gaining and holding territory from other dealers using brutal violence. Instead he gathered Baltimore's major dealers into a "co-op"; they would all club together to buy wholesale drugs from the same source, and share their territory instead of fighting over it. He ordered his low-level dealers, confused that rivals were now being allowed to sell on their turf, to abandon their customary intimidation and bloodshed and compete for customers using mainstream tactics: undercutting prices, for example, or throwing in freebies.

His theory was that having a high-quality product would make the Barksdale gang more money than controlling a specific area of territory. His approach had the added advantage of deterring police attention, since the police were principally interested in those drug dealers who were ordering or carrying out murders.

Meanwhile, Bell invested more and more of the organisation's money into property, aiming to amass so much that he and Barksdale could eventually abandon drug dealing altogether and become legitimate businessmen.

Yet Avon was always ambivalent about this move into the mainstream. Here we see his lack of interest as the two tour a building site and are told of problem after insurmountable problem. Avon's normal approach to problem-solving – aggressively ordering someone to fix it: "Y'all fucked up, so y'all supposed to take the hit, right?" – doesn't work; bored and irritated, he quickly leaves.

Later Barksdale and Bell discuss how to handle young turk Marlo Stanfield, who has taken over some of their territory. Avon wants to go to war, but Stringer tells him: "We *past* that run-and-gun shit, man … We find us a package and we ain't got to see nothing but bank … No corners, no territory. Nothing … I mean who gives a fuck who's standing on what corner if we taking that shit off the top, putting that shit to good use, making that shit work for us. We can run more than corners, B. Period. We could … run this goddamn city."

This is a powerful, seductive speech, and it almost looks like his message has got through. But then Avon looks up. "I ain't no suit-wearing businessman like you," he tells String. "I'm just a gangster, I suppose … And I want my corners."

Later we see state senator Clay Davis running rings around Stringer; this is the side of supposedly legitimate business Bell is unable to handle. Avon's eventual verdict that "they saw your ghetto ass coming" seems accurate. While his ideas for improving the drug game almost always have great merit, Stringer finds it difficult to negotiate the labyrinthine procedures of local government and the housing industry he seeks to join, and his ignorance is taken advantage of, particularly by Davis. So he is unable to take the final step into legal business that he desires – even as his past actions in the drug world begin to catch up with him.

QUOTE OF THE WEEK:

Marlo: "Sound like one of them good problems."

RUNNING TOTALS:

Murders: up three to 48 with the deaths of two useless Barksdale boys, and the killing of a Stanfield dealer by Slim Charles.

McNulty giving a fuck when it's not his turn: up one to 22, investigating D'Angelo's death, tracking Stringer, and sounding off to Bunny Colvin.

Bunk drunk: no, still five, but instead we get Bunk furious, in an incandescent scene where he really puts Omar in his place. Unusually, Omar comes out of the whole exchange quite badly, convincingly painted as a "predatory motherfucker", exactly the sort of charge he had attempted to put on Levy, the lawyer, in the second series. "Makes me sick, motherfucker, how far we done fell," Bunk tells him.

EPISODE 7 – Would legalising drugs be so wrong?

STEVE BUSFIELD

Bubbles is a man who has experienced the highs and suffered the lows, but his journey through Hamsterdam is particularly dark. So dark that he stays clean. Hamsterdam at night is portrayed as Dante's Inferno made real, a vision of hell, junkies shooting up in the street and public sexual favours for a score. It looks much worse even than the normally miserable scene you would associate with drug dens. Johnny, in his messed up state, calls it "paradise".

In the same episode, Bunny, whose brainwave all this was, gets new stats that reveal that crime is down in the district, and markedly down in the areas where the drugs business would be taking place were it not for the existence of Hamsterdam.

Later, when Carver is forced to tell Jimmy and Kima about the "free zone", Greggs can't quite get over the fact that drugs have been legalised, while McNulty is more understanding, either because, as real pOlice, he knows that there are more important crimes to eliminate than drug taking (such as murder, in a town with a horrific homicide rate) or because he just likes giving a fuck when it isn't his turn. When his old boss Bunny explains the situation – McNulty: "And the bosses don't know?" Colvin: "Fuck the bosses" – that's Jimmy's kind of language.

The Hamsterdam storyline follows a real-life Baltimore initiative, when mayor Kurt L Schmoke had the temerity to suggest decriminalising drugs.

America has a long and unhappy history with the criminalisation of substances that some (many!) people find enjoyable. In the 1930s, prohibition didn't stop alcohol, it merely drove it underground and created a criminal culture around it. The present-day war on drugs has had much the same effect. That is certainly The Wire's take on it. The show is loaded with dialogue about how the war can never be won and the story arc that sees one kingpin replaced seamlessly by another certainly suggests that the participants may change but the business goes on. And it is a business. A lucrative one. And because it is illegal it is accompanied by guns and murder.

Which of course raises several questions. Why fight a war that can't be won? Why decide that alcohol is fine but other drugs (notice I say "other drugs") are not? Alcohol, by dint of its legal standing, is considered socially acceptable, and yet is a major factor in significant levels of crime (domestic violence, road deaths) and social disintegration. Marijuana leaves its takers much less likely to fight than drunks. More likely to eat a lot of chocolate, but that is a much less serious social problem, I think.

Of course the drugs that are being taken on these mean streets are harder than marijuana. Cocaine in all its forms is highly addictive. But so is alcohol. Marijuana use does not necessarily lead to cocaine and heroin use, just as alcohol does not automatically lead to methylated spirits. And, were they legalised, it would at the very least force the organised crime around it to move elsewhere.

QUOTE OF THE WEEK:

"What are you, a fucking communist?" Herc to Carver after the latter forces dealers in Hamsterdam to take better care of their employees.

RUNNING TOTALS:

Murders: up one to 49. Snoop (dressed like a girl!) guns down Rico from the back of a motorbike.

McNulty giving a fuck when it's not his turn: up two to 24, having gone behind Daniels's back (again) and backed up Bunny.

Drunk: up one to 16: although we don't see him drinking, we know that it was he who got Kima legless before her domestic dispute.

Herc fuck-ups: up one to eight and a half (if we are being unkind and counting his inability to remember Avon's full name).

Bubbles attempting to get clean: up one to three (as long as we count his hesitant declining of Johnny's offer).

EPISODE 8 – In search of that second act

SAPTARSHI RAY

D'Angelo's memory causes many waves this week. Reliving the accidental gangster's death sees McNulty, Brianna, Stringer and, finally, Avon, explore and face up to many home truths. The boy's death will always be with them, and, as D'Angelo himself tried to grasp so eloquently in prison, there are no second acts in American lives. Not in these ones anyway.

D'Angelo's murder was a powerful slap across the face for the viewer back in season two. The warning was clear: don't get complacent; don't think anyone's too good to die. And it occurred just when things were looking up, relatively, for D. Deciding to finally cut his ties to his uncle, D was seemingly on a redemptive path before he was slain on Stringer's orders.

Jimmy is a man with two motivations in pursuing the truth about D's demise. First, he genuinely cared about him and believed he was in over his head. Second, his obsessive chasing of Stringer leads him to this seemingly overlooked detail that no one else seems to care about. McNulty may well and truly be giving a fuck when it's not his turn in this latest line of inquiry, but we give a fuck. How could we not? In this case Jimmy is the voice of morality.

Brianna's understandable distress at being shown pictures of her son lying dead and being accused of sacrificing him for her own lifestyle would appear distasteful and downright despicable, were Jimmy, damn him, not right on the money. He manages to figure out what happened and how it came to be by pushing the right buttons, and sends Brianna back to her brother as an agent of justice. Jimmy is not sure whether it was Avon or Stringer who inked the final contract on D, but he uses a mother's grief – and deserved guilt – to beat the bushes.

As he devastatingly tells Brianna: "I kinda liked your son, and it grinded me that there was no one to speak up for him." And when she demands to know why he went to Donette instead of her, he cruelly replies: "Honestly? I was looking for someone who cared about the boy."

For Stringer, D'Angelo's death was, on the surface, simply a business decision that Avon or Brianna could not possibly make. But, as we have discussed many times before, String's innate jealousy and animosity towards D suggests his dirty little secret is also a source of mischievous pride. He knows he did what was right for the organisation. The boy was soft; he would inevitably roll.

And as Stringer slowly and deliberately reveals the truth to Avon after receiving a barracking for being too weak, we are left in no doubt where his sensibilities lie. It is he, not Avon, who is strong. "You gonna tell me blood's thicker than water? You take that shit somewhere else!"

For best friends or brothers, it takes something extraordinary to break their bond – jealousy, a woman, betrayal, or, as in this case, money. As Avon says: "The difference between you and me? I bleed red, you bleed green." Their playground tussle and subsequent angry silence telegraphs what is to come later in the series: mutual betrayal resulting in one's incarceration and the other's death.

FAVOURITE QUOTE:

"A great village of pain and you're the mayor." – The Deacon strips away any pretensions Bunny may have had about Hamsterdam.

RUNNING TOTALS:

Murders: up one to 50, as one of Avon's crew gets taken out when Chris susses his honey trap for Marlo.

McNulty giving a fuck when it's not his turn: up one to 25 as he mercilessly preys on Brianna's guilt to sow discord among the Barksdales.

Omar stick-ups: up one to eight with an off-screen score.

EPISODE 9 – Is Hamsterdam realistic?

PAUL OWEN

Hamsterdam is probably The Wire's bravest and most radical storyline. Elsewhere the programme confines itself to describing problems – under-resourced and irrelevant schooling, sluggish bureaucracy, political corruption – but on the subject of the war on drugs it examines a possible solution. Over the course of this series, police chief Bunny Colvin establishes three drugs-tolerance "free zones" in derelict areas of Baltimore, and the programme carefully and even-handedly analyses how these would work and what the eventual political, media and public reaction would be.

Quickly nicknamed Hamsterdam – a corruption of Amsterdam, "one of those countries where drugs are legal" – the experiment is successful in clearing drug dealing off residential street corners that had been blighted by the dealing and its attendant violence for years. We see peaceful corners presented like a dream or a fantasy, or a trip to the past, with neighbours hanging up their clothes, the radio trilling softly, kids rushing past to play games.

In interviews, Simon has put his cards on the table, calling the war on drugs "a venal war on our underclass" and promising to vote to acquit any drug suspect if ever called up for jury service. "Since declaring war on drugs nearly 40 years ago, we've been demonising our most desperate citizens, isolating and incarcerating them and otherwise denying them a role in the American collective. All to no purpose. The prison population doubles and doubles again; the drugs remain," he wrote in Time magazine.

But The Wire does not present Hamsterdam as a simple answer. The free zones themselves, while largely violence-free, are shown encouraging addiction and promoting disease and prostitution. (Colvin eventually invites public-health charity workers and harm-reduction experts into Hamsterdam to deal with these problems – an impressively undramatic, realistic touch.) Young children formerly employed by dealers as look-outs are laid off, leaving them idle and in poverty. The viewer is also invited to sympathise with the one person who lives in the derelict area, an elderly woman who tells Colvin: "You say you've got a programme that can place me somewhere else, but you ain't got a programme for what's outside my door." The writers are not afraid to point out flaws in the plan.

In this week's episode Colvin's informal adviser, the Deacon – who has been harsh on Hamsterdam before – criticises Bunny for choosing to retire before seeing his experiment through. "You managed a truce," he tells him. "Keep it going, we're gonna reach some of those people chasing dope and coke, and maybe even some hoppers too."

There has been some criticism that the Hamsterdam storyline is unrealistic, with some even comparing it to McNulty's antics with the homeless in series five for breaking the show's informal rule that "nothing should happen on screen that hasn't in some fashion happened on the streets".

I concede it's unrealistic that the police bureaucracy wouldn't quickly get to hear of what was happening, but the policy itself echoes experiments tried by various governments and police forces, from Portugal to Argentina to Brixton, as they struggle with the problems arising from the fact that so many people want to take drugs. As Steve Busfield has mentioned, Kurt Schmoke, the mayor of Baltimore from 1988 to 1999, was a vocal advocate of drug legalisation, which may have had some influence on the storyline.

David Simon and Ed Burns's basic point is this: the prohibition of drugs makes the situation worse, just as prohibition of alcohol ramped up the problems caused by alcohol in the 1930s. It criminalises swaths of society, fills prisons with non-violent offenders, facilitates the creation and enrichment of violent gangs, forces those who use drugs to use adulterated, dangerous products, brings the law into disrepute, and costs vast amounts of money that could be put to better uses. In their book The Corner, Simon and Burns describe "the absolute futility of trying to police a culture with an economy founded on lawbreaking".

QUOTE OF THE WEEK:

An indignant Omar on his blissfully ignorant grandma, the shooting of whose hat causes much baroque outrage: "That woman think I work in a cafeteria – at the airport!"

RUNNING TOTALS:

McNulty giving a fuck when it's not his turn: up one to 26 for coming into work on a Sunday. It makes the rest of us look bad.

Dubious parenting: up one to seven. He sneaks off in the middle of the night while his kids are asleep to go and have sex with Theresa.

Herc fuck-ups: I'd call dropping a dime on Hamsterdam a big fuck-up – so up one to nine and a half.

EPISODE 10 – "Reform, Lamar, reform"

MARK SMITH

Reformation's the word as season three's dramatic setpieces are set in motion in a blink-and-you'll miss it episode of plot and character development, beginning with the revelation of McNulty's vulnerable side: "I feel like I don't belong to any fucking world that even matters ... First time in my life I feel like a fucking doormat – like I'm just a breathing machine for my dick." The scene, shared with an increasingly marginalised Kima, is the only time that I can recall where his characterisation blossoms much beyond the rather crude "cop show staple" stereotype that chagrins many Wire fans. Kima reacts with a stifled snort followed by an uncomfortable what-the-fuck-do-you-say-to-that silence.

The reformation of the episode's title can be applied to various themes within the episode, not least Carver's personal development. I think we can trace the emergence of Carver's tenderness and maturity that so defines much of season four back to his little pep talk from Colvin here. Colvin, of course, hits the nail on the head so damn hard that even Herc would probably have walked out of that room with something approaching a renewed sense of purpose and vocation.

Meanwhile, the reformation of the western district's drug policing is already having a profound effect on Rawls's beloved stats: a 14% drop in crime in just a couple of weeks. Information is also the thread that runs through Cutty's sub-plot, and that of the corner boys he's struggling to get into his gym. "I ain't got no idea how to come at these hoppers," he says to the Deacon. It seems to me that Cutty is living his own battle to go straight through the corner boys, as if, if he can manage to "save" just a few hoppers, then he will be absolved of his own demons.

Cutty's disbelief at the attitude of youngsters is another example of how things "ain't what they used to be" in Baltimore, of crumbling social structures and respect. On a number of occasions, Prop Joe, Butchie, Stringer, Avon and Omar all reminisce about a time when, even in the game, things were done with a little more respect, a touch more class, a bit more nobility. Cutty's history, his crimes and his time don't seem to have prepared him for the sheer shock of being treated like dirt by a hopper whom he's trying to help. He realises, with the help of the Deacon, something that Carver and Prez, principally, learn with greater fanfare in series four – that if you stick with Baltimore's young people, let them know you're in it for the long-haul, build their trust and weather the storm of their sharp tongues and surliness, you'll get through their defences to the real people underneath. And only then can you start making a difference.

FAVOURITE QUOTE:

"Why the fuck you coming up behind me?!" an anxious Lemar exclaims in the gay bar. It just made me chuckle. And of course we have Rawls's surprising appearance – surprising only because you expect to recognise gay characters on TV from their behaviour. But it doesn't always work like that in real life, so why should it in television? Raises the question though: why even show him in there at all?

RUNNING TOTALS:

Murders: up one to 51 with the death of Devonne.

McNulty giving a fuck when it's not his turn: up one to 27, though this time he's giving a fuck about what the women he sleeps with think of his career.

Bubbles attempting to get clean: earning clean money from his superb efforts with Squeak and Bernard, and he seems to have shaken off the irredeemable Johnny Weeks – up to four.

EPISODE 11 – Stringer down

JUDITH SOAL

If The Wire is the best television series ever made, this surely rates as the finest episode ever seen on the small screen. It earned writer George Pelecanos an Emmy nomination (one of only two nominations across the five series – neither won), although it's the director, Joe Chapelle, who really shines. The episode opens with a sepia-toned ode to the Wild West, as Omar and Brother Mouzone square up in a classic gunfighter duel. You can almost smell the tumbleweeds on the deserted street while the outlaws make small talk about their weapons.

Much has been made of the influence of Greek tragedy and Shakespeare on The Wire, but it's a different genre that's being referenced here. Bunny isn't the commander of the Western district for nothing, the sheriff who single-handedly tries to keep civilians safe from the bad guys. When he takes Carcetti around the post-Hamsterdam corners, it's no coincidence that he talks about having "shown you the good, now let me show you the ugly".

Like the opener, the most cataclysmic scenes in this episode discard The Wire's usual raw, naturalistic look in favour of a more stylised aesthetic. Take Stringer Bell and Bunny Colvin's meeting in the graveyard, where it's all back lighting and smoke playing off giant crosses and angels on the graves. Chapelle says the intent was Gothic, and of course it would have to be. Stringer meeting Bunny Colvin? To inform on Avon? Who would've thought? And where else could the meet take place but a cemetery, with its grim foretelling of events to come?

The episode is called Middle Ground, but the message seems to be that there's no such thing in Baltimore. You can't be half-gangster, half-businessman, and a mayor hoping for re-election can't half-legalise drugs. As the penultimate episode of the season, there's a whole heap going on, but no storyline can compete with Stringer Bell's. There's no middle ground for Stringer and Avon to resolve their differences, with Stringer believing Avon is threatening the business with his determination to make war for corners and Avon seeing Stringer as weak and unfocused for letting Marlo gain the upper hand. The relationship breaks when Avon ridicules Stringer for being played by Clay Davis. "They saw your ghetto ass coming from miles away," he mocks.

When the betrayals finally happen we watch them in concert, moving from Stringer and Bunny in the graveyard to Avon and Brother Mouzone in the barber shop and back. And the intensity ratchets up even further in the pair's final scene together (the best scene in the best episode of the best show?), with the balcony of Avon's apartment acting as a modern-day garden of Gethsemane. It's shot with a long lens, featuring tight close ups of the men's faces against a blurred but beautiful view of Baltimore. The coloured lights in the background add a magical quality to the scene, part of The Wire's extended love letter to the city. Each man knows he's betrayed the other without knowing he's been betrayed himself, but as viewers we can appreciate the emotional charge of every moment. They reminisce about the early years, trying to recapture past intimacy, but the poison beneath the surface keeps breaking through.

Stringer: Imagine if I had the money that I had now man, I could've bought half this waterfront property, god damn it.

Avon: Nah. Forget about that for while, man, you know, just dream with me.

Stringer: We ain't gotta dream no more, man. We got real shit. Real estate, that we can touch.

And in the last few, uncomfortable minutes, Avon extracts the information he needs to bring Stringer down.

We're back in the Wild West for the final, devastating encounter between Omar and Brother Mouzone and Stringer, which takes place at (high) noon. The set could be a run-down saloon in a small frontier town, with its dusty wooden floors, exposed staircases and roosting pigeons being disturbed on cue. For all that it's taken three seasons to set up this moment, Stringer's end comes suddenly. He learns the reason for his fate, finds out that Avon set him up, but isn't given a grand closing speech. "Get on with it motherf–" he says, without being allowed to finish the sentence. They do. It's beyond shocking, and, once it's over, eerily quiet. You can hear the shell casings hit the floor, as if in slow motion, and Omar and the Brother's footsteps as they walk away. The camera focuses on a battered sign for B&B Enterprises followed by a lingering shot of Stringer's body on the floor. The dream is over.

FAVOURITE QUOTE:

"That's it! Yeah! We got him!" Cheers and laughter from the detail after Stringer incriminates himself on the wire tap. Shortlived joy.

RUNNING TOTALS:

Murders: up two to 53.

McNulty giving a fuck when it's not his turn: it's a slightly different situation but I'm giving him one for protecting Bunny's Hamsterdam secret, even at the cost of a night with Theresa. This decision seems to mark a turning point for McNulty, as he finally starts to grow up. So 28.

Omar stick-ups: steady on eight; I don't think Stringer's death counts.

EPISODE 12 – Time for change

SAPTARSHI RAY

Hamsterdam is finished. Stringer Bell is dead. Prezbo is leaving the BPD. McNulty no longer wants to be a murder police. Bunny Colvin gets the boot. Tommy Carcetti wants to be mayor. It's all change in Baltimore as season three draws to a melancholy close.

And there is no sadder figure than Bunny, the likeable district commander of the western, undone by his attempts at making sense of the war on drugs, unhinged by his attempts to stop people finding out, and unwavering in his loyalty to his men – the trait that seals his fate.

As Rawls and Burrell make political hay out of Hamsterdam in securing their posts, for the moment at least, Bunny has to answer for his hare-brained scheme. As TV reporters descend on the vision of hell among the vacants, Mayor Royce realises his idiocy in believing voters would have approved.

In threatening to punish everyone under his command, Rawls strongarms Bunny into taking not only the blame, but leaving the force in ignoble fashion – a sad end to an otherwise stellar career. "What part of bend over didn't you understand?"

Burrell gets his full term from Royce while Rawls stand like a colonial officer in the trenches, shouting "Over the top, gentlemen!" as Ride of the Valkyries blares from his car. The BPD's humps do what they do best: bust heads. The buses roll in, the fiends and hoppers are rounded up, and, as the glorious strains of Solomon Burke's version of Fast Train plays over the final montage, Herc, Colicchio and the western's finest revel in returning to street rips and corner raids. Same as it ever was.

FAVOURITE QUOTE:

"This must be one of those contrapment things" – Bodie beats the rap over Hamsterdam.

RUNNING TOTALS:

Murders: no change at 53, though we say farewell to Johnny Weeks, who dies a lonely overdose death in Hamsterdam.

McNulty giving a fuck when it's not his turn: I'm giving him one this week, not so much for his police work as for his acknowledgement that he has to change in order to survive, and sees a future with Beadie. So 29.

Bunk drunk: up one to six: a hipflask of whiskey to the good.

Interview: Idris Elba

STUART JEFFRIES

Recently, one of Idris Elba's young relatives came up to him, rolled up his trouser leg and showed off some bite marks. "Man from another corner set his pit bull on me," he said. The kid is dealing drugs on London's streets, Elba says. "He needs help getting out of that world."

Elba is telling this story in a Soho screening room before an audience of hardcore fans of the cult TV series The Wire, in which the Hackney-born actor excelled in the role of the venal, disgusting, but utterly captivating Baltimore drug kingpin Russell "Stringer" Bell. After the Q&A, the audience will get to see Elba's favourite instalment of the drama. Most of the people here know his character better than Elba does: they know that Bell was shot in that episode by charismatic hoodlum Omar Little and bow-tied assassin Brother Mouzone in a hit commissioned by his boss, Avon Barksdale. Elba, if he ever knew these details, has consigned them to oblivion. He claims not to have watched much of his work on the series and to be immune to his character's allure.

"I like this episode because Stringer dies in it," Elba says by way of introducing it. "I celebrate the fact that he dies. I have a problem with the glorification of a drug dealer and America is fascinated with that world. We're celebrating the very fucking problem that America has in its hood. But Stringer Bell was no role model. He ruled the people who worked for him through fear. So it was good that Stringer died." The lights go down on a rather stunned silence: the audience, if not the man who played him, loved String.

A couple of days later I meet Elba in a posh East End members' club and ask about his relative's story. There's one word that intrigues me, namely "corner". It's the word, after all, that the slingers, junkies and narcos in The Wire use to describe a drug gang's territory. I know diddly about the slang of illicit pharmaceutical retailing in London, but it just strikes me that maybe London is imitating the Baltimore of The Wire, as dealers sort out their turf wars.

"That word was around here before The Wire," he says. "For me, the point of the story is that what you see on The Wire is happening here. I find it hard to believe, especially that a kid from an African family sells drugs. Africans, we hold on to our youths and whip them into shape." Elba, whose father is Sierra Leonean and mother Ghanaian, pauses. "But you know what? I can't judge now. I'm 36 and I don't live here any more. When I was a kid, I thought it was tough. I got beaten up. There was this bully who would nick your bike and ride it around and give it back to you messed up at the end of the day. Once he locked me and my bike in this 6ft by 4ft cupboard in the stairwell of the high rise we were living in. He lit a newspaper and threw it in. I was kicking to get out. That was terrifying, but I know it's harder for kids today."

Elba, who now lives mostly in Atlanta, Georgia, is visiting London, staying in his mum and dad's house in East Ham. "I'm back in the room I was in when I was 13 and started dreaming of making a mark as an actor like Marlon Brando or Robert De Niro." Today, Idris Elba is making a mark. When he presented some awards at the Baftas last month, someone whispered that his latest movie, Obsessed, had grossed a record-breaking $27.5m in its first weekend. "I looked around the room and there were all these stars – Jonathan Ross, Ross Kemp and Lenny Henry – and knew for the first time I was as good as them."

Obsessed's success means Elba's stock has risen through the roof – so much so now that critics are already talking about him as the first black James Bond. "There was this thing on CNN where they had a discussion saying that if there's a black president in the White House we now need a black Bond. And then the idea just spread like a virus. People kept coming up with ideas as to who should play the role, and then people in the blogosphere said what about Idris Elba. Even Daniel Craig said in an interview that the world is ready for a black Bond."

So would you fancy it? "Who wouldn't like to play Bond? Do I think it will happen? No, but I've got what it takes to do it. I can run around, flirt with ladies and drink. Plus I'm English."

The fact that Elba, the Hackney boy made good, is being considered for the role shows how far he has come. He credits his parents with making all the difference, but they couldn't do everything for him. "They were poor. When I passed the audition to get into the National Youth Music Theatre, my mother said: 'You can't go. We haven't got the money.'" So Elba went to see his school drama teacher, who advised him to apply to a grant from the Prince's Trust, the charity set up by Prince Charles to help young people. "Without that £1,500, I don't know what I'd have become. It got me into drama school."

When I first meet Elba, he is chatting to some young men and women, mostly aspiring actors, wannabe sports stars or musicians, who have also benefited from the Prince's Trust. In the room, there are people who are crawling from the wreckage of their earlier lives, from broken families, unemployment and the lack of confidence that comes with being from the wrong race or class in modern Britain.

Elba tells them about the book that helped him (Paolo Coelho's The Alchemist), about acting he admires (Meryl Streep in Doubt), and then takes questions. One young actor asks what she should do when she feels like jacking it in. "Don't be discouraged," says Elba. "It's easy to complain, but take that energy and use it and take that £17.50 you earned that week and spend it on seeing a play that will inspire you."

Did you connect with those kids, I ask Elba. "Yeah, but their stories are very different from mine. My parents kept me on the straight and narrow. Some of those kids weren't so lucky." Did your parents want you to become an actor? "No, they couldn't see any money in it." What then? "They saw me in something manual. I wasn't bad at school, but I was never a bookworm. My dad wanted me to be a footballer." Were you a good footballer? "Yeah. I could have done that. If it hadn't have been acting, though, I guess it would have been music." Elba still works as a DJ, using the name Big Driis or, when in the US, Big Driis the Londoner.

"I think the thing for talented people is that they can turn themselves in any direction. I'm one of those people who've been able to do anything." He doesn't say this boastfully, just in the pleasant realisation of the proposition's truth. Elba has an enviable confidence about him, even to the extent of talking of himself in the third person. "If Idris had been a footballer now, he'd have been coming to the end of his career now," he says. "I could have been like Vinnie Jones."

He tells me how he made his name as an actor. His first assignments were hardly glamorous. He worked the night shift at Ford in Dagenham and then, by day, played in burglary reconstructions for Crimewatch, nicely demonstrating the institutionalised racism of the

British media and society. "That was about the first on-screen acting I did. All the time I was trying to get agents to come and see me when I did pub theatre. Only one did, and thanks to her I got roles that weren't those roles just for black men. Even so, I could see my career being like those of black British actors I admire, such as Colin Salmon or Adrian Lester. I wanted something different. In the end, I realised that if I wanted to be all I could be, I would have to go to the US."

So he moved to New York. One problem: the accent. "It took me three years to get it right and during that time I wasn't working there at all. I kept flying back for acting jobs over here, but it wasn't exactly cost effective." Eventually, he nailed that accent and the roles started coming. He joined The Wire after impressing in Law & Order.

"I auditioned for Avon Barksdale, and when I didn't get it, it was a kick in the teeth. But on the same day my baby girl was born, they told me I'd got the part as Stringer." The role became infinitely more interesting than that of Barksdale. Bell had aspirations to leave the dealing behind and become a legitimate property developer. "He had the intelligence to take classes in economics, I'll give him that," Elba says of Stringer. It's symptomatic of The Wire's dismal prognostications for African-American men from Baltimore's mean streets that Bell had the most considered exit strategy of any of them, and died within a whisker of making his escape.

After The Wire, Elba decided he would make a career move. "Like I told those kids, you've got to move out of your comfort zone. I never want to play anything like Stringer Bell ever again."

Are you enjoying your success? "I'd throw it all away tomorrow for my baby girl," says Elba, who lives near his daughter and his ex-wife Dormowa Sherman. He gets his reality checks, not just from his daughter, but from his parents. "They're so removed from what I do. I tell them that Obsessed is breaking box-office records and that I'm going to be interviewed on the Paul O'Grady Show, and my mum says, 'Oh, that's good. Did you eat today?' I need that stuff more than ever."

Dennis Lehane on The Wire

INTERVIEW BY KILLIAN FOX

I'd known David Simon for a bit, and I knew George Pelecanos quite well. David asked me to write an episode for the third season and I said, "Sure," because I was a great fan. I'd never written for TV before. I was a little out of my depth at first – I wrote too long and too many speeches. In a script, less truly equals more. You have to be more judicious and your characters have to come out and act. There's no time to dick around with them sitting around thinking or talking about what they might do, which is the type of lassitude you can engage with if you're a novelist.

David talks a lot about how he thinks one of the greatest bits of dialogue in film is the line near the end of The Wild Bunch when William Holden says, "Let's go." The film is working by that point. That's not to say that brevity is always the soul of the scene. It's saying that if you're doing your job, you should be able to get to the point where you can write a line as simple as "Let's go" and it carries the entire weight of everything that went before it.

The scene in The Wire that people will be talking about in 100 years from now will be the "fuck" scene that David and Ed Burns wrote, with McNulty and Bunk doing nothing but saying the word "fuck" in all its variations for two minutes as they go through a crime scene. There are so many other ways you could have written that scene but none as fresh and original as that.

The people who have the original vision for a TV show do the architecture and build the structure, as David and Ed did for each season. Then they bring in the writers to fill in the room and hang the dry wall and lay down the floors. I wrote three episodes, one per season from the third to the fifth. I would fly in, because I don't live in Baltimore, and spend three or four days in the writers' room and we'd "beat out" my episode, then I'd go home and write it. In the writers' room, as well as David and Ed, you'd have the writers George Pelecanos and David Mills, Bill Zorzi, The Wire's political guru, and, when he was alive, Bob Colesberry, the executive producer who played a detective on the show. The meetings were wonderful but you had to know who you were as a writer before you walked into that room, because kid gloves were not in play. Nobody was cracking the whip but nobody was suffering fools either. If you came up with a dumb idea, someone would say: "No, that doesn't work." Why? "Because it doesn't." There was no hand-holding; I had some ideas shot down in flames.

I would come out with what's known as a "beat sheet", in which the major movements of the episode are all played out for you. You don't have much wriggle room within that, but David said he was always at his best as a writer when the beats were the least detailed. One of the beats I had was simply: Stringer Bell needs to discover that his crew are not as intelligent as he had hoped. That's when I got to write the "40-degree day" speech, which his crew just doesn't get. But nobody told me to write about a "40-degree day".

Baltimore's issues are the issues of any large urban centre in the US, but I wasn't prepared for the sheer scale of the poverty. Anybody who oversimplifies the issue of poverty in this post-industrialised alleged first world, should be forced to spend live in a tenement in west Baltimore. It looks like Berlin, April 1945. It was eye-opening for me.

What makes The Wire so good? I don't think there's an ounce of wish fulfilment in it, as there is at the base of most dramas. Every country has its central myth, and one of America's is that good will out. David and Ed just said "bullshit" to that. But nor do they indulge the flipside, which is that life sucks and then you die. It isn't that simple, it's just that we're all fucked up. Don't go looking for heroes or villains in this show because you'll have a hard time finding them.

Series Four

The next generation

EPISODE 1 – Education, education, education

JUDITH SOAL

Snoop at the hardware store buying a nail gun; you just know she won't be using it for a nice bit of DIY. Watching that same realisation dawn on the face of the sales assistant is one of those brilliant but uncomfortable Wire moments that shouldn't be funny but is, even though you suspect that by laughing along you might be celebrating violence. There are many such moments in this series, with its focus on children and schools, and David Simon has confessed that he sometimes felt ashamed at the words he put into the young actors' mouths.

But as the opening scene of the season it's a classic, setting up one of the most important storylines – the bodies in the vacants – while hinting at the theme of education with Snoop listening intently to the relative merits of the De Walt 410 and the Hilti DX 460. See how easy it is to get them to pay attention when you teach them stuff that's meaningful to their lives …

This is by far the most we've seen and heard from Felicia "Snoop" Pearson. The actor's personal history as a convicted murderer and Baltimore drug dealer lends credence and disquiet to a character described by Stephen King as "the most terrifying female villain ever to appear in a television series". She pulls the scene off superbly, although the audio commentary suggests it was hard work – particularly for the script supervisor.

But the real stars of the series are the four children we meet here and watch with our hearts in our mouths as the season progresses. Michael, Namond, Randy and Dukie, the Boys of Summer of the title and the classroom characters you might find in any school. Simon describes them as, respectively, the cool, quiet one no one seems able to reach; the wannabe gangster who can't really take the heat; the hustler with a scheme for every situation; and the smelly kid with social problems.

Not that they don't all have social problems, and that's why we're here. The series is going back to childhood to tease out where the street players have come from and why they ended up the way they did. For although Michael and co have already been touched by the drug trade to a greater or lesser extent, there's still a childlike quality to their games. How could these innocent young things end up like Marlo or Omar or Bubbles? Keep watching.

A lot of the blame lands at the feet of the school system, another vehicle The Wire uses to explore institutional dysfunction. There's a great scene where the teachers at Prez's new school are being lectured on how to communicate with difficult students – always remember IALAC (I Am Loveable And Capable) – intercut with a similar situation in the western district with officers being trained in counterterrorism. In both cases the lectures are so way off the mark as to be laughable.

By the end of the episode, some of that childlike innocence is already gone, after Randy inadvertently sends Lex to his death. He sits on the steps outside his home, the weight of what he's done bearing down his shoulders, and somehow we know that things are only going to get worse.

FAVOURITE QUOTE:

Bunk about Lester Freamon (unscripted addition from Wendell Pierce): "Look at that bow-legged mother-fucker. I made him walk like that."

RUNNING TOTALS:

Murders: up three to 56, although we could add another five for the jobs Snoop did off-camera last month.

McNulty giving a fuck when it's not his turn: perhaps we should start deducting points here. McNulty turns down a chance to help Bunk out on Fruit's murder. Still on 29.

Drunk: McNulty's gone sober. Steady on 16.

EPISODE 2 – Being schooled

PAUL OWEN

Series four is Ed Burns's season. Burns was a Baltimore policeman – in Homicide, David Simon recalls him working on a wiretap case rather similar to Avon Barksdale's – who left the force to become a comprehensive school teacher, a journey very much like the one made by Prez during this series. Of the episodes in season four, Simon co-wrote only four of them – Burns was involved in writing every one.

The change is noticeable; there is less of the lewd police banter that Simon seems to enjoy recounting, and in fact this whole season is much more serious in tone, tragic, even depressing, without the levity that made earlier series such a "hoot" (as the New York Times put it), but offering the greatest level of sociological insight.

The themes are unfashionable and unglamorous to the point of self-parody, one of the main ones being the ethics and practicality of setting in schools. But the result is anything but undramatic, and this is perhaps the most moving series of the five.

Incidentally, it's interesting that two of the key elements of the schools plotline read rather differently in the UK. Setting, or "tracking", is normal – though not totally uncontroversial – in Britain, but seems to be anathema in The Wire's Baltimore. By contrast, the concept of allowing students to move up to the next school year only once they pass their exams is unheard of in the UK, and the "social promotion" that Prez and others get so worked up about (allowing troublesome kids to go up to the next class anyway) is simply the norm in Britain.

We have discussed before how police officers in The Wire often talk about working in certain neighbourhoods the way an army would talk about occupying enemy territory. In this week's episode it seems that this attitude has spread to the teachers; as they sit around trying to establish consistent groundrules for their pupils, one of them, Grace Sampson, instructs Prez: "You keep them busy, you keep them off-guard."

This week also features a tense scene where Michael, one of the youngsters whose stories we have begun to follow, refuses to take the money that Marlo, west Baltimore's new drug kingpin, is giving out to establish his place in the neighbourhood pecking order. Michael's refusal gives the viewer some sense of his backbone – and Marlo gets the point too.

QUOTE OF THE WEEK:

Valchek to Herc: Just shut up and play dumb.

Herc: I can do that. No problem.

RUNNING TOTALS:

Murders: up one to 57 – the witness whose death will help win Carcetti the election.

McNulty giving a fuck when it's not his turn / drunk / dubious parenting: no sign of McNulty; this is the first episode of The Wire where he hasn't featured at all.

Herc fuck-ups: the episode starts with something he initially thinks is a pretty bad one – catching the mayor getting a blowjob from his secretary – but by the end he reckons it might just have made his career. Nevertheless, it is touch and go how Royce will react, so his total goes up by half a point to 10.

EPISODE 3 – Homerooms

AMELIA HODSDON

Summer is well and truly over in this episode, and the wannabe corner boys are swapping petty crime for their first day as eighth graders at Edward Tilghman middle school. Namond is told off within seconds of entering the building; Randy plays nice then skips class to sell snacks to other grades; Dukie is bullied by fellow pupils; Michael sits quiet and watches.

And their homeroom teacher? "Mr Pryzbylewski – but you can call me Mr Pryzbylewski." Prezbo, as he inevitably becomes, sees his careful preparation come to nothing in the face of these hardened teenagers and has to be rescued by another teacher twice, the second time after a girl slashes the face of a fellow pupil. His only high, over a single completed paper, ends with scrawled desk graffiti – FUCK PREZBO – and the return of that hard-to-chip-off bubblegum.

We've seen Prezbo deal with more stressful situations than this, though, and a piece of chalk is not likely to be accidentally discharged or used to shoot a fellow officer.

What's going on in the city's other homerooms?

The corner: Omar's usual uniform of Kevlar vest and diabolical trenchcoat is discarded in favour of a silky blue pyjama suit when he finds his boyfriend, Renaldo, has finished the Honey Nut, and the effect is no less terrifying for the corner population. "Omar coming!" "Omar, yo!" "Omar, Omar!" The bogeyman is bemused, and no more so than when a pause for a cigarette results in a stash bag being thrown to him from a window. Not that he is pleased: "It ain't what you taking, it's who you taking from, you feel me? How do you expect to run with the wolves come night, when you spend all day sportin' with the puppies?" he says to Renaldo, who breaks off from reading a copy of Drama City by Wire regular George Pelecanos.

That novel's main character, Lorenzo Brown, is a former criminal trying to stay straight doing social work. The obvious parallel is Cutty, but, in his absence, let's look at Bunny Colvin – former district commander trying to stay employed and within his moral code. His job as director of security at a hotel ends badly when he can't leave his police sensibilities behind, and he is persuaded by the Deacon into a job as a fixer "operating in the urban environment" for an academic researching criminal behaviour – as Colvin had earlier put it, one of those "downtown, tie-wearing, come-to-do-good, stay-to-do-well college-types". This work will take them into the middle school after the initial target of 18- to 21-year-olds are found to be "too seasoned".

Chez McNulty: peace reigns in the McNulty household. His dismissal of Bunk's pleas to go out "for a taste" in the first episode became an invitation to come round and have dinner with "Beadie and the ankle-biters". Bunk has recovered from the shock sufficiently to take McNulty up on the offer, and comes round to find "one domesticated motherfucker". McNulty – not Jimmy, not Jim, not Daddy, not Pops, "just plain McNulty" – is eventually persuaded to go out with Bunk for that long-awaited taste (only after he hands over the decision to Beadie), though this is not the railroad-watering classic drunk of yester-episode. Bunk confronts the new-style, non-excessive McNulty with an extended metaphor about fish, concluding: "All dressed up like something it ain't, you know what I'm saying." McNulty counters: "Sometimes it is what it is. It really is."

FAVOURITE QUOTE:

"Let me see who I don't love no more" – Rawls tries to find room in homicide for Greggs.

RUNNING TOTALS:

Omar stick-ups: up two to 10. The corner shop stick-up is a classic – Omar insists on paying for his carton of Newports, and getting the correct change – and the street stash bounty is completely accidental.

EPISODE 4 – The world according to Cool Lester Smooth

SAPTARSHI RAY

If ever there was a character that illustrated The Wire's complexity, gusto, humour, empathy and social message, it's Detective Lester Freamon. Illuminating this week's episode with his zealous pursuit of Chris and Snoop, and the murders he just knows have been committed to rule the west side, his breadth of talents come into sharp focus in comparison to some of his more lackadaisical comrades.

Blessed with the supernatural patience and concentration of a chess grandmaster, the investigative skills of a super sleuth and a fashion sense labelled "brash, tweedy impertinence" by his boss, Cool Lester Smooth, played by a sparkling Clarke Peters, is often the closest thing the show gets to a narrator, mentor and brain all rolled into one.

"All the pieces matter" is Lester's maxim, and his eye for the paper trail, money trail, surveillance trail and every other kind of trail bedazzles his superiors and peers. As the man himself says: "You follow drugs, you get drug addicts and drug dealers. But you start to follow the money, and you don't know where the fuck it's gonna take you."

Exiled to the pawn shop unit for 13 years (and four months) after disobeying the bosses over a politically-flavoured homicide, Freamon is seen as a "cuddly house cat who couldn't even find his gun" by Daniels when he takes over the detail in season one. But the enigmatic doll's house craftsman proves himself to be anything but by procuring the first picture of Avon Barksdale, after overhearing someone say the gangster used to be a boxer.

Lester is more like a detective from the annals of crime fiction than the street – his eccentric hobbies, his smooth demeanour, his measured, cognac-like voice, simultaneously reassuring yet confrontational, often lend him the persona of a dapper professor rather than a hard-boiled cop. Taking Prez, Kima and Sydnor under his wing, he sculpts the team in his image and makes them all better police. As Daniels tells him in season three: "Motherfucker, you are the major crimes unit, far as I'm concerned."

So what exactly did Lester achieve? While it is Pryzbylewski who actually cracks the pager code in season one, it's Lester who figures out the geography of the supply trail and identifies the main stash house. In season two, partnered with Bunk in homicide, Freamon investigates the dead women in the container, and, once transferred to the Frank Sobotka detail, immediately connects the two investigations – something the BPD is notoriously bad at doing in The Wire.

In season three, it's Freamon who figures out how to get a bead on Stringer and the operation – culminating in his star turn undercover as a phone-jacking con artist. In season four, his obsessive certainty about an unseen killing spree culminates in 22 bodies being discovered.

And of course, his traverse to the dark side in season five, when he not only chases Clay Davis with the single mindedness of a hitman, and follows Marlo and his lieutenants in his own spare time, but also joins McNulty in his doomed serial-killer facade. It seems totally out of character for Lester to do this – or does it? After all, when McNulty was a mere pup, Lester was already giving a fuck when it wasn't his turn – long before it was Jimmy's turn. Freamon's connect is with the craft, and whatever means are necessary to pursue it.

Jimmy and Lester have an understanding that eclipses ones they have with any other partners, even Bunk. The two know it and cannot resist it. McNulty sees in the older man the kind of police he always wanted to be and joined the force to become, while Freamon sees in Jimmy a younger, more hot-headed version of himself. The two often clash – over repaying Daniels's faith in them, over Jimmy's selfish traits, over "that chain of command bullshit" and over the best way to bring down Stringer Bell – but they always make up and come together to do police work. Their first proper chat sets the tone for things to come:

McNulty: Why'd you ask out of homicide?

Freamon: Wasn't no "ask" about it.

McNulty: You got the boot?

Freamon: Uh-huh.

McNulty: What'd you do to piss 'em off?

Freamon: Police work.

FAVOURITE QUOTE:

"A good churchman is always up in everybody's shit. That's how we do" – The Deacon.

RUNNING TOTALS:

Murders: up two to 59 as Kima joins Crutchfield and Bunk at her first crime scene as a murder police, becoming the victim of the unit's weird initiation pranks.

Bunk drunk: up one to seven in one of my favourite scenes in the entire show. Lester obsesses over the bodies in a bar, while the Bunk screams for his old wingman Jimmy, and crapulously trumpets the merits of "puss-i".

Omar stick-ups: up one to 11 as Prop Joe sets him up to rob Marlo and his poker buddies, beginning a long-running feud.

EPISODE 5 – In sickness and in health

JUDITH SOAL

This week's episode is called Alliances, with its reminder that relationships can both feed and destroy the seat of power. "If you with us, you with us," Chris tells Michael, but we're shown that the reality is more complex than that. Betrayal and manipulation are as likely as loyalty, and a union that serves a character well at the start might eventually lead to their destruction. (Think Prop Joe.) We see the beginnings of three alliances that will become pivotal: Chris and Snoop reaching out to Michael on the street; Marlo realising the advantages of joining forces with Prop Joe (the result of some very underhand manipulation from Joe); and the influential Delegate Watkins being convinced to throw his weight behind mayoral hopeful Carcetti (a development made possible by Rawls's own alliances in the mayor's office and his ruthless eye for an opportunity).

It's not how good you are or how hard you try that determines your success, but rather how well you are able to play the game. A prime example is Stan Valchek, the commander of the south-eastern district, who ends season five one of the few Wire winners despite being repeatedly exposed as vindictive, devious and incompetent. The only time Valchek appears to hold back is when Herc seeks advice after inadvertently catching Royce getting a blowjob from his secretary. Rather than using the information himself, Valchek gives Herc a lesson in the art of political gamesmanship. Not that this should be seen as an uncharacteristic act of selflessness, rather perhaps as an insurance policy in case Royce wins the mayoral race: then Valchek would have some leverage over Herc, who has leverage over Royce. A master manipulator at work.

So in the spirit of the episode, here are my top five relationship lists:

Top partnerships:

1. Bunk and Freamon

It may be controversial not to have Bunk and McNulty, but for me it is the Lester–Bunk relationship that really stands out. There's a crackle in the air every time they are on set together. Two gifted but idiosyncratic detectives; two talented and charismatic actors.

2. Prop Joe's drug co-op

Prop Joe is the only drug kingpin who appears in all five series, largely due to his success in pulling his enemies into the co-op – although even that turns sour in the end.

3. Omar and Brother Mouzone

Again, it's tempting to list Omar's bond with Butchie here, but the Brother Mouzone alliance is more compelling for its dramatic repercussions.

4. Rhonda and Cedric

One of the few (only?) functional couples on the show.

5. Bubbles and Kima

Very different characters, but it's clear that there's real affection between them. This relationship is also used to stress the importance of developing CIs (confidential informants) rather than relying on aggression and street busts.

Top rivalries

1. Stan Valchek v Frank Sobotka

I know it only lasted one season, but this rates top for me because of the extreme pettiness and massive waste of personal energy and official resources. Remember the painful fall-out from the competition to donate a stained glass window to the local church? The police surveillance vehicle being sent around the world, an international alliance of dockworkers adding to the misery of one policeman in Baltimore? Police officers being diverted from fighting crime to ticket cars outside the union offices? There's a lesson here for us all.

2. Stringer Bell v Avon Barksdale

Childhood friends and lifetime partners who turn against each other, they could just as easily feature in the "top partnership" list. Interesting that Marlo, who comes to replace them, combines their relative strengths of business acumen and toughness on the streets.

3. Omar v the drug hierarchy

First the Barksdale empire, then Marlo, Prop Joe and the co-op – Omar's vendettas are always compelling. And none of the major players is ever able to win one over on him – that's left to a hopper.

4. Carcetti v Royce

The election battle that forms the backbone of much of season four – and would have had its own show, The Hall, if HBO had let David Simon have his way.

5. McNulty v Rawls

Another example of the destructive power of personal rivalries – McNulty spends hours tracing tide patterns to relocate a murder into Rawls's district and Rawls refuses (for ages) to let McNulty work proper cases, despite it being his best shot at getting the murder rate down. The words "cutting off nose to spite face" come to mind.

FAVOURITE QUOTE:

"Wait until he turns the corner." A hilarious, if somewhat un-Wire-like, scene where Carcetti and his campaign manager Norman force themselves to stay composed until Rawls is out of eyeshot after being told that Watkins has cut ties with the mayor.

RUNNING TOTALS:

Murders: up one to 60.

Herc fuck-ups: up one to 11. Taking the police camera to film Marlo was a good idea, it just lacked something in the execution.

EPISODE 6 – Where's Jimmy?

PAUL OWEN

Why does Jimmy McNulty appear in this series so infrequently? Billed first in the credits, Dominic West began the programme as its star. As we have discussed, McNulty – at his most basic, a roguish, talented Irish-American cop – was an easy "in" for the viewer, a recognisable character you could latch on to in the first series as you got used to the unfamiliar settings and dialect and the relatively demanding style of writing.

Some readers have suggested West's absence in series four was due to his wish to expand his movie career – he appeared in Hannibal Rising and 300 in 2007, and Punisher War Zone in 2008. But I prefer to put it down to the same unsentimental instinct in David Simon and Ed Burns that led them to strangle D'Angelo Barksdale and gun down Stringer Bell. The city's the star. The script leads where it leads. Everyone's expendable. If a season primarily about education and politics has no place for a dogged, egocentric homicide detective, then he's out. They don't always act so ruthlessly (Omar, Bubbles), but in this case Simon and Burns credit the viewer with no longer needing McNulty to hold their hand.

Anyway, Jimmy is not totally absent in series four. He has swapped major crimes for uniformed patrol duty, stopped drinking, and shacked up with port policewoman Beadie Russell and her kids. This rather extreme change in character is a little underwritten, as his transformation into the dead-body-strangling "McNutty" is in series five. Although West carries each change off convincingly, in both instances we are presented with the finished product without ever being shown exactly how it was formed.

McNulty pops up in this episode when a warrant is issued for the arrest of Omar Little – the old informant for whom he has always had a soft spot. His sympathy for Omar is evident when he lets Little use his mobile to make a phone call. "You some kind of Democrat, or what?" asks a fellow officer.

Omar in prison is a gripping diversion which, as far as I'm concerned, could have run for the rest of the series. Seeing this fearsome character trapped with hundreds of his enemies put me in mind of the line from Watchmen: "I'm not locked in here with you; you're locked in here with me." Yet the viewer genuinely fears for Omar's life, especially at first, and it must be said that the two inmates Little's best friend Butchie sends to protect him toy with his feelings quite cruelly – playing threateningly with a knife etc – before finally revealing who they are.

In the world outside the prison, we finally reach election day for mayor Clarence Royce and challenger Tommy Carcetti. The programme admirably bows to realism in dramatising the hotly contested Democratic primary vote rather than the general election – a one-horse race in this heavily Democratic city – although that putative main event, which must have caused Carcetti at least a day or two of organisational sweat and toil, is rather farcically dealt with through nothing more than a line of expository dialogue later on.

The buzzing campaign scenes here have become very West Wing: very detailed, very fast-moving, with much plausible talk of districts, bases, endorsements and Photoshopped attack ads. Yet, for all the excitement, the result, when it comes, is a little underwhelming, announced over half a mobile conversation and greeted with ambivalence by Carcetti. It's also strange in terms of the pacing of this series – surely it would have made a satisfyingly dramatic climax to one of the later episodes?

Incidentally, it's an achievement for the programme that a storyline based around a white politician booting out a black mayor in order to get a majority-black city back on its feet never acquires any racist overtones.

QUOTE OF THE WEEK:

Donut to Randy, after the latter proves the only one of his friends willing to do an honest day's work for an honest day's pay: "Fool, if the motherfucker paid you out already, then why the hell are we still here?"

RUNNING TOTALS:

McNulty giving a fuck when it's not his turn: up one to 30: letting Omar use his phone.

Herc fuck-ups: up one to 12: Marlo outsmarts him good and proper with the sting at the train station.

EPISODE 7 – The rules of the game

SIMON JEFFERY

"The game" is The Wire's shorthand for the rules and conventions that govern life on the street, and by extension politics and the politics of police work. But sometimes the rules aren't clear and need to be restated. "A man got to have a code," an imprisoned Omar reminds Bunk in this episode. And sometimes the world is just murky. This week sees characters across all the major storylines turning to others for guidance.

Most prolific is Carcetti. Now set to be mayor, he has breakfast with a predecessor who explains the realities of the office in terms of being given a succession of silver pots – from the unions, the blacks, the Polacks – full of shit that you, as mayor, then have to eat. Luckily, outgoing mayor Clarence Royce is more on Carcetti's level. He calls it "a hell of goddamn job" and after the two laugh and joke about the primary campaign's dirty tricks a magnanimous Royce promises to do what he can to help the transition.

Likewise, Marlo and Herc turn to others to address their problems with the surveillance camera. Marlo wants to know how to find out who put it there, Herc how to get it back after Marlo steals it. But the choice of who they ask reveals volumes about them and their status.

Marlo turns to Prop Joe. With Avon and Stringer out of the way, Joe is now settling into his role as the sage of the Baltimore drugs gangs. From a park bench with the downtown towers behind him, he offers advice of such savvy you could imagine he has spent his whole life schooling the younger generation.

"Camera still there? Steal that motherfucker. If no one speaks to it then it's the feds sniffing you out. It's only federals be rich enough to lose a camera and not go to crying about it. You steal that bitch and someone comes knocking: it's local. Steal that bitch. See what comes."

Herc turns for his advice not to the older generation, but to his own – to Carver. This really is a bad episode for Herc. The theft of the camera begins the chain of events that sees him kicked off the force. But that he turns to his fellow sergeant, and not, say, a wilier older officer, cements a change between the former partners, and the onward rise of Carver.

More conventional mentoring between the generations has more success. Cutty is developing well – he gives up work rounding up truants if he cannot make a longer-lasting commitment to his boys; Prez's use of dice and a computer in the classroom warms the relationship between him Randy, Dukie and Michael; and it is in this episode that Colvin first encounters Namond, whom he will eventually take into his home.

Namond, Colvin possibly spots, wants rules. When his swearing and abuse fail to get him thrown out of school so he can go back to his corner dealing he shouts at his teachers: "I know the rules. You gotta suspend me. School gotta have rules."

If you know the rules you can use them. Levy – as always – is a great example of this. While Kima is unaware of the purpose of a polygraph test on Levy's client Wardell – "Leverage. To get him in here and fuck with him," a colleague tells her – the lawyer recognises it as the sign of desperation it is. But it is not just about absorbing the rules; the game will only take you so far. What is striking in this episode is that the most successful characters are the ones who strike out on their own. Prez's dice; Pearlman's promotion to the violent crimes unit because she risked offending the politicians; Daniels's disagreements with his superiors that catch the attention of Carcetti; and, in an impressive piece of pOlice work, Greggs going back to the scene of the crime to see who really did kill that witness.

FAVOURITE QUOTE:

Omar: "If I'd known I was going to be sharing quarters with all these boys, I probably wouldn't have robbed so many of them."

RUNNING TOTALS:

Murders: up one to 61. We don't know the victim, but Carcetti is impressed with how Daniels handles the crime scene.

Herc fuck-ups: up three to 15. Getting the camera stolen, aggressively interviewing Randy, and then failing to deliver him to Bunk.

EPISODE 8 – Political animals

HAROON SIDDIQUE

"How for real are you?" Lieutenant Daniels asks Carcetti at the meeting where he is anointed colonel by the mayor. Being "for real" may be a ghetto phrase, beloved of rappers eager to show they have not deserted the street, but it is a question that should probably be asked of every politician. Significantly, given what we know will happen in series five, it never gets a direct answer from the rookie mayor. "Well, I guess we're gonna find that out together," he says instead.

If Daniels were to look back on this exchange he would probably give it one of his wry smiles. At this point Carcetti is still the new, blue-eyed boy come to shake up the political system, with the run for governor that will eventually change his priorities still a distant thought.

The mayor is driven to act after he is treated to an unedifying spectacle of low-level street rips as he accompanies officers to see the reality of policing. Carcetti's introduction to "real" police work includes one of the funnier scenes of an overridingly bleak series, when the mayor, imploring the homicide detectives to act normally, prompts Jay to pull out a porno, Freamon to go to work on his models and Kima to slouch in her chair. "We catch a body, it's different."

But there are more serious aspects to Carcetti's wake-up call. When the mayor meets Rawls, Burrell's deputy blames affirmative action, a hugely divisive issue in the US in recent years, for the problems on the streets of Baltimore. This is an issue David Simon also tackled in Homicide and it re-emerges in The Wire with the need for a black commissioner to replace Burrell. Carcetti's deputy chief of staff, Norm, accuses Rawls of racism, but the mayor believes he is just saying it as he thinks it is. In Homicide, Simon details the often casual racism of detectives while also highlighting a system that does not always lead to the right man getting the job.

This is also the episode in which Prezbo learns that being "for real" and trying to do the best for his pupils is secondary to the requirement to "teach to the test", to deliver stats in a similar way to the police department.

And the pupils in Bunny Colvin's special programme become animated about the one thing that interests them – being corner boys (or a corner girl in the case of Zenobia). Namond offers Colvin a lesson in morality, pointing out that booze and cigarettes are not much different from illegal drugs, ironic given that the former major was turfed out of the force for his Hamsterdam experiment: "We do the same thing as y'all except when you do it, it's, 'These kids are animals.'"

No doubt: the adults are just political animals.

RUNNING TOTALS:

Murders: a New Yorker is shot by Chris for failing to identify the singer of Shake It and Jiggle It, thereby proving that he is from out of town. We also see Snoop and Chris disposing of the bodies of another two New Yorkers, although we don't see the hits. So up three to 64.

Bunk drunk: he's plastered again at the wake of Colonel Foerster and is disgusted by "mincing" McNulty being on the soft drinks: "Why don't I just suck your dick and get it over with?" Up one to eight. He's catching up with Jimmy.

EPISODE 9 – Gourmet moments in the game

SAPTARSHI RAY

Food has a pervasive existence in The Wire. While most shows think of meal times as an off-screen triviality, the trials and tribulations of Baltimore's residents seem to unfurl in and among their times of repast.

The melancholy scene in Ruth's Chris Steak House this week, where Bunny takes Namond, Zenobia and Darnell as a treat for their efforts in school, is a masterclass in studying the psychology of angry, confused and insecure teenagers from tough upbringings.

Their journey from "euphoria to abject humiliation to anger, without knowing the reason why" is played out among the white clientele and middle-class furnishings of an uptown restaurant. They are surprised there will be waiters, chastise each other for not using straws, mock each other for thinking "special" means a dish is on special offer and are too embarrassed and uncomfortable to ask for what they want to drink.

A mesmerising piece of TV, which illustrates how food, cuisine and habit are as much a part of your character as your actions or your language, and reminiscent of D'Angelo and Donette's visit to a similarly upscale eatery in season one, where a snooty maître d' plonks them on a puny table near the kitchen as they "don't have reservations".

Food in The Wire crops up in many ways, from the iconic Domino Sugars sign over the harbour in the opening credits to the Chinese food boxes constantly in the hands of the hoppers on the corners. Sometimes it is used as a visual metaphor, as when Wee-Bey scolds D'Angelo for talking in the car outside a takeaway – Bey stands under the sign that says "beef", while D is framed by the word "chicken".

At other times, it's a standpoint on which to proclaim your true identity. Bunk, at his most unsavoury, compares Jimmy to a recurring Baltimore speciality – lake trout – when he tries to clean up his act and settle down with Beadie. "They take something and give it a name to make it sound better, but it's still just a just a trash fish."

Lake trout makes many appearances throughout the programme, understandably, being a Maryland staple. When Marlo agrees to meet the honey-trap girl from the Barksdales it's at the Lake trout restaurant. Randy likes a lake trout sub with cherry soda while on the campaign trail for Carcetti. In fact, lake trout is such a signifier of project life that when Brianna drops off some spicy fish of a different variety from a downtown restaurant, Wallace has no idea where it's from or what the big deal is. "If it ain't in the west side, I don't know it, yo."

The cuisine is a part of the everyday fabric for the lives of our characters so there's no reason we shouldn't be privy to it too. Just as Martin Scorsese once famously described Goodfellas as "basically, a film about food", The Wire could be relatively labelled a "programme concerned with the consumption of chicken".

Oh the chicken, so much chicken. From the KFC feasts of Avon and Wee-Bey in jail, to Herc's apologetic chicken box for Bubs from Tyrone in season four, to the majestic chicken nuggets speech from D'Angelo in season one.

Herc and Sydnor arguing over where to get the best hot dog in Baltimore; Bodie and McNulty bonding over a burger and mutual hatred of Marlo; J-Bird's never-ending feasts that take in everything from sushi to quesadillas; Carcetti's cosy chats with Burrell and Daniels in Werner's diner; Duquan asking for "yakame with turkey grease" (which makes drunks throw up their liquor) in a decent Korean takeaway; and of course, Omar's enduring obsession with Honey Nut Loops. Something about everyone's eating habits leaves as much of an impression as their rhetoric or antics. Sure, all the pieces matter, but maybe all the ingredients do too.

QUOTE OF THE WEEK:

"You see anyone else in here all Fred Flintstone and shit?" Zenobia rebukes Darnell for tucking his napkin into his shirt.

RUNNING TOTALS:

Murders: up one to 65, as Chris and Snoop catch up with Andre.

Herc fuck-ups: up three to 18 – a bumper week for the BPD's answer to a never-ending migraine. One for carting off "anyone under 5ft 10 or under 160lbs" while looking for Little Kevin, who is a lot bigger than he sounds. Two for promising to help Bubbles then ignoring his call as he's getting pummelled, while interrogating the real Kevin. Three for, in said interrogation, claiming that Randy was an eyewitness to Lex's murder. All setting off a course of events that end in heartbreak and misery for Kevin, Randy, Bubs, Sherrod, Miss Anna, Carver, Herc himself, City Hall and the whole police force. That takes talent.

Bubbles attempting to get clean: up one to five as he is trying to keep it clean, but he has bigger problems in the shape of the thug that keeps knocking him out and stealing his hard-earned cash.

EPISODE 10 – Comedy in The Wire

VARUN KESAR (AKA WENGERBALL)

About six episodes into series one I realised I was into something very special and I did what I am sure every fan has done: I tried to convert the infidels. But how do you sell it? My way was by emphasising the humour.

An often forgotten aspect of The Wire is that it has some absolute laugh-out-loud moments: Bunk throwing up in the bin; McNulty and his partner surveying a murder scene using only the word "fuck". Naturally, as this is The Wire, some of the humour is dark and can leave you a little uncomfortable. Should we be laughing at Bubbles and Johnny when they are humiliated and stripped to their pants by Marlo's crew? Or when Bubbles goads the junkie bully, thinking he has Herc to come and back him up, only to be beaten severely? Was anyone else a little disturbed at the way in which the murder team played practical jokes on newbie Kima using a dead body as a prop?

In this week's episode we see a couple of good examples: the show starts with the tiny Donut driving another stolen car – always comic – but that scene culminates in the malevolent Officer Walker breaking his fingers. Later, a bitter Bubbles – having been left hanging by Herc and treated rudely by a minister – gets his revenge on both by tricking Sergeant Hauk into busting the clergyman.

One of the main ways in which The Wire uses comedy is to develop someone's character, because we never get a clearer picture of someone than when they are being funny (though not necessarily intentionally). So we know that Bodie's world is the game when the only fitting tribute he can give D'Angelo is a floral depiction of the towers, we know that Herc is a hump from his constant fumbling at work (his attempt to push the desk through the door, for example), we know that Ziggy craves attention and acceptance, but is ultimately not made of the right stuff for the game, when he tries to fight Maui and gets humiliated and is left on top of a stack of containers.

Steve Busfield has called The Corner "The Wire without the humour", but to imagine The Wire without the humour would be to imagine it without its soul. Yes, the plot, the characters and the realism are the main elements of the show, but the comedy is the glue that holds them together.

WITH THAT IN MIND, HERE ARE MY TOP THREE FUNNIEST MOMENTS:

3. The wiggers who exasperate Nick Sobotka in series two.

Ever since Ali G it has not been possible to watch a white man trying to act like a black gangster and not break into fits of laughter. Nice to see that The Wire shares this view.

2. Prezbo shooting the wall in series one.

Prez is far and away my favourite character. The way he redeems himself, twice, shows that maybe there is hope for us all. His first incarnation was as a hump in BPD and nothing summed him up more than this scene. I think this scene is only just funnier than the one where he hits Valchek, but both are classic.

1. The "fuck" scene.

A lot of the humour here is the face of the observer, the janitor showing McNulty and Bunk around. It's worth noting that the silliness and humour of the scene belies some real and very effective pOlice work.

QUOTE OF THE WEEK:

"Woulda enjoyed it that much more." Omar's response when asked if he would have robbed Marlo if he'd known who he was.

RUNNING TOTALS:

Murders: up two to 67: Little Kevin is murdered by Chris and Snoop, and Michael's stepfather is killed by Chris at Michael's request.

McNulty giving a fuck when it's not his turn: up one to 31 – ignoring the order to make small-time arrests.

Herc fuck-ups: up two to 20 – ignores Bubbles's cry for help for a second time, and then set up by Bubs to arrest an innocent minister.

EPISODE 11 – Fathers and sons

PAUL OWEN

This is a series about surrogate fathers and surrogate sons, a theme predicated on the lack of real fathers among the estates of west Baltimore.

None of the four kids whose stories drive this season have healthy relationships with their fathers. Randy (who might be the son of notorious gangster Cheese) lives with a foster mother. Dukie lives with a family of alcoholics; it is unclear whether his father is among them, but he is never mentioned.

Namond's father, Wee-Bey Brice, whom we know from previous series, is serving time for multiple murders. Namond lives with a mother who aggressively pushes him into a drug industry for which he is ill-suited with seemingly no regard for the danger this might place him in, let alone wider questions of its illegality or immorality. Wee-Bey is a more sympathetic figure, but for most of the series at least he broadly agrees with De'Londa's destructive approach.

Most interesting is Michael. In this week's episode we see his mother, a heroin or crack addict, begging Namond for a cut-price hit. She shows little regard for the welfare of Michael or his brother, Bug, and Michael acts as a parent to the little boy, picking him up from school, making sure he has enough to eat, giving him encouragement and helping him with his homework. We hear nothing of Michael's dad, but it is strongly suggested that Bug's father sexually abused the older boy, leading to his distrust of any well-meaning adults, such as boxing coach Cutty, and to a lesser extent Prez, the policeman turned teacher.

Cutty spots Michael's intelligence and maturity early, and he makes the most effort to be a father to him, as he does with many of the neighbourhood boys. He offers to train Michael personally, takes him to a boxing match and even follows him to the street corner where he has begun dealing to remonstrate with him one night. He is shot in the leg for his pains, while Bug's father meets a worse fate: Michael arranges to have him killed by Chris Partlow, the chief hitman of drug kingpin Marlo Stanfield. It is Chris who eventually becomes a mentor to Michael, whom he sees as a "puppy" to be trained up into a fellow killer and with whom he seems to bond due to his own memories of sexual abuse, although this is never spelled out. Eventually Michael will reject him too.

There are other father figures in this series. Prez's relationship with his pupils has matured: not only does he now command authority and respect – as we see in a classroom scene this week and when he breaks up a fight – but his loyalties have decisively shifted away from the police and towards his kids. Here we see him instructing Randy not to "snitch" and clamming up himself in the face of Lester and Bunk's questioning in order to protect his pupil.

Another father figure is Bunny Colvin, the former major who is now "a sort of a teacher". As a policeman he was a mentor to Carver, whose newfound maturity means he now joins Cutty as something of a surrogate father on the streets. But, in the classroom, Bunny's paternal instincts come to the fore. In this episode we see him begin to get through to Namond, the boy he will eventually adopt, first persuading him to play a trust game with his peers, and later being teased by the boy about his nickname. He is also very good with Albert, a foul-mouthed youngster who has just lost his mother but came back to school on his grandmother's instructions. "You wanted to be with your mom; course you did," murmurs Bunny.

Last, there is Bubbles, the heroin addict who has found a new apprentice following the death of his former partner in crime, Johnny Weeks. Bubbles is much more paternal to the callow Sherrod than he was to the unsympathetic Johnny, taking him to school and gradually giving him more responsibility within their business. His guilt and grief when Sherrod dies almost unhinges him.

QUOTE OF THE WEEK:

Bunk: "Lester do love listening to other people's phone calls, don't you? Bit of a pervert that way."

RUNNING TOTALS:

Herc fuck-ups: his worst fuck-up – hanging Randy out to dry – is behind him. This week he tries to make up for the damage this has done to his fellow officers, but the effect on the boy will be more long-lasting. Steady on 20.

EPISODE 12 – "Mike ain't Mike no more"

AMELIA HODSDON

If nothing before in The Wire has brought you to tears, this is the episode where you will crack at the sheer, epic shittiness of the hand our boys of summer have been dealt. George Pelecanos, who wrote the episode, has said of it: "We were at the top of our game here." It's hard to disagree.

The Michael who turned down work on the corner is long gone; his education at the hands of Snoop and Chris kicks off the episode, wrongfooting the viewer, and he is now a killer in training, as methodical with this as he was with his sporadic schoolwork: "One to the head, keep it quick." The puppy with the big paws puts his hands to different use when Kenard needs to be punished for stealing the stash – his violence, which leaves the tiny boy bloodied and silenced on the ground, terrifies Namond, who later says: "Mike ain't Mike no more."

Dukie is being forced to move on by the school system, away from the one place he had felt safe. Randy is confined to his foster mother's house, in fear for his life after Carver inadvertently gave him away. Namond is being punked by everyone he comes across – his reluctance to step up is ruthlessly exploited by his monstrous mother. "She expect me to be my father, but I ain't him," he sobs.

In the episode commentary, Pelecanos and director Joe Chappelle mention the "false moves" made by adults as they try to reach out to the four lost boys.

Colvin tries to console Namond, who ends up at the station after his mother declares: "Put that bitch in baby booking where he belongs; let him learn something" – before she can be told he has done nothing wrong. Bunny again reaches out, and Namond has nowhere left to go.

Prez tries to establish an understanding with Dukie, who responds blankly ("Did I do something wrong?") to talk of moving up a grade and away from the friend he has found.

Cutty tries to break through to Michael, and gets the most violent rejection – he is shot down by Monk on the corner.

Left with no home, friends or reputation, Randy shrugs off Carver's hand in the hospital, and along with it yet another offer of help. "You gonna look out for me, Sergeant Carver? You mean it? You gonna look out for me? You promise? You got my back, huh?"

One more shot of tragedy comes from Bubs. Searching for a way to get rid of the vicious junkie, he asks around, and leaps at the local Arabbers' suggestion of sodium cyanide. The apparent glimmer of hope around his excited preparations at bedtime seems too good to be true, and so it is. The tainted vial in his pocket is a loaded gun, and Sherrod duly pulls the trigger. The camera's lingering shot on the jacket forestalls the event, and we know the horror before Bubs realises that in his effort to escape his tormentor he has caused the death of his friend. What set this in motion? Herc's repeated failure to come to his aid.

FAVOURITE QUOTE:

"You do your piece with them and then you let them go," Prez is advised. We've spent a term with these boys, and seen how quickly the street takes them – I don't think we're ready to leave them just yet.

RUNNING TOTALS:

Bunk drunk: slurring about "another little taste" and J-Lo's "prime cut of ass", Bunk's on fine form: up one to nine.

Omar stick-ups: Omar pulls off an almighty heist, supported by his old soldiers. "The shit was unseemly, man," confesses Cheese to Proposition Joe. Up one to 12.

EPISODE 13 – The end?

PAUL OWEN

Should The Wire have finished here, at the conclusion of what a rough consensus suggests is its finest series?

How would we have left the characters? McNulty, happy, sober, in a stable relationship with Beadie, and hopeful about future involvement in complex, difficult cases like the ones that have defined his career, far from the drunken self-parody he will threaten to become in series five. "Maybe I'd be different, you know?" he suggests to Beadie, but the old McNulty is not far from the surface – witness the way he uses his guilt over Bodie's death as an excuse to rejoin Daniels's team.

Is it still possible at the end of series four for Carcetti to become someone idealistic and transformative for Baltimore, as he promised during his campaign? Not quite. He has already decided not to take Maryland's money to prop up Baltimore's school system, largely due to his own pride and ambition.

Prop Joe is still alive, the Greeks not yet persuaded of the wisdom of letting Marlo succeed him. "Joe, who I trust, who I respect, who I worked with for many years," Vondas intones to Marlo, who seems somewhat out of his depth. That will change.

Omar, having pulled off his greatest stick-up, is setting off for a peaceful new life in the Caribbean. If the programme ended here, we'd miss the happy scene of his new life down south – all he lacks is his Honey Nut Cheerios – but we'd also miss his dreadful decline.

The stories of Bunny Colvin and his educational experiment, Prez and his transformation into a teacher, and Cutty's successful attempt to go straight are all more or less wrapped up here. So, in a way, are the lives of Namond and Randy; we can see the future that's mapped out for them in the beating that Randy falls to in the group home and in the jangling of wind chimes that closes the series and suggests a better life for Namond, perhaps the least deserving of the four boys whose lives we have followed; perhaps that's the point.

But it was worth The Wire carrying on for it to complete two stories, at least. If we had left Bubbles here we would never have seen the heartening and hard-won scenes of his eventual redemption. In this episode, having just caused Sherrod's death, he is desperate, guilty, suicidal. "Like I don't know who I am," he says of his thwarted ambitions to make something better of himself. In series five, we get to see him find another, more positive side to his character, and work through some of the grief and guilt he is suffering from here.

Last: Michael. His is the story left least complete here. Intelligent, sensitive, and almost always aware of what the right thing to do is – witness the love and responsibility he feels for Bug, and his willingness to stand by Randy at his own risk – how has he fallen in with Marlo, Chris and Snoop, three of the show's most amoral, cold-blooded characters? Marlo rightly sees great potential in the boy but Michael will gradually come to see that the people who saved him from his abusive stepfather are not offering the life that he wants. If The Wire had stopped here, we would never have seen that final, heartbreaking moment when he says goodbye to Dukie and Bug, unable to even remember the person he once was.

FAVOURITE QUOTE:

Wee-Bey and Colvin's moving, sentimental conversation about the old days. "Our kind ... shit," says Colvin. "Man, we both know we're gonna go to our grave forever knowing what block Bentalou dead-ends at or who got the liquor licence over at the Underground or what corner Tater Man got shot on ... The west side we knew, it's dead, man."

RUNNING TOTALS:

Murders: up two to 69, and both traumatic in their own way: Bodie, then Michael's first kill. It's worth noting how bewildering it is that the guy who kills Bodie looks a lot like Michael, this following on from a scene where Marlo suggests Michael should do the killing. Chris talks him out of it, but the murder scene is lit and the killer's face concealed in such a way that it leads to confusion and probably undercuts the drama of the moment.

McNulty giving a fuck when it's not his turn: up one to 32: he gets Bodie's case dropped so he can turn him. But, in a fuck-up more typical of Herc than Jimmy, the two are spotted together, leading to Bodie's execution as a snitch.

Omar stick-ups: not exactly a stick-up, but he deserves one point for the audacity of his selling Prop Joe's own shipment of drugs – which he stole from Joe last week – right back to him. Up one to 13.

Bubbles attempting to get clean: up one to six – desperate to get off drugs, to go to prison or to kill himself for what he did to Sherrod.

Interview: Felicia Pearson

OLIVER BURKEMAN

The story of Felicia "Snoop" Pearson's life so far turns upon a single moment – a chance encounter that proved so significant, and might so easily never have occurred, it feels like a plot contrivance. In early 2004, she was 23, a mid-level operative in the Baltimore drugs trade who had been released from jail four years earlier after serving time for second-degree murder. One Sunday night, she was drinking at a nightclub, when she noticed someone watching her. "He was looking at me like he was crazy," she recalls. "He look like a thug, and I'm, like, 'Man, what you keep lookin' at me for?'"

Pearson had never seen The Wire, the TV drama that examines the life of Baltimore with a moral ferocity and a novelistic complexity that has won it near-universal critical adulation. So she had no way of knowing that the man watching her was Michael Kenneth Williams, who plays Omar, a freelance gangster who makes his living robbing drug dealers. "I remember just staring at her, staring at her, because I couldn't tell if she was a young lady or a little boy," says Williams. "I went over, and we started talking. And when I realised she was a young woman ... I just felt compelled to have her meet our producers. I thought maybe they could use her as a PA or something. I just wanted to be part of her having an option that wasn't going back to prison."

Pearson was sceptical. But, growing up in the ghetto, she'd long learned to stay attuned to opportunity. So the next morning she found the trailers housing the cast and crew, and almost immediately found herself ushered in for a screen test. A couple of weeks later, she had a part – as "Snoop Pearson", a character with the same name, same defiantly ambling gait and the same distinctive, smoky voice with its undulating, often-hard-to-follow Baltimore accent. The Wire's Snoop Pearson is a cold-blooded assassin, a soldier in the Baltimore drugs empire of Marlo Stanfield (played by Jamie Hector), who unflinchingly dispatches those who fall foul of her boss before boarding up their bodies in the city's abandoned buildings.

The real-life Pearson, meanwhile, felt as though she'd stepped through a looking-glass. Like Hector, she first appeared in the show's third season. But, until well into its run, in real life she was still dealing in hard drugs so she had a foot in two worlds, and the experience was disorienting. "I wake up in the morning," she writes of that period in her memoir, Grace After Midnight, co-authored with David Ritz, "get dressed, leave my work on the block to walk into a world about make-believe work on the block."

Pearson doesn't dress up her eventual decision to quit dealing in the language of moral repudiation: it was just that her old job became impractical. "If I keep hitting the block, I'll fuck up this acting business." But she's also keen to emphasise that her own life wasn't quite like The Wire's version. "We never put nobody in abandoned buildings or nothing like that. I sold drugs, yes, when I was younger. But, you know, I never, like, killed a lot of people, like Snoop on The Wire had. Nah. That's not me at all."

Four years later, Pearson still seems to be feeling her way in her new environment, treading with care, bestowing honorifics and using hyper-respectful "sir"s and "ma'am"s. She is dressed in baggy jeans and an outsized T-shirt, her hair immaculately braided. You're unprepared for her beauty – she and her fellow assassin in The Wire, Chris Partlow, played by Gbenga Akinnagbe, may be two of the best-looking hoodlums ever to terrorise a neighbourhood, but good looks aren't what you're focusing on while they're doing it. Also present is Hector, a professionally trained actor who is something of a chaperone to Pearson; I could meet her, her manager explained, only if he was free to meet, too. Together, they have launched a youth drama organisation, Moving Mountains, which works with young people in New York and Baltimore to devise and perform new plays. It is a matter of amusement for Hector that the Baltimore branch, which Pearson runs, is about to perform its first play, while the New York participants are still in the planning stages.

For Pearson, these are uncertain times: The Wire's fifth and final season has ended, and it is impossible to avoid the question of what she does next.

"I believe, if she puts her heart into it, that she can play other types of roles," David Simon says. "But she suffers from the same problem as any African-American actor: there are fewer roles than there is talent, and they're marginalised by the types of stories that the film industry tends to finance."

When Pearson was born, prematurely, in 1980, she weighed only three pounds; she was so small that she had to be fed with an eyedropper. Her parents, now dead, were both addicts, and she was born cross-eyed, she says, because of the drugs that had been coursing through her mother's body. As a baby, she was placed in a foster home in a neighbourhood she describes as the toughest in east Baltimore. It was a world of random violence, where everyday household chores might suddenly be punctuated by gunshots. Pearson describes one particularly gruesome day from her childhood: "I hear my cousin slipping out the back door ... I go back to washing a plate. Then Pop! Pop! Pop! Pop! I drop the plate. Someone's shooting. Someone's shot. Someone's screaming: 'Your cousin's down!'"

"I mean, trouble just always find you," she tells me. "You could try to stay away from it, but it'll find you, man, it'll find you."

Yet, for all the horror, there's an unmistakable sense that her life need not necessarily have veered in the direction that it did: her foster-parents were an attentive couple, who worried when she didn't come home on time and helped her become a high achiever in her first years at school. "I could have gone either way," she says. But they were already in their 60s when they adopted her, and their devout Christianity left her cold. She could not have discussed with them, for example, her dawning realisation that she was attracted to other girls.

Besides, the streets were calling. By the time she reached what she describes today as "the worst day of my life", she was 14, and no longer just working corners but running errands for senior dealers, charging $100 a time to pistol-whip people as a warning.

The way Pearson tells the story, she was walking through her neighbourhood when she saw a fight break out. "Didn't know the people," she wrote later. "Didn't know why they was fighting. Didn't know nothing except fights always drew me ... I wanted to get close and see what was happening. So I crossed the street. I fuckin' crossed the street."

According to an account in the Washington Post several years later, Okia Toomer, who was 15, had left her house to go to a nearby shop. But Pearson says Toomer attacked her with a baseball bat made of lead, "with murder in her eyes... If she caught me, I'd be dead." Pearson tried to get away, she insists, but the crowd was too thick. At some point in the struggle she fired the gun she was carrying. Toomer died on arrival at hospital.

In Pearson's mind, the killing was a clear-cut case of self-defence. True, she'd been carrying a loaded weapon, but "I used to always. That was the streets. Every time you turn around, somebody getting killed ... Sorry to say, you know, but I'd rather take somebody else's life than mine, you know. Back in the day." She was tried as an adult and sentenced to eight years in the Correctional Institute for Women in Jessup, Maryland.

Pearson's account of her time in prison is notable for its matter-of-factness. She seems to have given little thought, at the time, to the killing she had committed, a lack of feeling matched only by her lack of pity for herself. Arnold Lonly, a dealer who acted as a father figure, visited her regularly in jail, urging her to behave well, to study hard and to get her GED, the high-school equivalency exam. Then, a few days after one of his visits, news reached her that he was dead, shot in a drug deal that went bad.

Lonly's death seems to have changed Pearson profoundly: she describes a quasi-religious experience in her cell late one night that provides the title for her memoir, Grace After Midnight – a mystical sense of Lonly's presence. She vowed to change the direction of her life, studied for her GED, and was released almost as soon as the terms of her sentence allowed. But she lost two jobs, in a car wash and on an assembly line, after her employers discovered her record. By the time she met Michael K Williams that night in the bar, she was again making good money from drugs.

Her move from that world to the world of TV was not, she says, as easy as it might look in hindsight. But the swiftness of the transition was not lost on others, notably the family of Okia Toomer, who in a 2007 Washington Post article sounded distressed by the experience of having seen their daughter's killer playing a killer on TV. Sylvia Williams, Toomer's grandmother, recalled receiving a phone call from one of her daughters, crying. "She said, 'That girl that killed Kia is on The Wire,'" Williams said. "She's still acting violent."

Now, though, that old environment is completely behind her, Pearson insists: she's too busy, and doing too well financially, to miss the corners for a moment. She lives in a larger home now, outside the city, with her girlfriend and their dog. She has taken acting lessons, and has appeared on the quasi-reality series The Hills.

When you don't know what's coming next the trick is to be grateful for what you've got. She writes: "I wake up in the morning, yawn, stretch, get up, and look out the window. If the sun is shining, fine. If it ain't, that's fine, too. I'm saying a little two-word prayer. 'Thank you.' That's the whole prayer."

In defence of Marlo

BEN DAVIE (AKA STUPIDMANSUIT)

Many see Marlo as the most "evil" being on The Wire. He lacks the humour and profane wisdom of the more popular B'more denizens, but I believe he is key to understanding the show's themes. He is, in effect, the ultimate bureaucrat, one who plays the system without empathy or fear.

His sole aim is the increase of bureaucratic power – both his own power within the bureaucracy, and the power of the bureaucracy itself. Although he is certainly a person without a moral backbone, it is not really a question of good and evil at all, but of efficient success. Marlo's methods are the same approach taken by (say) Rawls; the only difference is the bureaucracy is the drug distribution system, so the brutality is more overt. The system itself is the evil, Marlo is just another player, albeit more successful than most.

He may come across as robotic and emotionally dead, but I don't think he's some unreal satanic bogeyman. He does still have feelings and desires, but he has obtained absolute control over them in order to succeed. Marlo allows himself to evince real care only with his pigeons. Emotional reliance of any kind on other humans is detrimental to playing the game so he has denied this to himself and uses his pets as a substitute, a means to safely bond with something.

The first time Marlo makes an impact is when his underlings are about to punish Bubbles and Johnny for leaning on their car, threatening them with a handgun. Marlo takes in the situation and says simply: "Do it or don't. I've got places to be." He instantly puts himself above trivial concerns; he shows neither anger nor compassion. He has merely sized the situation up, judged there is no threat or benefit to him therein, and leaves it as not worth his time. His decision-making is calibrated to winning "the game".

Marlo's utilitarian analysis is perhaps most marked when he decides Michael's fate. He clearly has a slight fondness for Michael (he chose him after all), and agrees with Chris he's unlikely to be the snitch. "But you willing to bet your life on it?" he asks, and the decision is made. He acknowledges his inability to put human relationships first in his last exchange with Joe, who he clearly also felt some bond with: "I treated you like a son." "I wasn't made to play the son. Close your eyes ... It won't hurt none".

On two crucial occasions rivals underestimate his ruthless efficiency: when Avon tries to set him him up by having a girl hit on him, and when Prop Joe presumes he can "civilise" him. Both Avon and Prop Joe believe they see themselves in Marlo and miscalculate as a consequence, fatally in Joe's case (and fatally for the set-up girl too). Marlo doesn't rely on heart and emotion like Avon, and he doesn't share Prop Joe's desire for friendship and community – and these traits which make Avon and Prop Joe so human also prove their undoing.

Marlo knows his name is everything for his power, so it is no surprise that the slur on his street cred provokes the one moment of genuine anger, the "my name is my name" speech played so beautifully by Jamie Hector. It is significant that Omar is the one who calls him out, as Omar is the other character who relies on his name for his power – "Omar coming" etc. Omar understands that the deathgrip Marlo has on the projects is inextricably entwined with his reputation and his name. He found Marlo's Achilles heel, calling him out and challenging him as a coward – trying to play on his street honour, like some modern gunfighter or samurai. If word had got back to Marlo it could have succeeded.

The value Marlo places on his street rep above all is shown when Herc tries to take him in to meet Bunny Colvin. He simply refuses with a stony "ain't gonna happen" and faces Herc down until Carver (wisely sensing the violence about to boil over) pulls him off. This was the only time in the series when someone stood up to the police in a face-to-face confrontation, as most of the underworld know the danger of hurting or killing a cop. Marlo knows this too, but his name on the street is more important than anything to him, and he was quite prepared to start something serious with the police to protect it. "My name is my name" trumps all.

A few words need to be said about Jamie Hector's masterful portrayal. He brings an eerily unsettling permanent stillness to the role, as though every little action has been perfectly measured in advance. The very absence of any distracting tics or movements make him mesmerising and terrifying to watch, a being of pure will who cannot be dominated. When he finally snaps, the impact is all the more profound for the absolute restraint that preceded it.

Lest you think I am celebrating Marlo for cracking the code of the game, I think he may be the classic victim of the system. In The Wire the overarching organisational machinery is geared to generate Marlos, people who have been forced to leave their humanity behind to succeed. I thought long on Joe's "It's hard work civilising this motherfucker". The systems we've created to live together in civilised society are the same soulless forces that create monsters like Marlo; paradoxically, civilisation itself is its own worst enemy.

Series Five

McNutty

NOTE: The articles for series five were published at the time of original broadcast

EPISODE 1 – My kind of news editor

STEVE BUSFIELD

So, Carcetti is eating mayoral shit, McNulty is back on the booze, Chris and Snoop are still free and Herc is still fucking it up for other people. And Omar, as always, is elusive so far.

The Wire has the beautiful knack of perfectly moving the story along between seasons: Herc now working for the bad guys (and probably not even realising it), Carcetti making the city pay for his political ambitions, and Bubbles turning his life around back in his sister's basement and selling the Baltimore Sun on the streets.

Speaking of the Sun, Gus is my kind of news editor.

RUNNING TOTALS:

McNulty drunk: back drinking heavily again – up two this week to 18.

Bubbles attempting to get clean: up one to seven: Reginald's making a supreme effort this series – and he looks well for it.

COMMENTS

EnglishRed Sheeeeeeeeeeeeeeeeeeeeeeeet... I hope Clay Davies gets his comeuppance, but The Wire being the Wire, and America being America I don't think it will be that simple!

foxtrotdelta I've always found The Wire a little strange, not because of anything wrong with it, but because of something right with it – for the first half of most seasons you kind of feel like you're being held back from the plot and they're never going to wrap things up, the second half it almost feels the other way round. But then when you get to the end you can see the whole story – how one small event in episode 2 shaped the outcomes of so many people. It's all about small knock on effects – if A didn't do that then B wouldn't have had to kill C, so D would never have found out E etc and so on. It's the ultimate butterfly effect I guess, and it shows how two events seemingly totally disconnected are inextricably linked.

silentbazz Cannot believe Jimmy's drinking again <Sigh>

EPISODE 2 – Getting away with murder

STEVE BUSFIELD

A strange and fucked up day for Jimmy McNulty: first he is the everyman, as flawed as the rest of us (who hasn't kicked an inanimate object when furious and ended up hurting themselves?), then he's going a bit far (whiskey at work) and then he crosses a serious line by tampering with evidence. This could be his undoing, or, in the weird world of B-more it could be the moment that it all comes together for the serious crimes crew.

Or maybe it will be Lester Freamon, who may actually nail Snoop and Chris the old-fashioned and legitimate way. Or they may be undone by Michael (it would be heartening if he returned to being a caring big brother instead of a young enforcer) letting the child/witness get away.

Or will it be Avon Barksdale? (Strange how pleased I was to see him back, even if he is still in jail.) Is he really going to help Marlo Stanfield, or is he setting him up for a fall?

Of course Marlo's gang may just keep on getting away with murder. Can anyone remember who it was that fucked off the FBI so much that they won't help solve the bodies in the vacants case? (Was that McNulty?)

Like politics in season four, the newsroom is already an excellent vehicle for reminding us that some more privileged people get away with murder too, just not the kind that leaves bodies behind. Who here believes there's a 13-year-old in a wheelchair called "EJ" who can't get a ticket to see the Orioles?

On a personal note, I'm relieved to discover that I am not the only news editor struck by late night anxiety moments ringing the office to check facts.

QUOTE OF THE WEEK: Avon Barksdale returns. "Up in this bitch here [prison] I'm what you might consider an authority figure." You don't say …

RUNNING TOTALS:

Murders: up four to 73. June Bug and three others killed by Chris and Snoop.

McNulty giving a fuck when it's not his turn: up three to 35. Bunk actually uses this immortal phrase when he rushes to catch a case, then Jimmy meets Fitz to try to get some FBI help on Marlo – and then he fakes his first murder.

Drunk: up two to 20: a trip to the bar with Bunk and Freamon, and then a taste or two as he fakes the murder.

Bubbles attempting to get clean: fifteen months clean, he reveals.

COMMENTS

joedoone why is McNulty boosting the murder rate in a city that isn't exactly short of murders?

Maikeru I think this goes back to the scene where McNulty and Bunk were discussing how nobody cares – it is just black bodies which keep piling up.

"This ain't Aruba, bitch."

So McNulty's thinking seems, to me, to be that if people think there is a serial killer targeting the white folk of Baltimore then they will not be able to brush it aside any more, and so the city/state/country/whomever will be forced to act.

jamie12 The McNulty stuff I could sort of buy. It's oh so easy to fall off the wagon, especially if you were never seriously on it in the first place and after 5 seasons (following String, Avon, Marlow etc.) without any sense of closure I too am getting annoyed and need a drink. Marlo, Snoop, and Chris will come unstuck I reckon, they are going after O-Mar rather impetuously and as David Simon said O-Mar has patience which is why he is so dangerous.

foxtrotdelta The thing I had to keep telling myself, is what have The Wire's writers ever done to lose our trust? Just trust them and see where the story goes... Also – as The Wire is there to mirror the state of America, and not just tell a story plain and simple, can you think of anyone else who may have tampered with or manufactured evidence?

I totally agree with McNulty going back on't booze – I think he's pissed off with the system, and not only that, I think he was hit hard by Bodie's death. He never gave up drinking so it was always going to be easy to hit the bottle hard again...

This is the fifth season where essentially the police are dealing with the same problem – the drug dealers and related crimes. Despite mammoth efforts on Jimmy & everyone else's part they haven't changed a damn thing in the city. Jimmy's spotted this and reasoned (while drunk) that this might be his chance to finally change things for the better, even if it's by going about things the wrong way... Good police don't always play by the rules, especially when the rules are set up for the good police to fail to do their jobs...

blstryker I have always felt that McNulty is the most typical of tough street cops from other shows – almost as if he is written to be a bit of a stereotype to juxtapose with the quality of the characterisation of the gangsters when contrasted. His fall from grace is not for me "out of character" but typical of him not following the chain of command. His counterpart was Stringer Bell and look where he ended. The wire is a metaphor for the thin line between them all – cops and robbers – both sides reflect the other. Every season holds Omar back...cannot wait.

Although Simon has referenced western influences and articles have frequently noted The Wild Bunch as a key influence for the show, Omar is pure samurai. It is a bit trite but he could also be the Grim Reaper. The blind oracle also makes clear links to Greek Tragedy which lends Omar something mythic by attachment. The character is supposedly meant to be based on a real figure from the B-More scene but surely it has evolved beyond that. I think it is only fair that the writers are excused a certain amount of artistic flair beyond the realism of other aspects of the show. He is like Duvall in Apocalypse Now's war in that he is above and impervious "the game". I for one would throw my hat in the ring and state Omar is the single greatest character in television. The court scene, Marlo's poker game heist, confrontation with Mouzone, the whistle, the shotgun – cannot think of another character with so many quality facets or scenes, including Tony Soprano et al. Any takers?

jamie12 … I know he drives his old lady to church on Sundays, that's all I'm sayin'.

I think it's interesting how they are now going after Marlo's crew on the pretext that they are serial killers, when given the fact that there is no rhyme or reason to their killings this is the logical extension of what they are doing.

foxtrotdelta Re: Omar – he's everyone's favourite character, fo sho, and he trained as a dancer, working with CC Peniston amongst others… Anyway – I've always taken him to be a mythic character rather than someone we're supposed to take literally. He invokes the element of chance and randomness that inhabits our lives. He is everything that is beyond anyone's control. He's almost superheroic, except he's not technically a hero. He also kinda feels like one definition given of Keyser Soze – he's the spook story on the streets, the scare story to keep everyone on their toes. He comes from nowhere, he can't be killed, keep your wits about you, be alert, never let your guard down…

EPISODE 3 – Unacceptable behaviour

STEVE BUSFIELD

So that's where Omar is! But will he come back for his High Noon-style shoot out with Marlo's boys (and "little girl")? Or will it be in the Caribbean? And is Prop Joe setting it all up? Or the Greek? Who will survive? How many votes for lots of loose ends being nicely tied up by the end of season five? Not many, I'm sure. We may get some closure but a lot of shit will still be going down in Baltimore when this show ends. And the only people we will know how it ends up for will be those who are already dead.

Now McNulty is dragging Lester into his madness. They have had five years (or are the five series over a longer time span?) of minor convictions: how far will they go to get what they want? And will this make them any better than those crooked politicians? Or the crooks? Or, indeed, the crooked hacks. One can only hope that the quote-cheat in the newsroom will come unstuck. If I was his news editor and I too thought his copy was too good to be true and yet so flaky, I'd be wanting more information on those quotes.

RUNNING TOTALS:

Murders: up one to 74: Butchie, horribly killed by Chris and Snoop.

McNulty giving a fuck when it's not his turn: up one to 36 – adding a red ribbon element to his fake murders scheme.

Omar stick-ups: no stick-ups for Omar as he goes about his pleasant life somewhere hot and relaxing. Steady on 13.

COMMENTS

darren73 I loved Michael, Dukie and Bug's Day Out. It was just great to see them smile, laugh and flirt like normal kids, even if it was just for one day, and they have to go back to their real world. Nice dolphin, kid.

jamie12 Marlo's naivety is a telling reminder that these characters are basically just kids with no other options and not the devil incarnate. It reveals the structural racism of B-More. This goes some way to explaining my increasing obsession with Snoop. In many ways she is the purest character in the show. Others have a romantic and I would argue misguided impression that the individual can change the rules of the game (most notably McNaughty) and that there can be some salvation or redemption (for Bubbles, for Michael etc). It's pretty impossible to imagine redemption for Snoop. What would she do? I suspect this is why she elicits such terror and animosity. She is a kind of limit case for liberal sentiment.

SaintSnowy It was fascinating seeing Marlo in a different context, wearing a Hawaiian-type shirt and getting confused about how to get to his money. Prop Joe's comment about trying to civilise him was brilliant. I can't wait for Marlo to get what he deserves but, of course with this being The Wire, I won't expect it soon.

I agree about Michael seeing Chris and Snoop almost like his saviours when it came to his stepdad/dad. I thought it was nicely done, the way in which they almost offered him an alternative family set-up, with money and a home and some sense of belonging to a "crew", which he certainly didn't get with his junkie mother and abusive (though we'll never really know) father. It was an interesting inversion of his situation. And he is a good kid essentially, so it's even sadder to see where he's probably headed...

jamie12 Suggestions for alternative career paths for Snoop: fronting daytime TV DIY programme; entering the Olympics in the synchronised 25M rapid fire pistol pairs event with Chris; teaching ebonics101 at Johns Hopkins Uni.

foxtrotdelta Re: Freamon getting involved in McNulty's scheme – Here's a man who was sent to the records library (or wherever it was) for years, but who is perhaps the best detective on the books, he's now got his chance to do some real work because people are trusting him, but there's no money to do anything with. So when he sees a scheme he can run which may give him the resources to complete his case he runs with it. Remember, he's not a young man, it's not like he's going to mess up the next 20 years of his career.

However, here's a question for you – Does Lester have his roots in the 'mystical/magical negro' character? I ask because of his background from the first season – he has been pulled from nowhere, very few people knew he still existed in the police force, he is smarter than the others, he often comes up with solutions that others are incapable of reaching. Sure, he's more three dimensional than this archetype usually is when presented, and given that the show features a predominantly black cast, it doesn't have the same racist overtones that this character type can often have. Or equally, could he be a purposeful twist on this archetype by The Wire's writing team? Just a thought...

Totus I like the way that Duquan is looking a lot healthier since the street money started flowing in from Michael. The show has described this a few times, that the corner drug trade doesn't merely 'force' youngsters into it, it also provides a (seemingly) far more attractive alternative to a legit existence. Anyone remember all the trouble that Cutty went through trying to fund his gym legitimately in Season 3, before going to see Avon and getting more money than he'd even asked for in less than 10 minutes?

jamie12 I am nonplussed too by McNulty's success with B-More's women. There was that scene a few series back where he wandered into a diner and picked up the waitress when half-cut in the middle of the night. I have tried this any number of times (as a form of social experiment you understand). It does not work. Indeed, I submit that this has never happened to anyone. And people complain about the lie detector sequence in terms of realism.

"Give me some eggs, will ya?" "You can have anything you want."

–That's never happened to me in The Little Chef.

EPISODE 4 – In defence of McNulty

STEVE BUSFIELD

Bloody hell, who here thought that Prop Joe wouldn't make it? Remembrances please.

Twenty-two bodies in the last series; Chris, Snoop and Marlo are back into their stride this series. They've bought Cheese. And he's given them his uncle. But Omar wants Marlo. McNulty wants Marlo. Herc may yet even get them Marlo (has he got the brains for it?). Lester, it turns out, wants Rawls.

The newsroom story arc is enjoyable in its own right – Gus and Twigg's old school and Templeton's Washington Post ambitions belittled – and I'm not quite sure where it's going. But it's all the better for that.

Clay is so far up shit creek that he doesn't even have the energy for a sheeeeeiiiiiit. Just one more for old times' sake please.

Carver has grown into proper pOlice. McNulty started this show in a bedsit. I think he's going to end it in one too. Kima wishes her life could go the other way.

QUOTE OF THE WEEK:

Prop Joe: I treated you like a son.

Marlo: I wasn't made to play the son.

RUNNING TOTALS:

Murders: up two to 76: Proposition Joe and Hungry Man.

COMMENTS

ShangoDan Prop Joe remembrance: Season 2, responding to Sergei's ("why always Boris?") point about tolerating Ziggy – "Family, what are you going to do" – Joe responds: "I got motherf**ing nephews and in-laws f**king all my shit up all the time, and it ain't like I can pop a cap in their ass and not hear about it Thanksgiving time".

Fontane The Wire once again illustrated that family ties can blind a character to weaknesses. As with Avon and D'Angelo, Prop Joe tolerated his nephew Cheese without his usual strategic acumen. It broke my heart when the sociopathic genius of Marlo sauntered into the room.

But as stunning as his demise was it was all illustrated in political slow motion as Nerese Campbell acted as both a traitor and friend as she padded out Burrell's fall from grace; lining her pockets along the way. Cedric Daniel's smile in his new office was the dark twin of Prop Joe closing his eyes.

I love this program. It's so complicated, layered, unpredictable and heart breaking. I like the speechless scenes which seem to be a nod to us faithful fans like when McNulty and Freeman who were "getting a feel" to their case when they visited skid row and we see Johnny Fifty (Ziggy's partner-in-crime in Mercedes appropriation) from Season Two drinking in vagrant hell.

joedoone Colicchio gets his hands on some serious shit. Carver is much more mature and sees the bigger picture. Carver once said, after a round-up of young hoppers, "I like to think that, until the cuffs actually fit, there's still talking to be done." He gave Colicchio a chance to get out from under his moronic behaviour at the top of the episode, but Colicchio was still boiling at the effrontery of an innocent citizen who merely wanted to get his car past Colicchio's sloppy parking. Carver realised that Colicchio was never going to stop being a fully paid-up, card-carrying member of the Assholes Trade Union, and decided to write him up, and, hopefully, to get rid of him. Dominic West said, in an extra for Season Four, that The Wire is about realising that you can't change the world, so you have to change yourself; it's a pity that McNutty is so resistant to self-improvement.

darren73 The look on Daniels' face, when just for a second he thinks Burrell is going to brain him with the putter.

quipu the look on Marlo's face as he seems to get what he wants. Ever since Season 3, he's been after the crown, fighting the Barksdale organisation for dominance of the west side. He's even warned by his bank, Vinson, that usually the King only gets to reign a short time, and they all usually end up dead or in prison, to which Marlo simply replies, "It's my time now." And you realise that Marlo isn't motivated by money, but by power and his reputation. Now he has control of the drug game in Baltimore, and has effectively removed anyone who stands in his way... and yet it remains ambiguous as to how much satisfaction Marlo is deriving from this moment. A ghost of a smile plays about his lips, and the eyes remain as expressionless and dead as they have always been. It really is a unsettling image to end the episode on. The face of the future.

PaoloT I think Marlo was enjoying himself a little bit too much as he watched Chris blow Joe away. He certainly appeared in more danger of slipping into genuine arousal, emotional or otherwise, than when we saw him have an encounter with Avon's honeytrap girl in Series 3.

I doubt Mr Stanfield is a man of letters but I'm sure if he read the Origin of Species he'd have had no problems twisting the theory of natural selection to his own ends in the way Richard Dawkins was despairing of on C4 last night. He truly is the nightmare of social Darwinism gone bad, the living embodiment of The Game and, since he appears to have given up looking after his pigeons, utterly devoid of any compassion.

All the big players in The Game have had a "weakness", in the sense that some factor other than pure profit seems to have motivated them. Avon, String and Joe were all driven by a desire to improve themselves, having come from so little. The fact that, in their eyes, The Game was the easiest way of doing this is the show's damning indictment of the lack of opportunities society offered these men. But, whether it was Avon and Stringer reminiscing about back in the day or Joe proudly looking at the picture of his grandfather (both these moments of weakness taking place before The Game/Marlo bit back hard at the sentimentality) they had an awareness of where they'd come from and what they'd been. Where does Marlo come from? Maybe he's had wrongs visited upon him that make the upbringings of Michael, Dukie and Randy pale into insignificance but I don't think the writers have any intention of letting us know. He'll just be left as he is, Mr The Game.

joedoone The Burrell/Daniels scene reminded me of the scene in The Untouchables where Al Capone casually walked round a conference table until he stood behind a guy who had disappointed him, whereupon he bashed his head in with a baseball bat. An effective tactic at boring meetings.

Totus ErrorGorrilla: "why is KT Tunstall working at the Baltimore Sun?" Brilliant.

Re: Burrell's golf club. He was doing the same in-office putting practice when he promoted Daniels to Major, only that time he managed to get the ball in the hole. This time, he didn't, and the conversation went a very different way. Jesus. We could spend all day just on the symbolism in this show, and never get around to discussing our favourite Prop Joe moments...

...such as when he acts as guarantor for Stringer's and Omar's meet at the end of Season 1, and explains his role to the pair of them. "y'see, I'm like one of those marriage guidance motherf*ckers, I tell him to buy some flowers every once in a while, and tell her to suck some d*ck every once in a while, then they both give me some money"

Proposition for you indeed...

blstryker Been reviewing series 1 and think it goes some way to contextualising Lester taking on McNutty's serial killer efforts. He floats quietly in the background lumped in with the fools recruited to the Barksdale detail – old pensions chasers and gun totin' Prezbo. When Lester secures D'Angelo's pager number and the Barksdale Golden Gloves poster McNutty has his eyes opened. This comes shortly after his porn-watching/food-eating boss makes a speech to save him in Rawls's eyes within homicide – basically McNutty always thinks he is the smartest in the room and cannot help himself. McNutty's look towards Lester and his hearing from Bunk that Freeman is "natural pOlice" is the first moment where he seems not to seem himself as the smartest in the room. They then share a drink and Lester informs him of a McNuttyesque past chasing the truth and not following the chain, leading to him in the pawn-shop. There is also a cruelly funny moment where Lester tells McNutty not to say his least favourite posting, where there is the dramatic irony of knowing that McNutty has already told people about the boats (Series 2 is set up). All of this I believe establishes the Freeman and McNutty Series 5 collaborative working outside the system and it is pre-dominantly in Episode 4.

seanca The more I think about it I think Michael is going to be pivotal to how the show ends, since he first appeared (although still a kid) he was the strong but silent type but when called upon he stood up for his little gang, the Deez Nuts/Water balloon scene, standing up to Namond when he bullied Dukie, looking after Bug, f**king up Kenard when he obviously stroked Namond over his supposedly lost / stolen drugs, giving Dukie a home. His sense of doing what's right, no matter how shitty the situation has always shone through.

Now he's deep in the big time, and what he's seen what he's seen, no matter how much Marlo has looked after him I think his conscience will kick in big time, we've already seen him having doubts.

Maybe Marlo, Snoop, Chris et al will get the mother of all double crosses from Michael.

CodProfundity In fact as David Simon has repeatedly stated HBO were more than helpful when it came to how many episodes were needed, although they did initially offer 8 Simon told them no fucking way and HBO then offered them 10 to 12, Simon took 10 and decided to cut Cutty and Prez's stories as they were already much done. I hesitate to use the word "main" when describing the serial killer and Sun storyline, if the Wire does anything it demonstrates how all stories in the show influence each other but anyway … The main story lines were not truncated. I've seen the whole season and it's prominent mood is blackly comic, it's like that from the opening episode, but black comedy has always been a strong element of the show and as such the twists and turns the stories take work perfectly in that context.

And finally I find it interesting so many people are incredulous with the serial killer plot when Hamsterdam seemed to attract almost no similar reaction and that involved an entire district of police keeping it quiet for months.

I often think people praise The Wire for realism when what they are actually recognising is accuracy in terms of dialect, procedure, incidence and so forth. In reality, Omar wouldn't walk 3 blocks over to a corner shop in his PJ's with stash houses dropping the re-up in his wake, but it works in the context of the show. The important thing, for me, is that it works thematically with the rest of the other 4 seasons. And it does, wonderfully so.

KatharineP Ah, one of my favourite scenes CodProf, from his shrug at the failure of the gloriously turquoise pyjama trousers to hold his gun, to the scattering of the children warning "Omar coming!", and his stroll through the deserted streets to buy his favourite breakfast cereal. Both hilarious and a great contribution to the Omar myth.

I think it's because the context is painted in such convincingly naturalistic detail that they can then make imaginative leaps into the improbable and make it feel possible, especially Hamsterdam, which is surely – like the special class for corner kids – a "what if". What would happen if we tried this? How would the drug dealers and politicians and bureaucrats respond? That it's not realistically "credible" is beside the point; it's not a documentary. And it's actually at these moments that it seems most like the Dickens novels with which it's so often compared, which combine a horrifically realistic representation of Victorian London with wonderfully grotesque hyperbole. That night scene when Bubbles walks though Hamsterdam, which till then had seemed relatively benign (within limits!), was a vision of hell worthy of Gustave Dore.

EPISODE 5 – Pulling on the heartstrings

PAUL MACINNES

It's not often that The Wire opens on a tender scene in bucolic surroundings. So it's perhaps not surprising, then, that it's ultimately a performance; Marlo and Vondas sitting solemnly in a park, paying tribute to Prop Joe while setting out the ground rules for their future business relationship. "In business, in life," muses Vondas, "you learn to appreciate the most dependable man, one day to the next." Dependable until they're dead, that is.

It's an incongruous scene, made odder by another appearance from Marlo the technophobe, baffled then bemused by Vondas's gift of a snazzy mobile phone. But it does, in a way, set the tone for the episode as, over the course of the ensuing hour, there are more tender moments than you have a right to expect from the Wire. Heck, there's not even the death of a major character!

Bubs and Dukie are always the characters most likely to pull a viewer's heart strings, and in this episode they come into sharp focus. Dukie, goaded by the pre-teen thug Kenard, ends up accruing a beating and is sent, by Michael, to see Cutty at his now well-appointed gym in an attempt to give him some chops.

We see Dukie get in the ring and, inevitably, fail – seemingly lacking even the instinct to defend himself properly. After the bout, Dukie looks to Cutty to offer him first some advice – "What now?" – and then some hope.

Cutty does his best: "I guess what I'm trying to say is not everything comes down to how you handle it in the street. That ain't the only way to be." But it isn't enough. "The world is bigger than that, or so they tell me," says Cutty with the air of a man who may have escaped the corners but is still trapped in the west Baltimore ghetto.

"How do you get from here to the rest of the world?" asks Dukie, with wide eyes.

"I wish I knew," says Cutty.

Dukie looks lost, unable to survive on the streets, but unable to escape them; at least, though, he still has Michael. Bubbles meanwhile has Walon, his Narcotics Anonymous sponsor and the man who persuades Bubbles, at last, to take the test – the test for the bug. It becomes clear this week that the dark brooding air that has accompanied Bubbles into sobriety has been caused in part by his fears that he has HIV and, worse, his fears that he deserves to have it.

Walon is there, though, to leave his work when asked, to escort Bubbles to the clinic and wait for the results. The test, it turns out, is negative. "Shame ain't worth as much as you think," Walon tells Bubbles. "Let it go."

These scenes, in their emotional range and depth, show once again the Wire in its full glory. This, it has to be said, is probably just as well, seeing as what goes on in the rest of the episode. Clay Davis (who has uttered his first "sheeeiiiitt" of the season) might just get away with his corrupt activities thanks to the support of ex-mayor Royce. McNulty's phantom serial killer has won him the wiretap he has always been after. Finally, the hour ends with Omar escaping the murderous intentions of Snoop, Chris and Michael by jumping out of a fifth storey window and, apparently, surviving. Yeah, he's the closest the Wire has to a superhero; but not that close, surely?

RUNNING TOTALS:

Murders: up one to 77 as Omar's pal Donnie is killed by Marlo's crew.

McNulty giving a fuck when it's not his turn: up one to 38 – now adding a sexual motive to his serial killer scam and getting it on to the front page.

Dubious parenting: up one to eight, missing his son's play.

COMMENTS

joedoone WireWorld mixes realism with satire and parable and myth, the myth applying to the apparently indestructible Omar. The satire and parable apply to McNulty & Freamon, aided independently by Templeton. "Oh what a tangled web we weave, when first we practice to deceive." McNulty's bullshit will come undone because of Templeton's bullshit; when McNulty and Freamon set their madcap scheme in operation, they didn't know that another exponent of fact-free largesse, desperate to make a name for himself and escape Baltimore, would make the job of catching Marlo even more complicated, and God knows it's complicated enough already, even without whatever spin that Flatcap Greek and Marlo have put on proceedings. McNulty and Freamon are hoping that calls from the "serial killer" will be few and far between, and that they can concentrate on Marlo's phone, but they must already have twigged that Templeton is a lying bonek**ker, just as Templeton must know the same about McNulty. As Bubbles's workmate said to Bubbles, Templeton is "not exactly Bob Woodward", but he does possess a certain ratlike cunning. Never bullshit a bullshitter. And, to top it all, the "serial killer" story will keep Clay Davis off the front page; I love the way Davis talks about himself in the third person, always a sure sign of a bullshitter. Has Gus laid aside his doubts about Templeton's veracity in the greater cause of a good story? "If it bleeds, it leads."

EnglishRed Omar's leap from the balcony was awesome – the man is developing into B'more's very own Dark Knight- his failed plan would have rattled him though, a sign of things to come?

I liked the scene at the Sun's office when McNutty realised Templeton was also telling fibs about the "serial killer" – it will be interesting as to who gets found out first – Jimmy is arguably much better at it but is impaired by his self-destructive lifestyle.

Can't wait to see how/when Lester works out Marlo's new technique of contacting his cronies either..

stephenD Olympic Gold to Clay Davis for the longest "sheeeeeeeiiiiiiiit" ever in a TV series. And a 10 out of 10 to Omar Little for the best jump off a balcony.

joedoone McNulty's spiel about the sexual impulses of his imaginary serial killer, and the "evolution of his m.o." into biting homeless men in the ass, means that his own ass will bear the odd bitemark before the series wraps up.

KatharineP "How do you get from here to the rest of the world?" One of the crucial questions of any season, and in itself an example of what makes this show so good – absolutely simple in its phrasing, yet poetic in its effect, and completely unanswerable. (Loved seeing Cutty again, though.) Normally we only see the corrupt and powerful connect to the rest of the world – Carcetti with his eye on Annapolis pretty much the second he becomes mayor, Burrell paid off to DC, Marlo going to the Antilles and (gasp) Atlantic City. Perhaps Dukie should ask Omar? But even Omar never really left.

I fear for Dukie. Of the four boys, I imagine there only ever was going to be room for one redemption, and it's interesting that they chose to make it the one who was not only least likeable, but appeared least vulnerable. (A matter of degree, I know.) By choosing Namond, the writers, as always, showed that reality tends to triumph over sentiment; and besides, they could cause their viewers more pain by not rescuing Randy, Michael and Dukie. We must be masochists.

darren73 I can't help feeling that the increasingly outlandish serial-killer plot is not only a comment on what is deemed to sell papers, but also what is thought by TV execs to attract ratings. This plot, with the ribbons and the bite-marks belongs in Law and Order or CSI, where sensationalism will inevitably give way to easy resolution after 42 minutes. This obviously won't happen here, because in The Wire, there are always consequences.

foxtrotdelta Re: Omar's leap: It wasn't so far that it wasn't survivable, and survivable quite easily, you have just got to know how to land. Has no one seen parkour (or whatever it's called – the free running) – that demos how to land a big jump with minimal injury...

saisteve The firefight this week had my pulse racing like nothing I've ever seen before on TV, I was so sure that was it for Omar, he looked genuinely scared and vulnerable for the first time in the entire show. Cornered behind a sofa by 3 stone-cold killers with automatic weapons, and that leap into oblivion was characteristically awesome. It seemed believable because he had no other option, reminded me of those poor people jumping out of the world trade center to avoid being burned alive.

How he survived it, or if he survived, I just don't know but the look on Snoop's face was priceless, another first as she actually appeared surprised rather than her perpetual dead stare. It gives me hope that Omar survived though because in a sense Marlo took his shot and missed, he outsmarted Omar as he has outsmarted every player so far but in this case Omar got away and he won't be so careless next time.. or will he just give up and retire to his beachside lifestyle?

I fear, like with all great criminal heroes, he won't be able to walk away from that last job that needs completing and it will be the end of him.. but then every time the writers trick you into expecting some cliche to unfold something else happens so who knows..

CodProfundity This was the episode where it all coalesced this season, last year it was "Refugees" and before that "Straight and True". I couldn't stop laughing at the turn the Serial Killer/Sun storyline took, it's audacious to say the least but "the bigger the lie, the more they believe" after all.

Totus Re: Michael/Dukie being the new Omar/Bubs. This theory has a great deal going for it. One of the running themes throughout all the seasons has been how the game never changes. There will always be plenty of Bubs-a-likes on the streets of Baltimore (and any large city for that matter), so even if the man himself gets, and stays, clean this season, the element of Baltimore that he represents will continue.

The same is true for Omar, though to a lesser degree (there only being room for one mythical Robin Hood figure). I would like to see Michael use his obvious skills and his integrity to break free of Marlo's crew, and stepping into Omar's shoes would be the best way of doing that within the context of the show. Remember that Omar is the only character free of the shackles of institution. If Michael were to escape institutions, (Marlo, prison etc), then he would redeem himself in the context of the Wire, if not on a simple-minded moral level.

And if you want simple-minded moralising, this is not the show for you...

lifelister A first for me: I dreamt about Omar last night. He swooped down, told my husband and I that we needn't worry – he would take care of everything gave us some money to go out to the pictures. He then proceeded to stage a burglary in our house so that we could claim the insurance money.

EPISODE 6 – Chris's loyalty

PAUL MACINNES

Compared to previous episodes, the end of The Dickensian Aspect is rather low-key. No drug lords murdered in their own offices, no daredevil leaps from halfway up a tower block, just Jimmy McNulty watching a mentally damaged man trying unsuccessfully to finish a sandwich.

Still, it's not without its drama. McNutty is watching Larry, a homeless man he picked up from the streets of Baltimore and then dumped in Washington, with a degree of disgust. No doubt this is partially due to Larry's preference for tearing up his food rather than eating it. It's also true, though, that for the first time the orchestrator of B'more's big serial killer scam might just be having second thoughts. Was kidnapping really part of the plan when McNulty first set out to dig up resources in the hunt for Marlo Stanfield? Probably not, it seems fair to suggest.

Just as McNutty begins to doubt himself, though, his plot is achieving real effects, just not in ways he expected. For example, Scott Templeton's career is on the up and up, even if he's covering up his fabrications with even more lies. Mayor Carcetti, meanwhile, might just have found an issue to help his ascent to the state house.

Never one to flunk a media opportunity, Carcetti turns the interest in the homeless killer into a chance to wax oratorical on society's responsibility to support the vulnerable. It's a brief speech, but apparently it's a winner, Carcetti's advisors Wilson and Steintorf (Statler and Waldorf?) claiming he could now make the homeless a campaign issue.

That's the difference between being a local politician and a dominant player in the heroin market: in the game words only get you so far. Omar, semi-crippled and enraged after last week's leap, is staggering around west Baltimore creating chaos and sending a message. The message is simple: Marlo can't handle the streets. He might talk tough – viz his handling, and practical disbanding, of the co-op this week – but when it comes to the gritty, grisly side of his business, says Omar, Marlo is nowhere to be seen.

Whether Omar gets his wish – a showdown in the street, a gunfight at high noon – very much remains to be seen. Marlo may well be a "straight bitch" when it comes to applying violence himself, but he has never had need to be anything else, seeing as he has Chris Partlow in his employ.

How the relationship between Marlo and Chris actually works remains curiously unclear. Chris's respect for Marlo is unflinching, his obedience total. But why? He takes on all the physical risk for the Stanfield crew and it's Chris who is blamed by Marlo for Omar's escape ("We missed our shot. Now it'll be on us.") And it's not as if the monetary rewards seem to excite him much either.

We know from watching Avon and Stringer that even the tightest bonds can be broken by the pressure of the streets and how long Chris will unquestioningly do Marlo's bidding will be interesting to see. Even more interesting, in fact, when Bunk Moreland begins to bear down on him. Bunk has begun to dig around in the death of Michael Lee's stepfather again and the trail goes straight to Chris.

The irony of this development is that Bunk only began to work the case again out of a desire to prove there is one murder police who does things by the book. Indirectly, therefore, that's another point to McNutty.

QUOTE OF THE WEEK:

"Why don't you promise to get me out of here? That's what you all do, ain't it? Lie to dumb-ass niggers?" Randy, hardened by his time in the group home and his betrayal by the police.

RUNNING TOTALS:

McNulty giving a fuck when it's not his turn: up one to 39, grabbing his homeless victim still alive.

Drunk: up one to 24.

COMMENTS

Joedoone Templeton's bullshit will catch him out as sure as I am Irish, and Gus is on to him, telling him his stuff "seemed real this time." Because it actually was. Gus meanwhile has to wrestle with the bullshit of his higher-ups – "the Dickensian aspect" of homelessness – while Daniels listens to Carcetti's stirring speech about how everything "in our power" will be done to catch the serial killer, and then listens to Rawls telling him the police have no power. Omar has survived his "Spider-Man shit", albeit with a busted leg, and has hidden out in the basement of the very building from which he jumped. Marlo has blamed Omar for the deaths of Butchie & Prop Joe, but his story is not universally believed, and the co-op is growing restless at how prices are going up and at the fact that Marlo has assumed command. Thanks to Flatcap Greek, Marlo is using encrypted photos via his cellphone; perhaps he should beware of Greeks bearing gifts.

Gimplord I get nervous every time we see Omar on screen now. Seems like he's been tipped over the edge and isn't too concerned about his own safety. Bad vibes.

I'm loving the way the McNulty's serial killer story is spiralling out of control. Bunk's face when he found out he'd have to wait in a queue behind those murders for lab tests.

Prop Joe's death was a sentence buried deep within the Baltimore Sun. Such a significant character to us and yet just another sad statistic for the inside pages.

PaulinYork love the irony of McNulty's made-up homeless case being appropriated by Carcetti, for political gain as a campaign issue when running for governor.

Fontane I feel that Bunk is onto something now with Michael's stepfather. I was horrified by the savagery of Chris when he killed him but I was curious why it was given such prominence and now I'm beginning to see why. Apart from the fact it is alluded that Michael and Chris may have sexually abused by men ("you can look 'em right in the eye") this murder was different. It was driven by emotion and when that gets in the way you get careless. They took DNA samples of Chris.

ShangoDan "If you have a problem with this, I understand completely." Is this line supposed to be directed at the viewer as well, as a sort of apology/explanation for the crazy McNutty story line?

joedoone After initially rejecting McNutty's faux serial killer nonsense, it has come to fit in ever better with what is probably the most satirical season yet (though, of course, how it all ends will determine whether it has worked or not). When Gus wanted his boss to commit to a series on education, showing the whole picture, his boss shot him down, saying readers weren't interested in a lot of fuzzy background and big picture stuff. Last night, Gus's boss told him to shelve education in favour of the much punchier serial killer story, while at the same time championing the world of the homeless, the big picture replete with The Dickensian Aspect. Just as The Baltimore Sun is using the homeless to sell papers, Carcetti is using the homeless to further his political career. Homeless Larry is just a particularly vivid example of how the homeless are shafted. McNulty is very far from being the biggest bullshit artist in town, and he is far from being the only police to elevate bullshit to a whole new level, as with Rawls telling Daniels "Don't look so surprised; you're playing with the big boys now." Templeton is strictly Junior League.

Totus I'd been wondering where I'd seen Reg E Cathey (Norman Wilson) before, and it occurred to me that he played "Al", the homeless guy in American Psycho. He's murdered by Patrick Bateman after the latter makes false promises that he'll help him get off the streets.

Thought this was interesting, given this season's storylines.

If they pursue this connection, what do we reckon about Omar killing Marlo with an axe while dancing to "Hip to be Square" by Huey Lewis and The News?

verrochio I'd just as happily see Omar tip an avalanche of Crunchy Nut cornflakes over Marlo's head.

ShelfsideAndy The real Dickensian moment was Randy – institutionalised and brutalised.

Libby66 I don't think we will see a fairytale ending of Omar killing Marlo. I think Omar's time is running out, he is becoming careless and seems tired of living.

EPISODE 7 – A shot at redemption

STEVE BUSFIELD

McNulty is back: once it became clear that Jimmy wouldn't kill his "victim" last week, you had to laugh. There was method in the madness. Politicians and the media have bought into this bullshit. And sadly we know they would. Thus the police department has been given all the resources it needs to find a non-existent serial killer.

And Jimmy "Boss" McNulty is now running the police department's finances – to run real investigations. Can that last? Meanwhile Bunk and Carver are acting like proper pOlice. They might get to Chris 'n' Snoop yet. Especially now that Omar has scared the bejesus out of Michael. And at the rate that Omar is working through Marlo's army, if Chris 'n' Snoop go, then Marlo might yet find himself alone at high noon with Omar.

Good to see Bubbles getting a shot at redemption. Some proper journalism coming on the back of the serial killer nonsense too.

And, call me a sucker, but that was a sweet shot to fade as Kima found herself a real life.

QUOTE OF THE WEEK:

"Gimpy as a motherfuck'." Kenard's verdict on the limping Omar.

Who thinks this horrible urchin could be Omar's downfall?

RUNNING TOTALS:

Murders: up two to 79: Savino and another Marlo man are killed by Omar.

McNulty giving a fuck when it's not his turn: up two to 41: now imitating a serial killer on the phone to the press, and giving out overtime left, right and centre like he's running the place.

Omar stick-ups: up one to 15. He stole Marlo's stash and flushed it away.

COMMENTS

lifelister There is so much I need to happen in only 3 episodes and although tonight was great, my concern for Omar is starting to get in the way. He's in no condition to take part in the High Noon showdown with Marlo that he seems to want so badly.

I can't get that sofa image out of my head – it reminds me of times I spent behind the sofa watching Dr Who etc. OK, no one was shooting at me but you know what I mean. He's a wounded animal. He's not his usual self – that's for sure. I'm surprised at how he's gone downhill so fast and seems so desperate. My other half reckons he is suffering from blood poisoning, maybe that explains his change in behaviour. Has he even been home? Has he seen Reynaldo? Does he have a plan? It doesn't seem like it. At the beginning of this series I had so many hopes for many of the characters (Bubs and the young boys) but I was pretty sure Omar would be OK. In a few episodes all that's changed. Maybe I shouldn't care so much now that he seems to have lost his code?

I'm starting to get so tense when watching The Wire now that I almost feel like watching from behind the sofa. Tonight's episode was wonderful in so many ways and so funny but I think I'll only be able to appreciate the rest of this series after it's over when I watch the DVD and I already know how it all works out.

mwanauta Anyone else who got in to The Wire via Homicide: Life on the Street will have been delighted by the John Munch cameo in the bar.

"I used to own a bar, you know."

Yep, it was definitely Munch, not just Richard Belzer. Loving it. Obviously they can't go too far down this line, in case Meldrick Lewis showed up and bumped into Gus, causing the universe to implode.

joedoone Templeton, somewhat taken aback by his call from the serial killer, says "That was him." Quickly followed by "Again." McNutty enjoyed winding Templeton up over what the killer sounded like, but he knows he could be all too easily caught out himself, e.g. over his distinct lack of understanding of Freamon's technical wizardry. And, of course, by his new "boss" status and his ever-growing reputation as the go-to guy for getting things done: careless talk costs freedom. Maybe he should stick to assembling IKEA furniture; I thought he was going to go round and help Kima, having wrestled with beds for his own kids. How long will it be before Kima, a good cop, susses out McNutty? However crazy he might be, McNutty started out on his wacko scheme with good intentions, but, as with Clay Davis and his Prometheus Unbound, "No good deed goes unpunished." Another classic was referenced with Templeton's "Street Odyssey"; press prose has never been so purple. As with other posters, I'm wondering how on earth they can wind it all up in three episodes; at least the finale is extended. I think Michael is going to be a key player.

Episode Seven was laugh-out-loud funny, written by Richard Price and directed by McNutty's alter ego. He said, in an interview, that when he was directing Bunk, Bunk said "Are you trying to tell me how to act?"

SaptarshiRay I think Omar has been living under a hex ever since the shootout with the Barksdales when one of his crew died, the same girl who asked why they kept hitting the Barksdales even though they know they'd be coming. Omar put his team in unnecessary harm's way and one of them got killed and since then he's been moving from one problem to the next (hitting the card game with Marlo, being set up, landing in jail, Butchie etc) so that now he's wondering what the point of having a code is when no one else has one. After all, Bunk expected Omar to keep his promise of no more bodies and Omar fully intended to until he heard about Butchie, another death on his hands.

I do have to say 'shiiiiiiiiiiiit' what a barnstorming performance by Clay, those who ever thought he was going down must have been asking how they could have underestimated a snake so slick and shiny. "Playing not just the race card but the whole deck" – class.

joedoone A thieving, corrupt sod like Clay Davis comparing himself to Prometheus takes chutzpah to a whole new level.

Totus I liked the ending with Kima and her kid. I disagree that she has suddenly decided to take an interest in the young 'un – this was clearly developed (albeit briefly) in earlier episodes, not just when she faced the kid who survived the massacre, but also in the way she looked at Cheryl's home life when she went round to visit a while ago. I don't think that it was unnecessarily schmaltzy, and it did manage to put a smile on my face as the credits started to roll. I doubt that I'll be quite so heartwarmed at the end of the next few episodes...

CLM76 For the first time last night I picked up on the parallels between Gus and Bunk. Both bemoaned the lack of resources they were forced to work with and the lack of respect they and their colleagues received. But now that things are going too far the other way they are both dubious about the situation, Gus because he suspects there's something dodgy going on, Bunk because he knows there is.

ShelfsideAndy Regarding the aforementioned limp, isn't Omar's shattered leg a metaphor for his broken mental state; ever since his mentor and moral compass got a right earful our favourite coke redistributor (I'd like to teach the world to bling) has been spiralling like a Spitfire with one wing. Without the civilising Butchie we're now seeing the true beast.

Second metaphors: Surely the whole crazy McNulty serial killer storyline is David Simon's reaction to the lie told to the American people about Iraq; the very first message of season/series 5 – in the shot following the photocopier confession – was "the bigger the lie, the more they believe": For McNulty's serial killer read "WMD".

And just as Bush found his War on Terrah, so Carcetti has found his War on Homelessness – events fashioned and then co-opted to serve greater political agendas. The whole mad thing is crazy. Except it's not, the money tap has been turned on and Lester's back up on the wire.

ShelfsideAndy I wonder if the more pertinent point about the Baltimore Sun, the Police Department and City Hall is the theme that David Simon has used throughout, the inherent dysfunction of institutions. This time around the focus is angled more towards the ease with which they can be manipulated and the people within morally compromised. Templeton, McNulty and Carcetti are running the show for their own ends, stoking the fire as appropriate.

What we're exploring in this season is how institutions are used and manipulated.

Maybe think about Alistair Campbell's "dossier" and presentations of evidence to the UN Security Council by Colin Powell.

I'll offer this as an indication of David Simon's political subtext. From S3, Slim Charles to Avon (in the wake of Stringer's death):

"Don't matter who did what to who at this point. Fact is, we went to war and now there ain't no going back. I mean shit, it's what was is you know; once you in it, you in it. If it's a lie then we fight on that lie, but we gotta fight"

ShelfsideAndy In relation to the point about the profile the Sun is giving the story surely, from their point of view, now it's gone national it's about promoting the paper by feeding that national interest. That's the point I think, every institution has an agenda of its own – and it's those distinct agendas that drive the story regardless of the story's credibility. The story itself, such as it is, is secondary to: Carcetti for the Senate; Promotion of the Sun; Self-promotion of Templeton; McNulty's desire for overtime; Police credibility

You can replace a lot of those words with others like Bush, CNN, dossier, military – industrial complex, re-election.

No matter how absurd or crazy are the things McNulty gets up to in relation to his serial killer, he can never match what Cheney, Bush and Rumsfeld did.

David Simon's angle on all of that resonates so well, the bigger the lie gets, the more people do believe. Or perhaps, the bigger the lie the more able are institutions to find an angle that allows them to benefit and so they, in turn, perpetuate and grow the lie for their own good. Before you know it . . . it's the truth.

Who of the mainstream media seriously questioned the bonkers WMD hypothesis, who in the military said this is wrong – every institution was on board, because it was in their interest to be. As Templeton says "It's got legs".

KatharineP The amount of paralleling going on in the episode seems at first sight a bit heavy-handed: Bunk, Kima and Carver / Gus and Fletch – the good guys, doing things the right way; Templeton / Clay Davis / McNulty – the scammers; police/press hitting the streets; McNulty / Carcetti both learning more about the law of unintended consequences. But thinking about it, it's not that straightforward, because motive counts. McNulty's actions have made me cringe, but nothing he's done is for personal gain; it doesn't make it right, but it makes it comprehensible. As always (and like Omar), he doesn't quite fit into any category; he has a rather tangential relationship with morality, but at least is aware that such a thing exists. And perhaps it will need the scammers and the good guys jointly to bring down Marlo (unless the serial killer plot wholly buggers it up), if indeed he is legally brought down.

I think another layer of paralleling is going on in the episode, in structural terms – there's the marshalling of the press and police, ready for action; and similarly the final positioning of the different narrative threads before everything really kicks off. So I thought the final scene (potentially horrendously sentimental) was perfect in providing a moment of quiet and gentleness in advance of the storm. (Apparently it was a scene in Richard Price's book Clockers which he was specifically requested to incorporate – till I read TwOP, I didn't pick up that 'Goodnight Moon' was based on a classic American children's story.)

I guess David Simon isn't very good with flat-pack furniture…

Totus I've always had a lot of time for Slim Charles, but have never really given him that much thought. The comparisons with Landsman are really insightful, and definitely say a lot about middle management. The people at the top change frequently (everybody comin' at the king), as do those at the bottom (pawn-ass bitches).

It's interesting to note that both Slim and Jaybird always seem to be doing exactly the same thing throughout the seasons, whether that is sitting in a blacked out SUV or consuming kebabs and nudie cuties at their desk. Although they've both taken the opportunity to speak their minds (and have had/dished out the occasional ass-chewing), they are both essentially aware of where the line is, and never cross it. They, or rather their roles, are the inert constant at the heart of their institutions.

I get the strong impression that were Jay to be offered a promotion he would refuse it, just like Slim did. Their current positions are among the safest in their respective worlds, and deep down, they both know it.

This has to be one of The Wire's more subtle comments on institutions, and wonderfully done. I work in middle management. I'd have to say that this is also written really accurately. I sit in an enviable position here, not low enough to be wading in crap, not high enough to have it rain down on me.

And if that's a lie, then I fight on that lie…

EPISODE 8 – Obituary: Omar Little

STEVE BUSFIELD

Omar Little. Rest in peace (?).

We could talk about how McNulty can feel the web of his own lies tightening around himself (successfully profiled by the FBI), or we could debate whether Gus or Templeton will be the one looking for a new newspaper to work for very soon, or we could talk about the solution to the clock riddle, or whether Lester can scam Clay, or whether Bunk's police work will be enough to send down Chris. Frankly I am now so disillusioned with Carcetti that I don't even want to discuss how even his wife can see through his rampant careerism.

But what we should talk about is Omar. He deserves it. The Baltimore Sun didn't even grant him a news in brief, let alone an obituary.

I had long feared that Omar's end was coming. But it was still shocking when it came. As many of you had pointed out in recent weeks, he was getting reckless, careless with his own safety. Tonight he was even Don Quixote-like, throwing challenges out into an empty street. So no High Noon with Marlo. Capped, in the back of the head. By that horrible little kid. I think we owe it to the Baltimore gunslinger to spend some time recalling our favourite

Omar moments. I'd like to nominate the silk-pyjama-ed breakfast re-up, the execution of Stringer Bell and his be-tied performance in the witness box.

QUOTE OF THE WEEK:

"They're in the ballpark." McNulty on the FBI's unflattering psychological profile of his made-up serial killer.

RUNNING TOTALS:

Murders: up one to 80. Omar.

McNulty dubious parenting: not really, but he's in danger of driving Beadie and the kids away. Still eight.

COMMENTS

Marwelldezueew Omar, gonna miss you.

jamie12 Terrific episode. Things really coming to a head. Desperately worried now for McNaughty and Freamon who both seem hopelessly out of their depth. Am beginning to think that the whole process of major crimes is interminable, there will always be another connection, a bigger fish to fry, a "final" lead to follow, another wire to tap (war on terror allegory no doubt). Suppose that's the point of institutions as networks; they ultimately only reveal your own complicity, as evidenced in the psychological profiling of our ass-biter. Better to deal with the prosaic approach of Bunk, who let's not forget was not really involved in uncovering the crime of the century but just managed to get someone to eventually process the DNA. Dread to think what the significance of the final scene is.

Gimplord When Omar got popped I happened to be dangling a can of Coke Zero from my hand over the edge of the sofa. It was a a near miss that it didn't land on the beige carpet.

paintyface am still buzzing. So many brilliant scenes. McNulty listening to the FBI guys reading their profile of the serial killer and realising they are describing him. The vet catching Scott out in front of his boss, Carcetti doing a deal with Clay Davis and Omar being shot 20 odd minutes in and Marlo smiling! Most other shows would have killed him at the end but it just shows you how far ahead of the game this is.

joedoone It is obvious that no one at The Baltimore Sun watches The Wire. First, Prop Joe's death gets buried, and now Omar's. Gus should know better.

KatharineP The sheer prosaicness of it was perfect – no great shoot-out, no catharsis, no myth-making, and no room for him in the Sun, just a brutal small boy (who nevertheless was scared of what he'd done) and some souvenir seekers. (I saw elsewhere that Kenard was one of the children playing at "being Omar" in season 3 – does anyone with a better memory than me know if that's right?) Marlo was so horribly smug about it, but it was interesting that no one had actually given him all the details about Omar's messages. Chris seemed pissed off, though – will that have repercussions?

Dominic West was so good in this – McNulty clearly sober again, and beginning to think straight, but too late. He was hilarious as he listened to the profilers produce a spot-on description of himself, and heart-breaking as he finally understood what he's done to Beadie, and, indeed, to himself. I'd go to his wake. However, I suspect that his dying in the line of duty would be a touch too redemptive for The Wire; prison seems more likely (bet Avon would be glad to see him).

Is Kima going to give the game away?

Damascus Take a hit of a Newport cigarette for Omar, you feel me? Oh snap I guess smoking can get you killed.

Marwood1974 R.I.P. Omar Devone Little. You will always be my peoples, you feel me?

Busfield – even if the pOlice call had told Alma that the vic was Omar, the man most likely to ID the name was Roger Twigg (the news reporter who got "bought out" but did one last favour for Gus?). No accident, I feel; the people capable of laying out the Bigger Picture are all being discarded by the new media culture – a theme of the series so far.

Katherine P – yes, Kenard is indeed one of the kids playing at "being Omar" in the wake of the street shootout in S3. (I think he is the one who says, "It's my turn to be Omar now!" but I am not sure…)

as for Kima not going along with McNulty, she has always been good pOlice in that way, as far back as S1. She refuses to ID the other shooter (aside from Little Man? I think it may be Savino...) even though Bunk explains that they have all the forensics on it and just need her to nod when he points to a photo. "Sometimes it's good to play hard" she says – and isn't that what makes her one of the "good guys"?

Yes, I have been watching them all again from the beginning – what of it?

Favourite Omar Moments:

5) His first raid on a Barksdale stash house: "Don't make me huff and puff now!" followed by the stash dropping out while his back is turned.

4) His night-time hunt of two Barksdale boys, whistling "Farmer In The Dell" in S1, panicking them like teenagers in a Wes Craven movie.

3) His confrontation with Bunk in S3, with the big man managing to rattle Omar's cool and prick his conscience a little.

2) Omar & Brother Mouzone – shoot-out at the motel, Omar phoning him an ambulance, the face-off in an alleyway, the cat-and-mouse pursuit of Stringer. "The Wire" equivalent of Batman and Wolverine teaming up against you...

1) Courtroom. S2. Everything about it. "One day at a time, I s'pose..."

R.I.P., Omar.

ShelfsideAndy Talking of flouncing; Templeton. You can feel in every line David Simon sneering at the values of modern, corner-cutting news journalism.

Second favourite humorous moment; Kenard trying to set a cat alight with lighter fuel before following Omar to the store. Damn, that was a tight hour; less fat on that than Cedric Daniels.

joedoone Omar Moment: when he held up the store, then asked for ciggies and waited for his change. Kellogg's should use him to promote their Honey Nut Cheerios.

CLM76 Loved the irony in Carcetti's pseudo-impassioned speech about the homeless. "People are disappearing! People are dying!" Yeah, like the 24 people killed and shut up in those houses. But they didn't have a kinky serial-killer narrative attached. They were just bangers.

Oh, and bless Dukie. Glad to see Poot got out. It gets old, you know?

joedoone McNulty's incredulous catchphrase, "What the f**k did I do?" no longer applies. He knows exactly what the f**k he did. I still want him to avoid jail, though, because as twisted as his motives were, they came from some sort of a good place. There has been nothing good at all about Templeton's motives, or those of Clay Davis, but which of the three is likely to be called to account? That's what I thought.

Marwood1974 I think it's because we've come to know and love Jimmy for all of his faults that we are willing to turn a blind eye to the moral grey area he's walked into. Would we be so forgiving if it were Rawls telling them to do all of this for his purposes? (Not that he ever would.) The simple fact is that there are rules in society governing what pOlice can do to apprehend a suspect for a reason; Jimmy has – because he's not getting his own way again – thrown his toys out of his pram and broken those rules. It's not without precedent either – he forges a surveillance sheet when he and Prez are listening in and there's nobody on the rooftop to witness the other end of the call.

How would we all feel if we found out that a pOlice here forged evidence in order to pursue a prosecution against someone he "knew" was guilty? (I'm not castigating Jimmy here; I'm just pointing out the lovely moral ambiguities that "The Wire" can make you ponder on a Tuesday morning…)

Totus Now that Carcetti has jumped on the bandwagon and made it a political issue, it's not going to be so easy to sweep away. Be interesting to see if it impacts on his gubernatorial ambitions, and what mess is left behind.

It's all making sense now, with the media playing a significant role. It's not just about seeing what goes on in the newsroom, but how the media reaction can affect the other publicly accountable institutions. This was hinted at in the Hamsterdam storyline, but it is so much more clearly illustrated here.

SaptarshiRay Fave Omar moment for me is when after sticking up Cheese & his crew in the last season – leading to one of my fave quotes in the whole 5 series, from Cheese: "He had a girl pulling a gun out of her pussy, the shit was unseemly man" – Omar decides to sell Prop Joe's stolen stash back to him on Butchie's advice.

Omar: 20 on the dollar

Slim Charles: 10 Nigger.

Omar: Don't make me say 25 now.

Totus Anyone else notice that each season has featured the death of somebody just as they realised that they wanted out of the game, or had started to question it?

S1: Wallace

S2: D'Angelo

S3: Stringer

S4: Bodie

In each case, we saw the character discuss the game and its implications with somebody else. Wallace spoke to D. D spoke to the cops, (and his reading group in prison), Stringer spoke to Bunny, while Bodie and McNulty shared a moment.

Shall we chalk one up for Omar this season, given that he had ceased his stick-up game, and just came back for Marlo after Butchie bought the farm?

AxxB Omar moment – In season four, in prison. His two bodyguards have just fitted him with the encyclopedia of stab-vests, and they're coming out of the cell for breakfast, knowing that the hit is coming. Omar turns to his bodyguard and asks "Y'all reckon they got Honey Nut Cheerios up in here?"

ShelfsideAndy I was contrasting the two occasions we've seen CNN (as representative of the national media); the first occasion – the 22 bodies in the row houses – wasn't sold to the media as a serial killer story, but it effectively was. The second is sold as a serial killer story and is entirely bogus. So we better understand packaging and 'news consumerism'.

ShelfsideAndy It seemed to me the point about firstly Lester, then Sydnor, now Kima and Bunk being drawn into the conspiracy is that is exactly what happened with Iraq. In the end every relevant US and British agency was drawn in to, and poisoned by, the bogus reality. Further, so were non-government institutions, like the mainstream media.

Take, for example MI6 and the CIA, if you go back to 2001/2002 both were arguing in public documentation that Iraq posed no foreseeable risk. Which was, of course, an accurate assessment based on seven years of the (then) still on going UNSCOM inspections.

CodProfundity FUCKING KENARD?!?!?!?!

As fitting an ending as could be devised for Omar unfortunately and as with many of Omar's story lines a powerful metaphor for the series as a whole and that of course means for America too. It was the look of terror on Kenard's face afterwards that, for me, made it one of the very best moment of the series. His shock and awe at what he'd done was horribly real and it slammed home the point about just what the destruction of a huge swathe of the population is breeding.

It's a good job we also got one of the funniest scenes of the season later on with McNulty's deconstruction. I was laughing so loudly I'm sure my flatmate heard. But it really hit him didn't it? It's funny how people told Jimmy basically the same things as the profiler all the time, but when he heard it once removed it resonated with him in a very different way.

ShangoDan About Kenard I have to say I find it very hard to treat him as a villain (even though he's always been quite the scoundrel). He reminds me of the kid Michael Moore talks about in Bowling for Columbine who got access to a gun and shot a girl because no one was taking care of him. Kenard's is a heart wrenching tragedy, and I wonder now what would happen to him. I find it unlikely that he would escape the cops – CCTV plus a witness would see to that. I guess it's some form of juvie for him, but whatever happens will not be good. Bunk would obviously not know that he's seen him previously playing as Omar and that he inspired him to lecture Omar on "how far we done fell". If there's a tragedy here in American society – and there is – it is surely Kenard's story.

EPISODE 9 – Unravelling before our eyes

STEVE BUSFIELD

The Wire is unravelling before our eyes. McNulty has been grassed up by Kima. Michael has gone on the run, abandoning Bug and Dukie.

On the flip side Snoop got what was coming to her. Marlo is in a police cell. And Gus is on to Templeton's trail of nonsense.

I feared for young Michael but, as Snoop said (in one of her rare utterances that could be translated from that thick Baltimore brogue), he was always smart. He's dodged the first bullet. But he's either on the run now or facing a lifetime in witness protection or he turns and fights. That farewell scene with Michael's family was heartbreaking. Little brother has lost his brother, his father, and where is his mother? (Who was he left with?) Dukie is even worse off. That little speech about "remember that summer past ..." is on the Wire soundtrack album and I have been waiting for it to appear, unaware of its resonance.

Lester's wiretap and code-breaking have put Marlo's crew on remand. But will Herc mess it up for them by telling Levy about the wire? Surely Lester doesn't have enough time or evidence to get the better of the skanky lawyer, even with Clay's indiscretions.

Gus is gathering evidence of Templeton's lies. But the Sun bosses are dreaming of Pulitzers for their exposure of "Dickensian" homelessness. Daniels has enough evidence of McNulty's subterfuge. But Carcetti is claiming the credit for McNulty's (indirect) efforts.

QUOTE OF THE WEEK:

" ... I don't ... " Michael's response – after a long pause – when Dukie asks him if he remembers their innocent adventures: "You remember that one day summer past?"

RUNNING TOTALS:

Murders: up one to 81. Snoop is killed by Michael.

COMMENTS

pdmalcolm That is, quite simply, one of the best episodes of The Wire ever!

1) I knew nobody had told Marlo about Omar! And his reaction has set up a crazy Hamlet-esque situation amongst his lieutenants in the last episode

2) Bubbles finally coming to terms with the "hot-shot" and letting it all out. I think Bubs is basically the lyrics to the theme tune embodied... it's through hard, honest effort rather than hustling he has attained redemption.

3) Michael and Dukie... So poignant! Mike is clearly going down, but he read Snoop's move and got his retaliation in early, at least he looked out for his people. Although, looking at the Steptoe-esque yard he just walked into, Duquan is, sadly, doomed.

4) McNulty is boned. Gregg's conversation with Carver sealed his fate

5) Herc has made the case against Marlo and then destroyed it. knowingly, if you asked me... he used Carv there,

shakermaker82 Kima Kima Kima what have you done you snake?! I cannot believe she has snitched on her two pals. I even commented on here last week that I didn't think she would do it, that she would realise the end (Marlo in prison) would justify the means (McNutty's crazy serial killer idea). If Daniel's goes public with this it would bring everybody down, maybe they'll just give McNutty and Freamon the American equivalent of the P45. However it appears Levy is on the scent...

Tesswood The "my name" bit reminded me of John Proctor in The Crucible.

Strange how one scene can totally change your view of a character. After that scene I sort of like Marlo in a weird way. I'm rooting for him a bit now.

SaptarshiRay I think it's blackly comic that Herc will end up playing such a pivotal role in Marlo's, Jimmy and Lester's fate. Basically he's created a legal conundrum as his giving the cell no. to carver set the chain of events off, which Carver will know when it all comes out. What I found interesting was him telling Levy that he had it "off the record" that it was a wiretap when we don't see anyone say that to him.

Ultimately Herc has become Fuzzy Dunlop in a different scenario:

Carver could legitimately say that he was the "source" of the info, which has Marlo, monk and Chris scratching their heads in the jail. That ultimately means if Levy tries to play the illegal wiretap route, Pearlman could say in court the CI was actually Levy's employee, Herc. And what criminal lawyer would want the reputation of having a record of leaking info to the pOlice?

Jimmy and Lester always said the wiretap was merely a way of catching Marlo or his gang in possession, which they did. It would never be admissible as all they have is a series of photos of clocks on a number that was signed off in the belief it belonged to a serial killer. Which is why they've fudged the info on the affidavits as a "source". Any good lawyer would be able to unravel the case if they knew that but that's why if Ronnie says the initial tip off came from a CI and then surveillance led to the bust, they could theoretically win, as neither Herc nor Levy would want to admit to giving Marlo's number up. What they have to do is prevent Levy from connecting Marlo's case to the homeless one, otherwise he could go on a whole "how can we believe anything the BPD says" rant.

Like I say it's a legal maze where both sides know the other's cheating but can't call each other on it. Reminds me of the card game in The Sting when Robert Shaw knows Paul Newman cheated but can't call him out without being revealed as a cheat himself.

"What was I supposed to do, say he cheated but he did it better than me?!"

Tesswood Kima did the right thing in my view. Stuck to her principles. Didn't support her mates just because they were her mates. Incorruptible.

ShangoDan I'm going to say this even if I'm going to be hated – *RIP Snoop*. I remember fondly her "schooling" in the nail guns store, it was a hell of a scene – great way to start season 4. "The man say Cadillac, he mean Lexus but he don't know it". She then tells Chris, "F**k jus' nailin' up boards, we could kill a coupla mutha f**kers with this right here."

ShangoDan One interesting contrast between Marlo and the Greek – when the Greek fled Baltimore last time round, he says "my name is not my name" – the Greek is in a position to not run his business by rep (after all, he's working in a foreign country) – Marlo does not have this choice, his name must be his name.

Totus watching The Wire has affected my views on systems and institutions, and it has made a solid argument as to why such organisations cannot change, and simply perpetuate themselves. A necessary corollary of this is that change/reform/redemption is possible, but primarily (sometimes solely) on a personal level. In each case, personal or 1:1 intervention is required, the cold, megalithic institution isn't up to the task.

My favourite examples over the four series have been:

Freamon's mentoring of Prez in the first season. What a total fuck-up he was, but now we've had repeated demands (in this forum at least) for him to return to help out the investigation.

Carver's development, with guidance from Daniels and (particularly) Colvin. He could have gone either way, this one, but over the five seasons he has come to earn those stripes he wears. He carries himself like a leader, and does the right thing, whatever the personal cost. Contrast his attitude over the Colicchio incident with his pocketing of the stashhouse cash in Season 1.

Bunny's patient handling of Namond. To quote Simon, "A 15 year old drug dealer is still 15". Bunny's trick was to treat him like a 15 year old, encouraging him when he needed it, gently chiding him when he needed it, and loving him whatever. He needed a home. Give him an institution, like his pal Randy, and look what you get.

Finally, back to Bubbles. He's had Walon's infinitely patient guidance and support to help him, and he definitely needed it in the early days, but ultimately, he had to take the final step himself. His comments about not finding anyone to call, but still not getting high are among the most significant words spoken in the whole series. He's come the furthest of anybody there, but has had the furthest to travel. We all love Bubs, and I guess we all want him to come out OK. His has been among the most important of all the little stories in The Wire, and I for one feel better for having followed it.

jamie12 Snoop. Miss her. People have complained that she had no code. In my opinion she did; it was not one I subscribe to but there was an utter allegiance and loyalty. Perhaps her greatest performance was in the last scene when she made Mike come across as alien, disloyal and code-less. At least through the Snoop lens, and, momentarily, my own.

Hulegu Re: Kima: In the 3rd series McNulty continues chasing Stringer Bell even when the MCU has been reassigned to investigating a mid-level dealer called Kintel Williams. McNulty gets Kima embroiled in his little scheme before Freamon finds out and flips his nut, He accuses McNulty of burning everyone and everything to get what he wants and then turns on Greggs, saying "I'm disappointed in you girl – Daniels raised you from a pup". Daniels finds out and predictably carpets them both – although the MCU does eventually refocus on Bell.

However, it seems to me that may be when Kima starts thinking seriously about her career and issues of loyalty. As we have seen in the 5th series, Kima is investigating REAL murders – a home invasion by Marlo's people – and not some made-up s*it like McNulty's homeless-people-mass-murders nonsense.

Moreover, she realises the legal implications of a fraudulent case against Stanfield better than McNulty – although Freamon's role is hard to fathom. In my eyes he was "real police", doing good work and tutoring all the others throughout the 5 series – and now he's up to his neck in McNulty's fantasy world. Words desert me …

suziebee Hope Cheese is gonna get it. One death that I wouldn't mourn.

EPISODE 10 – The end

STEVE BUSFIELD

Well, that had everything: tears of sadness as we saw Dukie become Bubbles, tears of happiness as Bubbles was invited to his sister's dinner table, cheers as Slim Charles took out Cheese, and laughter as Valchek took the top job.

Everything made sense but was never the easy way out. Everything that could be concluded was, but the circle of Baltimore life goes on:

Marlo is the new Stringer, Michael is the new Omar, Pearlman is the new Phelan, Sydnor is the new Lester/McNulty.

Some folk just got to carry on being themselves: Lester carving his miniature furniture, Landsman speechifying over departed comrades accompanied by the Pogues, Levy introducing drug money to property development, the Greeks getting a new connect, Prezbo finding his vocation (and facial hair).

The conclusions were the right ones: Chris takes the fall for the vacants (he did commit them, after all), McNulty had to take the rap (he got away easy considering), and the courthouse leak was grand jury prosecutor Gary DiPasquale, a man we have probably seen dozens of times, but never noticed.

We can't be happy with all the outcomes, but we know the truth in them:

Templeton and his fool senior managers got their prize (we can but hope down the road they will get found out), Carcetti will probably become governor, Marlo and Levy don't just wriggle free but flourish (unless, of course, Stanfield can't shake his love of the streets).

We were at least given the dim and distant hope that Michael will one day finish Marlo like Omar ended Stringer.

And McNulty got a proper Kavanaugh's send off. As Jimmy acknowledged Kima, I was proud of the readers here for consistently arguing that she is proper pOlice.

Before the truth was out McNulty told Landsman: "I can't make shit up." Bunk's face was priceless. But McNulty knew what the fuck he did. We were as sad as McNulty to say goodbye to that side of Baltimore. All those wistful shots of the city and the people. But can you take a homeless person home? At least Beadie took McNulty back.

FAVOURITE QUOTE:

"That was for Joe." Slim Charles does the right thing by his old boss.

THOSE RUNNING TOTALS IN FULL:

Murders: up one – Cheese – to make a grand total of 82.

McNulty giving a fuck when it's not his turn: one last bucking of the system, as he refuses to falsely implicate a mentally ill man in all of his fake murders, taking him up one to 43.

Drunk: doesn't even get drunk at his own "wake". Is he turning over a new leaf again? Twenty-four drunken misadventures in 60 episodes.

Bunk drunk: up one to 10 for a celebratory drink for Jimmy, who over the course of five seasons has categorically outdrunk him.

Herc fuck-ups: one last fuck-up – helping Levy get Marlo off scot free – taking him to 21.

Omar stick-ups: RIP Omar. Seventeen. The torch has passed to Michael.

Bubbles attempting to get clean: the perfect ending: Bubbles has finally made it. Seven.

Dubious parenting: none: steady at eight.

COMMENTS

TrudyKockenlocker Now we're at the end, I've realised the main thing I love and admire so much about the show is how it manages to portray every point on the morality spectrum. Only by having such well-drawn and complex characters could you achieve this – it's what makes us respect and feel affection for Slim Charles, why we simultaneously understand Kima's actions yet kinda resent her for doing the right thing, why Omar was arguably the heart of the show. Such indeed is life, and why The Wire is simply the finest serial drama of them all.

prezbofan Prez and Dukie outside the school was simply heartbreaking.

joedoone As with the best novels, The Wire will always be there to go back to and get something more out of every time you open it up. The Wire is dead, long live The Wire. The game goes on. Many of the most guilty survive and prosper, while the relatively virtuous get eased out – we never did get to find out what was in Daniels's file, though he told his wife he didn't think it was enough to indict him. Freamon is back carving miniatures, and he has Shardene to give him some serious loving. Cheese gets his, Levy doesn't, and Marlo, who I thought for a moment was going to get mugged in his smart suit, shows he has the cojones to rescue his name from the dissing it received from Omar. Michael is the new Omar. Dukie is the new Bubbles. Bubbles has made it beyond the top of the basement stairs at his sister's, and has seen his life make some kind of sense in the Baltimore Sun. Alma pays the price for supporting Gus, and Gus is sidelined, while Templeton goes on to Columbia University. Daniels finally makes lawyer, Rhonda makes judge, and Judge Phelan looks set to start the cycle all over again with new McNutty, Sydnor. Bunk and Kima are still murder police. The City Hall mole is uncovered, to no great effect. Prezbo has a beard. We have another drinking session, for McNutty's "wake", and another outing for "I'm a freeborn man of the USA". McNutty gets to say "What the f**k did I do?" He and Freamon don't blame Kima for blowing the whistle, and he is at peace with himself, and "at home" with Beadie. Both McNutty and Daniels found lines beyond which they were not prepared to cross. Herc doesn't know what a line is. Slim Charles, who told Marlo he wasn't CEO material, steps up to the plate, both with the co-op and with avenging Prop Joe. Marlo, told by Levy that he has to get out of the game, tells Slim Charles and the co-op "I'm done with this gangster shit. I'm just a businessman." Not enough of a businessman to put up with Levy's redevelopment fat cats, and itchy to pop a cap in an ass or two. As with David Simon's script for the first episode of Season Five, points are sometimes less subtle than they might be, as when McNutty is struggling to wind up the serial killer bullshit and Bunk says "It's like a war. Easy to get in, hell to get out." Later, McNutty says to a cop, who is in on Templeton's bullshit over seeing an attempted abduction, "If you lock up every liar …" I felt like Carcetti, busting the telly and asking "Did someone not get the message?" Templeton is an empty notebook, but he prospers. Valchek is the new commissioner; all the shit he pulled to bring down Frank Sobotka goes unpunished. The Greeks quietly endure. Chris quietly does his time. Omar's killer is in cuffs. McNutty says to his homeless passenger "Let's go home."

Gimplord Highs – Michael disappearing into the shadows, the demise of Cheese, Prezbo's beard, Rawls impressive C-bomb.

Lows – Levy oozing smugness from every pore, Templeton's prize, not knowing what was in Daniels's file. This all pales into insignificance next to seeing Dukie shooting up. Crushing.

ShangoDan Love Slim's moment – like the eulogy, I felt as if I had seen Cheese's statement about the nostalgic past before, and from whom? Slim Charles of course: the thing about the old days, them the old days. What a way to be a critic, Slim – I like your way of thinking!

And how wrong was Beadie Russell that no one would attend McNulty's wake (he deserves not to be called Nutty today) – well, sort of.

Nice to see that Marlo ain't a spring chicken (even though Busfield rightly points out that his muscle does matter), and though we've all (?) been wishing his demise (at Michael's hand?), I'm glad how it ended – it was the lies that freed him, though of course he ain't really free – he lied when he said he was a "businessman, not a gangster" (as his foray into the street proved). He's now trapped in a world he doesn't understand or have a connection with, at the mercy of the gangsters with suitcases ((c) Omar). There are worse gangsters than the ones who've graced (sic) our screens most of the time on the street for 5 years – the point of the circularity and symmetry is I think indeed this – the structures are binding, constraining – one person escapes and another replaces her or him ad infinitum – until the structure is broken, if it is. Watching the buildings and the city, from McNulty's perspective, the people on the streets merging into the city and its buildings, organically co-existing or living with its streets, the question is, how does one break out of this world where the watchers are simply themselves agents of something above, where the watched are not per se their "enemies" but in a sense both are subservient (largely, not wholly) to a larger force.

So, I love the shot of the stone breaking against the camera – has always been my favourite of the opening montage and I'm glad they repeated it in a different context.

As far as I'm concerned, this is the greatest ever TV show, in fact because it went beyond the medium and asked the questions no one had ever really asked on the screen. It will be sorely missed.

paulcunningham enjoyed Gus's put-down, while sifting through some copy, of a reporter's phrase, mentioning Tom Wolfe, as I've always seen The Bonfire Of The Vanities as a bit of a companion piece to The Wire, with very similar themes, narrative construction and consequences.

Benches How this show has enriched my wife's vocabulary. I suggest we exit the motorway at the next junction and she's "Yeah, let's take that f*cking sh1t, man." Query into the size of something, and "it was 'yay' long/big etc". She one bad ass mutherf*cker.

funkitup I like the idea that there are roles in society and that someone will always fall into those roles. There are always leaders, there are always lieutenants, there are always parasites, there are always consumers, etc – a common social structure runs through every institution in our society. It's all part of the game!

That said, Dukie is not the next Bubbles, Dukie is Dukie.

churchdog I have to take issue with the analysis of some of the characters' end points in this review. Marlo doesn't flourish or become Stringer Bell; by the last scene he is completely lost, a paradox caught between two personalities that he can never be. He cannot ever deal in the drugs trade again, but he is not equipped to exist as a property tycoon. His 'taking back of the corner' is a frustrated act of self-defiance. The thwarted, almost childlike confusion in his eyes shows us that he can never be Stringer Bell but he can never be Avon Barksdale either. Though he has escaped jail, he cannot ever be what he set out to be – The King.

Also, I agree that Sydnor is the new Lester, but not the new McNulty – that position is surely filled by Kima, the hounding, commitment-phobic, real pOlice that exactly takes his place by the side of the steadfast Bunk.

CLM76 I think I shall now return to the start, and enjoy all five seasons again – with the added bonus this time that I don't have to worry about the fate of Reginald Cousins. I know he will end up eating dinner in his sister's kitchen. Of all the wonderful acting we've seen across 60 episodes, Andre Royo's achievement is surely paramount.

oohteenmusic Wee-Bey and Chris. probably responsible for about a hundred bodies between them, leaning against a fence shooting the breeze

sydneysider28 I really wanted Clay and Levy to get what was coming to them – almost made me feel sorry for Marlo when you see that

Levy is about to do to him what he had already done to Stringer.

And Dukie's story was maybe the worst.

And I am not sure what kind of job McNulty can do now.

And the Greeks never got any comeuppance at all, and the politicians all proved to be either self-serving and corrupt, or self-serving and ineffective.

I think Lester was the only one who had a happy ending, and even he didn't get to bring Clay down.

OmarLittle I would like to think that Michael could have the sense to make some money and then get out. Surely $100,000 would be more than enough to set up in NYC?

lastgeneration Agree about Kenard becoming the next King, he had one of my favourite scenes when dealing out on the corner in series 4, Michaels mother approached looking for a discount:

Namond: That's Michael's moms yo.

Kenard: The f*ck she is, she a f*cking dope fiend.

DogManStar 5 seasons and 63-odd hours of TV heaven. You'd have to have a heart of stone not to be touched by Bubs having dinner with his sister.

And to think it won around 0 Emmy awards. Because, as we all know, Boston Legal and Desperate Housewives are better shows. In the words of Mark Kermode, "I'm sorry, but I'm right and they're wrong".

SaptarshiRay What are we supposed to do now?

SpoddyFundunglus Cheese's death is the one single death in five seasons that I felt uncomplicatedly good about.

century As someone who works in TV at a fairly high level, I guarantee that we will never see anything as brilliant as The Wire in my lifetime.

ElizaClifford Christ how I love "The Wire". One of the best in-jokes throughout series five was the way in which senior members of staff at the Baltimore Sun kept urging Gus and the other journalists to write "Dickensian" stories, when it was obvious they had no idea what they meant by the term. Dickensian is of course the adjective that a lot of critics have applied to "The Wire" itself and I think it's pretty apt up to a point. Dickens' later books – Bleak House, Little Dorrit, Our Mutual Friend – are strident attacks on the corrupt and corrupting nature of social institutions (the law, the prison system etc) and this is obviously at the heart of "The Wire".

CodProfundity The irony of Marlo's position at the end of the series is that he's exactly where Stringer Bell wanted to be – in with Krawczyk etc but also with sound advice from Levy keeping him from getting scammed – and Marlo doesn't really want it, he wants the respect of the street. The fact it doesn't bode well for Jimmy or Lester is an ominous note playing under the final moments of the show.

AxxB I loved to see the way Pryzbylewski basically let Dukie play him while letting him know that its the only time that he would manage it – like this is not only the moment at which Dukie sacrifices his last link to the outside world, but its also the death of the last bit Prez's naivete, a bit of naivete that he really wanted to be able to hang on to. But is it realistic that Dukie would go straight from being clean to being on the needle? Where were all those gateway drugs that we hear so much about?

ChuckSchick The fact that the politicians and lawyers all seemed to get away with it was brilliant in my opinion. Let's face it, they usually do.

saisteve Watched the last episode late last night and sad as I was to see it go, in a way I'm glad it's over! Never have I been so obsessed with a TV show and have caught myself thinking about the characters and story lines at the strangest and most inappropriate moments. Is anyone else feeling that they can finally get on with their lives now that they know how it all ends? Found it very hard to sleep last night as I tried to digest all that had happened in that final episode..

Think the final scene should have been Marlo standing alone on the corner in the dark, caught between 2 worlds, having gained a fortune but lost everything that really mattered to him. I don't believe it was ever about the money for him and though he seemed to get away with it all in reality I think the worst end for him was to realise his name on the street was gone (as Michael said: Marlo ain't around no more) while Omar's legend clearly is growing.

For a moment there I though Chris would turn on Marlo as it seems to me that Marlo sold him out, life without parole? He ain't never getting out and he committed all those murders for Marlo who walked away scot free. Wish they'd shown us just how Marlo convinced Chris to go for that, would have loved to have seen that final conversation between them.

IrishDiaspora a couple thoughts on themes from this season:

Some people thought that this was a little heavy handed on the newsroom. I beg to differ. You see, many of us in the US read BBC or the Guardian for news because we simply don't get it in our local papers or on TV. I think the points made were very decent and I really appreciated the thoughts they kindled in my brain.

second, why would Chris Partlow take the fall for Marlo? I think it's probably the same as with Wee-Bey. He was tied to a murder with very strong evidence and it was unlikely that he'd ever get out of prison anyway. There would be no way the prosecutor would plea down a case as strong as those. So, since he was going to go to jail for the rest of his life anyway, what would be gained by ratting out his boss?

joedoone It can't be long before Gus – can't he get a job at the Guardian? – finds out the full truth behind the Ass Biter, how much of the lie was down to empty notebook Templeton and how much to McNulty. Gus, of course, won't be able to sell the facts to his higher-ups.

jamie12 Gus already has a job at the Guardian, his name is Steve Busfield. Child as I am, they occupy the same head-space.

AxxB As far as the serial killer thing goes, I think it was actually a veiled attack on serial killer culture – on the entertainment media's preoccupation with serial killers. Take the way the FBIs top serial killer guy is presented as a media whore, the way Dexter is shown as frivolous entertainment next to the reality of Michael's life, the way the media didn't make a big thing of the bodies in the vacants but their eyes lit up when they hear about someone killing white guys with a sexual motive. The idea of the serial killer being bullshit is tied to the idea the the whole concept of serial killers is a small piece of truth over-exaggerated to the point of meaninglessness. Meanwhile the drug trade kills many more hundred or thousands of people a year and is considered to be an inner-city urban issue with no bearing on the comfortable middle class world most newspaper readers live in. The real Dennis Wise (the one Cutty is named after, not the footballing pariah) killed far more people than Ed Gein, but nobody considers him to be a serial killer – just an executioner.

Pigtown Please, please remember that Baltimore's just not The Wire! It's but a small part of our lovely city! Look at this… a perfect early autumn evening, watching a baseball game, at a stadium set in the heart of the city… This is what Baltimore's about, not the gun-slinging, drug-dealing low-lives that The Wire portrays.

DesignerBaby I think Bubbles personifies a lot of what Simon tries to say about the human side of living in Baltimore (as well as the Bodie and Herc characters, for completely different reasons) – that you have to learn the hard way (or sometimes not at all) and are bound by your surroundings, but can find redemption in the most unlikeliest of places. He's got so many scenes of note, but I think his lecturing of Sydnor in the ways of the junkie in Series 1 and his casual summing-up of Season 3 at the end with Colvin are personal highlights.

Also: Vandelay – for some reason I took real exception to the photocopier scene when I started on Series 5. The first scene of each series normally goes some way to explaining some of the more cerebral themes to come – remember the classic "because this is America, man" line that started Series 1? and the way the blowing up of the high-rises (ie, 9/11) gives way to Marlo's occupation of the Barksdale empire (ie, US in Iraq) in Series 3? – so if the theme for Season 5 is simply "don't believe everything you read" then they seem to have dumbed down a bit!

I'd even argue it hints at a bit of cockiness coming into the writing of The Wire in the last series – if you'd believe a kid would fall for that prank, then just maybe an audience would fall for an invented serial killer plot…

Interview: David Simon

OLIVER BURKEMAN

People are occasionally surprised, David Simon says, to find that he still lives in Baltimore, the city that is the lead character in his epic television series The Wire. They assume that the man behind all those box sets would have found himself a luxury penthouse in LA, or Manhattan at least, far from the devastated neighbourhoods his show portrays. But on a cold, bright morning at the headquarters of his production company in downtown Baltimore, he seems as enmeshed as ever in the life of the city – bemoaning the latest antics of the police department and the failure of the Baltimore Sun, his former employer, to cover them. "If I want to find out what's going on in this city, I've got to go to a fucking bar and talk to a police lieutenant and take notes on a cocktail napkin," he says. Simon is 48, bald and stocky, and prone to grumbling aggressively in a manner that is, for some reason, wholly likable. "That's what passes for high-end journalism in Baltimore these days."

One irony of The Wire's global success is that there are now, presumably, plenty of middle-class Britons more familiar with the drugs economy, failing schools and corrupt politicians of Baltimore than they are with any part of inner-city Britain. So faithful is The Wire to the specific vernacular of its setting, indeed, that there may be Londoners or Mancunians whose knowledge of west Baltimore drugs slang exceeds that of dealers in Philadelphia or New York.

They will have a new opportunity to embellish their vocabularies next month with the first UK publication of The Corner, the 1997 non-fiction book that inspired The Wire. Written by Simon and his collaborator Ed Burns, a former Baltimore police detective, it is a forensic document of one year in the inner city, told through the prism of a single street corner, and the addicts and dealers for whom it's the frontline in the struggle to survive. The publication is part of a high-profile year for Simon in Britain: he will appear at this year's Hay literary festival, while BBC2 will give The Wire its first airing on mainstream television.

Simon purports to be amused by his British success – "It's hilarious to me that there are two people walking through Hyde Park right now, arguing about The Wire" – but it would be wrong to imply he's surprised by it. Modesty isn't part of the Simon repertoire. He freely describes The Wire as revolutionary television, capturing "the truth" about the "universal themes" of life in the era of unrestrained capitalism; you sense that, ultimately, he considers the global adulation only fitting. When people call The Wire Shakespearean, he demurs, but only because he considers it a Greek tragedy instead: Aeschylus updated, with urban institutions as the Olympian gods, destroying human lives on a whim. "It's the police department, or the drug economy, or the political structures, or the school administration, or the macroeconomic forces that are throwing the lightning bolts and hitting people in the ass for no decent reason," he has said. (In a show loaded with symbolism, it's no coincidence that the coldest expression of pure capitalism in The Wire is the criminal mastermind of season two, The Greek.) You can watch The Wire, of course, as no more than a gritty soap opera, charting the lives of the alcoholic-but-brilliant detective Jimmy McNulty, the sociopathic kingpin Marlo Stanfield or the heartbreaking dope fiend Bubbles. But don't imagine Simon isn't also operating on another plane entirely.

It's part of the price of admission to Simon's worlds, both fictional and non-fictional, that you'll have almost no idea what's going on for the first few episodes, or the first few hundred pages. Turning on the subtitles will help you only marginally with the Baltimore-speak of The Wire; within the first few pages of The Corner, Gary McCullough, the real-life inspiration for Bubbles, is shown concluding that "the issue is 30 on the hype", no explanation provided. The soldiers of Generation Kill – Simon's Iraq war mini-series, based on a Rolling Stone journalist's book-length account of being embedded with the US marines during the 2003 invasion of Iraq – speak for minutes on end in impenetrable military lingo, and Treme, a show about the New Orleans music scene on which he's currently working, promises similarly opaque music jargon. This is quite deliberate. The key principle of Simon's storytelling was encapsulated in a remark that caused raised eyebrows when he uttered it, late last year, on BBC2's Culture Show: "Fuck the average viewer."

When you want to write the truth, Simon argues, writing for those who know nothing sets the bar too low. "That's how they taught us to write at the Baltimore Sun: 'For the average reader with a seventh-grade education.' " But when he took a leave of absence to write Homicide, his account of a year with Baltimore murder detectives – it later became an acclaimed TV drama of the same name – he realised it was time for a new approach. "There came this point where I sat down with all my notebooks and I had to start to write," he says, "when I thought: this whole notion of writing for the person who understands nothing, the average reader … He has to die! I can't have him in my head. And so the person I started writing for was the homicide detective." He wasn't aiming to please his subjects themselves, he insists; many of the detectives emerge from the book as racist, homophobic, sexist or some mixture of all three. "My guy in my head was some guy in Chicago I'd never met. Not the average reader. Fuck him! I want to write for the guy living the event. When I criticise him, I want him to think, 'That was fair.' When I don't criticise him, I want him to think, 'He gets it.'"

For the average reader or viewer, "the promise is that, as they go along, they'll understand more and more, and maybe by the end they'll understand most if not all of it". This sounds daunting, but watching The Wire or Generation Kill, that's not how it feels: the ingenious effect is to leave the viewer with the smugness-inducing sense of being smarter than before. "I love people who get to the end of the first episode and say, 'That's the show they're calling the greatest show in television? What?'" Simon says. "The first season of The Wire was a training exercise. We were training you to watch television differently."

The startling narrative compression of The Wire and Generation Kill means that no scene is ever a throwaway: miss a 10-second plot point in episode three and you'll regret it in episode nine, when it's suddenly crucial. "Even with shows that are somewhat sophisticated, you can take a phone call, you can have a conversation with your boyfriend or your spouse, and still pretty much grasp the show. The Wire will fuck you if you do that."

Isn't it arrogant to presume to retrain viewers in the art of watching television? "You know what would feel arrogant to me? What would feel arrogant to me would be asking you to spend 10 or 12 hours of your time a year watching my shit, and delivering something where we didn't hold that time precious. Last year, with The Wire and Generation Kill, HBO gave me 17 hours of uninterrupted film – almost $100m of production value. What would be arrogant would be to waste that – to tell anything less than the most meaningful possible story. Whenever I see a good subject ruined with a bad film or a bad book, I feel: shit, now it'll be harder to go back there again. How dare you presume to tell me a story, and then not tell me the best possible story?"

When he started researching The Corner, Simon had covered crime for the Sun for 13 years, but examining the drugs trade from the inside presented fresh challenges: two white guys hanging around the corner of Monroe and Fayette in west Baltimore were hardly inconspicuous. "We were initially regarded by many of the corner regulars as police or police informants," Simon and Burns write. It didn't help that some older dealers remembered Burns from his detective days. The police posed a different problem: those who didn't recognise them kept threatening to arrest them, assuming they were buying drugs; those who did recognise them stopped to chat, incurring the suspicion of locals. It took five months until the corner regulars "were convinced that whatever else we claimed to be, we weren't police. No one could recall seeing us buy or sell anything, nor did we seem to do anything that resulted in anyone getting locked up." By the time The Corner had become first its own mini-series and then, along with Homicide, source material for The Wire, west Baltimore had come on board to the point that throngs of spectators got in the way of filming. According to rumour, real wiretaps went silent during broadcasts, as dealers suspended operations in order to watch.

If there's a fault with Simon's work, it's that his characters can be so compelling, you forget to be angry about the situations he portrays. You find yourself laughing at the war-hardened wisecracks of Generation Kill's Corporal Josh Person, say, or wondering at The Wire's Marlo and his cold-blooded cool, without stepping back to take stock of the modern nightmares they're enduring. Simon, on the other hand, is very angry indeed. "You are sitting in the deconstruction of the American Dream," he says, indicating Baltimore. "Which is to say there was a fundamental myth that if you were willing to work hard, support your family, stay away from shit that ain't good for you, you'd do all right. You didn't have to be the smartest guy in the room. The dream wasn't that everyone could get rich. It was that everyone gets to make a living and see the game on Saturday, and maybe, with the help of a government loan or two, your kid'll go to college." His anger is wide-reaching: deprivation in Baltimore, imaginary WMDs in Iraq and Wall Street scandals are all part of the same betrayal – of capitalist institutions "selling people shit and calling it gold".

Simon doesn't respond well to the criticism that perhaps things aren't entirely bad – that his shows' unremitting pessimism distorts a world where some people do defeat the crushing force of social institutions. Last year, the journalist Mark Bowden made that charge in the Atlantic magazine, and Simon hasn't forgiven him. "This premise that The Wire wasn't real because it didn't show people having good outcomes in west Baltimore ... I don't know what to tell him. We didn't spend a series in a cul-de-sac with people barbecuing; it was the story of what's happening at the bottom rungs of an economy where capitalism has been allowed free rein. And if he's telling me it's not happening, I want to take his fucking entitled ass and drive him to west Baltimore and shove him out of the car at Monroe and Fayette and say: 'Find your way back, fucker, because you've got your head up your ass at the Atlantic.'"

Behind Simon's general disillusion is a disillusionment with journalism, the only work he ever wanted to do. Raised in a secular Jewish household in the Washington suburbs, he wrote for his school magazine, then was so busy editing the University of Maryland newspaper that it took him five years to graduate ("with terrible grades"). In his final year he began stringing for the local paper, the Sun; his wife, the novelist Laura Lippman, is another former Sun reporter. The way he tells it, the central betrayal of Simon's life is the gutting of the Sun by profit-obsessed owners and Pulitzer-obsessed editors. One of those reviled executives, Bill Marimow, gets an obnoxious police lieutenant named after him in The Wire; Scott Templeton, the weaselly fabricator of season five, is modelled on a Sun colleague. (Other former staffers describe Simon as a perpetual picker of fights.)

The collapse of the US newspaper industry has left politicians free to pursue their unethical schemes unscrutinised. "The internet does froth and commentary very well, but you don't meet many internet reporters down at the courthouse," he says. "Oh to be a state or local official in America over the next 10 to 15 years, before somebody figures out the business model. To gambol freely across the wastelands of an American city as a local politician! It's got to be one of the great dreams in the history of American corruption."

The way Simon sees it, The Wire and Generation Kill are, above all else, an exercise in reporting: the pulling back of the curtain on the real America that should have been undertaken by newspapers, transposed instead into the multimillion-dollar world of TV drama. "It's fiction, I'm clear about that. But at its heart it's journalistic." Newspapers, he says, launching into a new tirade, "have been obsessed with what they called 'impact journalism' – take a bite-sized morsel of a problem, make a big noise, win a Pulitzer. It was bullshit! But it was the only thing they knew. But what America needed in the last two decades was not 'impact journalism'. What they needed was somebody explaining what the fuck was happening to the country." The phrase he uses to describe the role newspapers should have been playing is also, you can't help feeling, one Simon would like to see as his own epitaph: "A counterweight to bullshit."

The Wire is not escapism

JEREMY KAHN

When you walk through the garden, better watch your back. That lyric, from the Tom Waits song Way Down in the Hole, was constantly running through my head last autumn when I began reporting a story about witness intimidation in Baltimore.

The song serves as the opening theme to The Wire, producer David Simon's brilliant urban drama. The Wire is both set in and filmed on the streets of Baltimore. And, like so much of the show, Way Down in the Hole is spot on – an anthem that perfectly captures the danger that permeates almost every block in Charm City (a Baltimore tourism slogan that stuck but which seems purely ironic today). Baltimore is a place that encapsulates all of the intractable problems of urban America: drugs, violence, race, poverty and secular economic decline.

It is difficult to overstate the realism of The Wire. Simon, a former journalist for the Baltimore Sun and still a city resident, is dedicated to authenticity. He spent a year following Baltimore homicide detectives for his 1991 book Homicide. He spent another year hanging out on one of the city's drug corners for a 1997 book, The Corner.

It also helps that one of his co-writers and producers, Ed Burns, spent two decades as a Baltimore cop and then seven years as a teacher in its decaying public school system. The incidents The Wire portrays – and even many of the character names used on the show – are drawn from life. (For instance, Stringer Bell is a composite of two infamous west Baltimore drug lords, Stringer Reed and Roland Bell.)

To an outsider, particularly someone unaccustomed to America's inner cities, the exceptional violence depicted in The Wire might seem pure Hollywood. But, as I discovered during my reporting forays to the city, this too is real – with devastating consequences for many of the city's residents.

According to the census takers, east Baltimore lost a third of its residents between 1990 and 2000. This was on top of already steep population declines stretching back to the second world war, the cumulative toll of white flight, the late 1960s riots, job losses and the twin epidemics of crack and heroin. The people left, but the blocks of low-rise apartments and rowhouses remained.

In some portions of east Baltimore, 50% of the buildings are vacant. Others have been demolished, leaving behind rubbish strewn lots. In these vacant and abandoned properties, the drug trade – and its incumbent addiction, prostitution and violence – have flourished. Only 45,000 people live in east Baltimore and in some years the police have made 25,000 arrests.

I had come to east Baltimore to follow the story of John Dowery Jr, a 38-year-old former heroin addict who had become a witness in a murder investigation. Dowery's story is one that would not seem out of place on The Wire. He had watched from his porch as a friend robbed a drug dealer named Reds who worked out of vacant lot down the block. The friend timed his escape poorly – just as he was leaving he ran into Boo-Boo, an athletic 20-year old with his hair in corn rows and his thin beard and moustache meticulously groomed.

Boo-Boo was allegedly a key enforcer in the local drug organisation. About 30 minutes later, the friend was dead: pumped full of lead on a nearby corner. His was the 229th murder of the year in a city that would rack up a body count of 278 before the clock struck midnight on 31 December. (This is typical for Baltimore, which consistently has one of the highest per capita murder rates in the country.) Dowery would claim he later heard Boo-Boo and his younger half-brother, whose nickname is Moo-Moo, boast of murdering the man.

In the hope of getting a lighter sentence on an existing handgun charge of his own, Dowery had agreed to testify against Boo-Boo and Moo-Moo. In Dowery's neighbourhood, people soon became suspicious: they accused him of being "a snitch", which can be tantamount to a death sentence in east Baltimore and many other inner-city neighbourhoods where cooperation with the police is seen as an act of treason against the community.

Dowery largely shrugged off the accusation – and the risk. But then one day in October 2005 two men met Dowery in his front yard as he was returning from work; one of them had a gun. They chased Dowery around his house, shooting him six times before leaving him for dead.

Remarkably, Dowery survived. The police helped relocate him and his immediate family outside of Baltimore. And he went on to testify against Boo-Boo and Moo-Moo. But the other witnesses were not so brave. Many changed their stories on the witness stand and in the end the jury deadlocked. The judged declared a mistrial and the case soon became part of a larger federal drug investigation. Meanwhile, Dowery had gotten his life on track: he had kicked his heroin habit, had a new job and a new house in the suburbs.

But he missed his old neighbourhood. Like many in Baltimore, he had spent his whole life in a few city blocks. All his friends were there. So too were most of his family. So this past November, he decided to go back to the old hood to celebrate Thanksgiving at his aunt's house.

After dinner that night, he nipped across the street to get a beer and a smoke at the Kozy Korner, a local dive. There he ran into a former girlfriend and began chatting with her at the bar. He apparently didn't notice when two men slipped into the bar behind him. They levelled guns at his head and opened fire. John Dowery was dead. And, though the bar was crowded that night, no witnesses have come forward to say they saw a thing.

Today, Boo-Boo and Moo-Moo are facing federal charges for a host of drug-related offences along with several co-defendants who allegedly ran a large east Baltimore drug ring, fittingly called "Special Heroin". It's not far off the Barksdale organisation depicted in The Wire.

So yes, The Wire is great television. But it's not escapism. In fact, it's exactly the opposite: a journey into a violent and tragic world from which too many Americans cannot break free.

The end of The Wire

Charlie Brooker meets the cast

How good is The Wire? Put it this way: The Wire's so good, I've lost count of the number of people who've approached or emailed me just to thank ME for convincing THEM to watch it. The Wire's so good, I'm jealous of anyone who hasn't seen it yet, because they get to discover it anew. The Wire's so good, it's come to an end. Because that's what good things do, the bastards.

I went to New York for the premiere of season five and got to interview several members of the cast. It's odd meeting them in the flesh because they're simultaneously like and unlike the characters they portray. Wendell Pierce speaks with Bunk's voice – baritone, like an oak blowjob – but also discusses his recent stage appearance in Waiting for Godot. And Andre Royo sounds like Bubbles – that signature stuttering slur – yet seems scarcely recognisable in sharp clothes and designer specs. Incidentally, both Bubbles and Omar recognised me, having seen the Screen Wipe Wire segment on YouTube. And yes, I'm bragging about that. As Wire devotees will understand, it was possibly the most thrilling moment of my life.

What's the secret of the show's success?

Andre Royo (Bubbles): It makes people think. And they're so happy to fuckin' watch a show that makes them think.

Wendell Pierce (Bunk Moreland): The humanity. The more specific you are, the more universal it becomes. People want to know the truth, and there's authenticity to our show. That's what people are responding to; that's why there's such diversity in our audience too. Everyone thinks the show speaks only to them, for them, because of that authenticity.

Sonja Sohn (Kima Greggs): It validates the experiences of a large group of people. Walking down the street I could be approached by lawyers, cops, dealers all saying: "That's exactly how it is. Finally there's something that shows what we go through, every day."

In fact, it's so true-to-life, some of the criminal tactics portrayed on the show have been copied in real life.

Jamie Hector (Marlo Stanfield): The cellphone strategy was used in the Queensbridge Projects in Brooklyn.

WP: Dumping phones? Yeah, the cops got mad. The New York cops called HBO and said: "Wait a minute man, they're using that."

JH: And vice versa, because the cats on the street were like, "Damn, I see how we're getting set up now … "

WP: Some cops visited the set and said: "You know they talk about you on the wire? On the real wire that we have?" One time, they were sitting on this wire, and it was quiet for a real long time, and finally somebody called, and the first thing this guy said was: "Motherfucker, what did I say? Don't call when The Wire's on."

So the show's authentic. It's also complex. By taking in so many aspects of society – with characters ranging from corner boys (young street dealers) to schoolteachers to congressmen, all intermingling within this immense, malfunctioning social machine, battered by each other's agendas – The Wire offers a bleakly convincing portrayal of both Why Things Mess Up and Why That Won't Change …

Clarke Peters (Lester Freamon): It doesn't answer any questions. But in holding the mirror up, you get a broader picture of how one aspect of your local government affects another aspect of your local government and so on … It allows you to see how these have a knock-on effect in Baltimore, and how the same stuff might be resonating in your own environment.

What's more, with each season, The Wire adds an additional institution to its already sprawling virtual Baltimore, bringing an influx of fresh characters with it. This time round, it's the media's turn: a fictional version of the (real) Baltimore Sun newsroom lies at the heart of the story …

Lance Reddick (Cedric Daniels): One of the questions that's always asked in the show is: how do you reconcile ethics with necessity? This season, with the media – what's their responsibility? To tell the truth or sell papers? It's the same compromise between the two. And it's the same thing with the police department, with City Hall, the streets ... This season, they're all intertwined.

So is The Wire proof that fiction can sometimes be a substitute for journalism?

LR: I'm struck by the question and can't help thinking it's a sign of the times. Art is art, and journalism is journalism. But David Simon is a journalist. And historically, when you think about how many great novelists were journalists – did Dickens have a political agenda when he wrote Oliver Twist? Absolutely. And did he try to make it as realistic as possible, based on his experience? Absolutely. It's not journalism ... but the show is unique because as a piece of art it does its job amidst a sea of entertainment created to pacify people and get them to buy stuff. I can only speak as an American, but most journalism here isn't doing its job any more. It's about selling stuff.

Not many actors get to work on a bona-fide masterpiece. Has the show spoiled you?

WP: Oh, definitely.

AR: I did an episode of Law & Order ... My character's got a gun in the house. Now when the cops come in, and I see a clear hallway? I run out. And they're like, "Cut, cut ... Listen ... We're not as smart as The Wire." You know, I get it. It serves its purpose and it's a great show. But when I read a script now? I'm a little spoiled. Because not only was [The Wire's] writing great, but I don't know if you're going to see this many people of colour on one show. With characters. Not just walkbys. It felt great, man. You didn't really realise for the first couple of episodes. You're just happy to be working. But then you're looking round the table one lunchtime, and you're like: hey, there's a lot of black people here, wow! And we all have characters. Will it ever be like this again? I don't know, but you gotta hope.

If nothing else, The Wire's roll call of well-rounded black characters – making up the majority of the cast – highlights just how clueless most TV shows are on this front…

WP: To see the images of young black folks in the inner city coming from Hollywood? Pfff. Those little paper dolls they send out, those one-dimensional stereotypes of us … That's bullshit compared to the real in-depth investigation of these people. Sometimes it's little things, you know? I had a part once on a show, and one of my lines was "I came home that day and I saw mother dead." That got a rewrite to: "I came home that day and I saw momma dead." And I said, "Black people say mother! You don't have to be afraid of that! It doesn't have to be momma just because I'm black!" And they were like, "Are you sure?" Now that may seem silly, but I've been on shows where we literally had executives ask, "Uh, do black men kiss their kids?" They actually said that! It's like – do you think we're not human or something? So if [The Wire] actually changes people's perceptions, that's very important.

And now it's finally over? Clarke Peters describes it as "like experiencing a death". Lance Reddick admits to "crying like a baby" after his final scene. Sonja Sohn is more upbeat …

SS: We all felt that this was a mission. We all realised how important this show was. And that we got to be a part of it, we got to bring some sort of enlightenment … We got to move people. Just knowing that you served a brilliant purpose in your life for five years – on a television show? It was tremendous.

Pity about the lack of awards, though.

WP: It'd be great to get the awards, but you know man … years from now, when people look back and start calling off the best shows? We're gonna be on that list. We're gonna be like The Bicycle Thief of television.

When he says that, everybody laughs, Pierce included. Partly because the tongue-in-cheek way he says it is just naturally funny. But also because it's true.

My last week on The Wire

DOMINIC WEST

Tuesday, August 28 We have four more days left on The Wire. We've all been together for five years and 60 episodes. There have been 949 speaking roles since we started in 2001. With every shot this week, we do something for the last time: last scene in a rat-infested alley; last time someone throws up/shoots up/gets shot. It's the glamour I'll miss the most.

Today was Ed Norris's last scene. He acted in the first season when he was the chief of the Baltimore police. Then he fell foul of the FBI and they jailed him for falsifying a mortgage application. He's one of several actors with jail terms the writers had to work around. "For the past five years The Wire's been the only constant in my life," he said.

Wednesday Today we shoot a wake in a dingy downtown basement bar. It's a David Simon fantasy of how the police mourn their dead. We've done variations on the scene twice before, but this time it's really swinging and there's real whisky circulating, not the usual tea, and everyone's plastered.

At around 2am I have to direct a pick-up scene from the seventh episode, which I did in July. Clarke [Peters, who plays Lester Freamon] is acting. It's just a small scene and the last shot is an insert of the newspaper he's reading. "You don't need me for that," says Clarke, "use Lloyd" (the stand-in). "Lloyd's thumb is lighter-skinned than yours," I say and make him stay.

Thursday Work hungover all day and then have scenes with the great Amy "Cryin'" Ryan [Beadie Russell] and her on-screen kids. A raucous board game with the pre-teens, which we don't shoot till 11pm, when everyone would rather die. Amy does it without crying and we all feel cheated.

Friday The last day of shooting. Twelve pages instead of the usual eight to get through. We're not called till 3pm, so Cat and I go to an antiques fair downtown to get an engagement ring. The fifth attempt. We run out two hours later, our eyes sparkling with the diamonds we've ogled, but no ring. Dora, our baby, is howling. It takes the cheesiness out of engagement rituals when there's a bawling baby in tow. Jewellers lie less. The coffee man recognised me and someone else made me name all the films I'd been in, so she could remember how she knew me: "No ... no, not that one ... nope." My favourite conversation.

We're late for the call. Dora crawls all over the make-up trailer, then darts around the set. We start filming, Clarke calls "action" and Cat strides on set and dumps Dora and a letter on my lap and screams, "You'll be hearing from my lawyers!" I was astonished. I felt sick. Oh Christ. Then everybody laughed and I realised Cat was joking. I never get her jokes.

Saturday Fourteen and a half hours and many valedictions later, we wrap after a scene between me, Bunk and a mad murderer. Wendell [Pierce, who plays Bunk Moreland] makes a great speech which starts, "It's all about the work you do, the people you meet" and ends with " ... the family we've created and there's nothing more important than family". I foolishly try to be philosophical and start meandering into "this great country" and Bush and Iraq and oh fuck, why didn't I just say how much I'll miss everyone.

We pop champagne and one after another the crew stand up and make a speech. David Simon recalls a troubled 15-year-old boy who'd asked for a job when we filmed on his street in the hood during the first season. Duane, who was the boy, was listening and started bawling. The wardrobe department had taken him on and he's been with them ever since.

Robert Parker, the world's most influential nose, lives in Baltimore and gave us a bottle of 80-year-old armagnac, to drink "the moment we wrapped". So after the Dom Perignon, David popped it and we all had a long, hilarious knockabout with the Balti-Bard. The Bald Bard of Baltimore. I can't remember any of it.

Got home around 8am. Clarke went for 18 holes of golf with Rodney, the key grip. I got back to the antiques fair. Cat finally settles on a beautiful, damaged Victorian diamond ring. The first ring we saw yesterday. We all meet up for the wrap party at around 4pm. Barbecues and bands in a park, then an after-party at a downtown club where all of Baltimore seems to have shown up. At about 4am Wendell starts rapping. We all cry with laughter.

Sunday Take Cat and Dora groggily to the airport for their flight home. I'm joining them in two weeks after a 500-mile horse race in New Mexico. Sonja Sohn [Kima Greggs] invites me and Wendell to her house for dinner to keep our spirits up.

Tomorrow is labour day and we're all back without a job. Summer's over, the show's over and we'll never work with better people or writing that good again.

Two Americas

DAVID SIMON

Baltimore – It's been an ordinary week in Maryland's largest city. The August heat broke and one can nearly sleep with a window open; the Orioles are again down in the cellar in the American League East; the city murder rate is a bit behind last year's blood-letting, and, if it holds into the fall, politicians and police commanders will compete to claim credit.

The stories in the Baltimore Sun remain fixed on the surface, each of them premised on the givens: schools will open next week and provide more or less the same inferior education as previous years; Johns Hopkins is building its biotech park expansion where the east Baltimore ghetto used to be and the ghetto is migrating due east and north-east; the biotech park will be great for white folk with college degrees; for those with union cards, the factories are still closed and the port is still losing cargo to Norfolk; a shooting here, a cutting there …

All in all, an unremarkable summer.

Save for one lonely headline the other day – something that genuinely intrigues. It's a curious item – a draft report by a local non-profit foundation, a simple statistical study of the difference between Baltimore criminal juries and those of the surrounding, suburban counties.

It seems that in Baltimore, one of the most violent cities in America, jurors are far more reluctant to convict criminal defendants than in the suburban enclaves that ring the city.

The report upset the city's chief prosecutor; she thought its conclusions "politically divisive" and asked the foundation to either amend the draft study or kill it entirely. The press mocked her for this, of course, and rightly so, while on the radio here, white talk-show hosts had fun speculating about why city jurors – read "black people" – won't do their civic duty when it is, in fact, their communities that are so overwhelmed by crime.

Everyone had something to say for a day or two, and of course, after that brief span of time, the entire issue disappeared into the glowing mediafest that was Michael Phelps and his remarkable collection of gold medals. Phelps is from Baltimore, by the way. As he is not wrapped in crime-scene tape, hampered by a budget shortfall or unable to raise his standardised test scores to the national average, we claim the great Olympian with considerable pride. The boy can swim, yes he can.

In any event, the story about the reluctant city juries slipped quickly below the waves in the Beijing pool without anyone ever seriously inquiring into the why of it, much less attempting to do any actual reporting on the matter.

Anomaly noted. Half-assed speculation offered. On to new business.

But here's the thing of which we can all be certain, the thing that fuels all the dramatic arcs of The Wire, in fact: the why is the only thing that actually matters. The who, the what, the when, the where, even the how – every other building block in which journalists and policy planners and political leaders routinely trade – amount to nothing beyond the filler, interchangeable with the facts flung a year ago, a year from now and decades hence.

The why is it. The why is what makes journalism an adult game. The why is what makes policy coherent and useful. The why is what transforms bureaucrats and footsoldiers and political leaders into viable instruments of rational and affirmative change. The why is everything, and without it, the very suggestion of human progress becomes a cosmic joke.

And in the American city, at the millennium, the why has ceased to exist.

When I read reviews and commentary on The Wire in the British press, I am usually moved to a peculiar and conflicted place. I'm gratified by the incredible amount of verbiage accorded our little drama and I'm delighted to have the fundamental ideas and arguments of the piece discussed seriously.

But at the same time, I'm acutely aware that our dystopian depiction of Baltimore has more appeal the farther one travels from America. The Wire is, of course, dissent of a kind and it is true that there are many of my countrymen who are in fundamental disagreement with the manner in which the nation is being governed and managed. But somehow, it sounds better to my ear when it's my own people talking trash and calling our problems out.

At the same time, it's not just a question of standing, but of nuance as well. I get that we've been the bull in the china shop internationally, that we've been arrogant and tone-deaf in so many arenas for so many years, and now, with the margins of the American empire being pressed, everyone is ready to embrace the requisite number of I-told-you-so moments. Fair enough. We had it coming. But the emotion in all of that sometimes leads the overseas commentary about Baltimore and The Wire toward something that I don't recognise as accurate.

Baltimore is not the inner circle of hell. It is not entirely devoured by a drug economy that serves as its last viable industry. It is not a place in which gangsters routinely fire clip after clip, spraying the streets in daylight ambushes. It is not unlivable, or devoid of humanity, or a reservoir of unmitigated human despair.

I live in Baltimore, in a neighbourhood that is none of these things. I am vested in the city and its future and I can drive you to places in this city that would transform even the most devout Wire fan into a fat, happy tourist. Baltimore's charms are no less plentiful than most American cities.

And yet there are places in Baltimore where The Wire is not at all hyperbole, where all of the depicted tragedy and waste and dysfunction are fixed, certain and constant. And that place is, I might add, about 20 blocks from where I live.

That is the context of The Wire and that is the only context in which Baltimore – and by reasonable extension, urban America – can be fairly regarded. There are two Americas – separate, unequal, and no longer even acknowledging each other except on the barest cultural terms. In the one nation, new millionaires are minted every day. In the other, human beings no longer necessary to our economy, to our society, are being devalued and destroyed. Both things are true, and one gets a sense, reading the distant reaction to The Wire, that Europeans are far more ready to be convinced by one vision than the other.

I used to quote Churchill as declaring that a first-rate mind was one that could maintain two opposing ideas at the same time. It certainly sounded Churchillian to me, until someone better read pointed out that this notable quote is by F Scott Fitzgerald.

At first this disappoints, because the quote, to me, seems to argue for political nuance, for subtlety and precision in state affairs. For a long while, the literary origin of the credo made no sense.

But then, The Wire.

As with Fitzgerald, we were selling story only. And at all points, when filming our drama, we understood that we were arguing the case of one America to the other. We were not saying everything, showing everything. We focused on the urban dynamic of drugs, crime and race. We argued the fraud of the drug war and offered an elegy for the death of union labour and the working class. We ruminated on the political infrastructure and its inability to reform. We picked a fight over the decline of public education and the lie behind our national claim to equality of opportunity. And lastly, we suggested that, in the end, no one in our media culture is paying attention or asking hard questions.

We did not contemplate immigration. We largely ignored sex-based discrimination, feminism and gender issues. We spoke not a word about the pyramid scheme that is the mortgage crisis, or the diminishing consumer class, or the time bomb that all of our China-bought debt might prove to be. Nor did we glory in the healthy sectors of the American economy, in the growth industries of the information age. We did not embrace Brooklyn Heights and West Los Angeles, Silicon Valley and Marin County. Hell, we didn't even rest for more than a day or two in Roland Park or Mount Washington or Towson – those Baltimore neighbourhoods that define a viable, monied America. We spoke to the other part of town, the forgotten place, the one they don't tell many stories about, at least not in the medium of entertainment television. It was a story rooted in truth, but it wasn't the only story or the only truth. Who, but a second-rate mind, would claim otherwise?

Yet in my country, they actually argue the point. While British audiences might believe The Wire to represent more than it does, Americans – many of them, at least – are quick to argue that it doesn't represent everything and is therefore, somehow, not representative of anything at all.

Was The Wire myopic? Should it have been allowed to dwell for five seasons on that in America which is broken and brutal? Was it not obliged, as an act of journalistic equanimity, if not dramatic power, to display portions of the America where human lives are not marginalised and discarded?

Well, there are about 350 television shows about the affluent America, the comfortable America, the viable and cohesive nation where everyone gets what they want if they either work hard or know someone or have a pretty face or cheat like hell. That America is available every night, on every channel in the Comcast package.

For a brief time, there was one television drama about the other America.

Are we really going to debate whether it was one too many?

Which brings us back to this week in Baltimore and that jury report, the one that everyone had something to say about, but no one actually bothered to analyse. The draft study, which tracked jury trials in Baltimore over a one-year period from July 2005, found that jurors in surrounding, predominantly white suburban counties were 30 times more likely to convict defendants of the most serious charge. Overall in the surrounding counties, the acquittal rate was 27%. In the city, it was 43%. And the disinclination of Baltimore juries to convict drug defendants on serious charges was even more pronounced, according to the Baltimore Sun.

The Sun's coverage indicated that the report's author had speculated vaguely as to "population characteristics and socioeconomic factors" being relevant to the statistical variance. The Sun itself provided no additional analysis, reportage, thought or speculation as to why city juries behave as they do.

Again, the why of the thing. The only part that really matters.

Because in my city, we have fought the drug war to the very end of the line, with sergeants becoming lieutenants and majors becoming colonels and city mayors becoming state governors. We have done so for decades, one day into the next, one administration after another, each claiming progress and measuring such in arrest rates, drug seizures, crime stats. And no one asks: why?

No one asks why, with all the arrests and seizures, the availability and purity of narcotics and cocaine has actually increased over the past three decades. No one asks why, with all the law enforcement committed, whole tracts of the city have nonetheless degenerated into free-fire war zones. No one asks why police commanders are routinely able to reduce the rates of robbery, or rape, or assault significantly in any time period prior to an election, while the murder rate – in which the victim can't be obscured or clerically "unfounded" – stays as high as ever. And now, this week, no one asks why men and women from Baltimore, upon being given a chance to strike a blow against disorder and mayhem by convicting those charged criminally, would shirk their responsibility.

Well, here it is, plain as day…

In order to elect Baltimore's mayor as Maryland's governor, crime had to go down. And when that mayor was unable to do so legitimately, through a meaningful deterrent, his police officials did not merely go about cooking their statistics, making robberies and assaults disappear by corrupting the reporting of such incidents, they resorted to something far more disturbing.

For the last years of his administration, Mayor Martin O'Malley ordered the mass arrests of citizens in every struggling Baltimore neighbourhood, from east side to west. More than 100,000 bodies were dragged to Central Booking in a single year – record rates of arrest for a city with fewer than 700,000 residents. Corner boys, touts, drug slingers, petty criminals – yes, they went in the wagons.

But school teachers, city workers, shopkeepers, delivery boys – they too were jacked up, cuffed and hauled down to Eager Street – hundreds of them a night on the weekends. Some were charged, but few were prosecuted. And in 25,000 such cases, they were later freed from the detention facility without ever going to court; no charges were proffered because, well, no crime had been committed.

I wasn't arrested. Nor was Ed Burns or Dominic West or Aidan Gillen. Nor were my neighbours or the Baltimore Sun's editors or the members of the Maryland Club. But then, we're all white. Among the black members of my cast and crew, it was often impossible to drive from the film set to home at night without being stopped – and in some cases detained or arrested – on nonexistent probable cause and nonexistent charges. The crackdown came wholly in black neighbourhoods and it landed wholly on the backs of black citizens.

And now, just a few years later, comes this document that causes the state's attorney to deny the obvious and leaves everyone else wondering weakly and vaguely as to the why of it. Is it so hard to understand that the same people who had their civil rights cleanly dispatched, who spent nights in jail because police officers lied on them and dragged them off without charge – that these people might be inclined to disbelieve the word of law enforcement in any future criminal case?

In places like west Baltimore, the drug war destroyed every last thing that the drugs themselves left standing – including the credibility of the police deterrent. To elect one man to higher office, an entire city alienated its citizenry and destroyed its juror pool.

Mayor O'Malley is now Governor O'Malley. The police commanders have all been promoted. A daily newspaper that had no stomach for addressing the why a decade ago when it had 400 editors and reporters, a newspaper more consumed with prize submissions and gotcha stories than with complex analysis of its city's problems, now has 220 bodies in its newsroom and is even less capable of the task. And nothing, of course, changes.

Yes, such a scenario is grist for The Wire. We could have easily built half a season out of the collapse of the Baltimore jury pool and the inability of city prosecutors to bring cases into court.

Yet there is also something appalling in the suggestion that a television drama – a presumed entertainment – might be a focal point for a discussion of what has gone wrong in urban America, for why we have become a society that no longer even recognises the depth of our problems, much less works to solve any of them.

But where else is the why even being argued any more? Not in the stunted political discourse of an American election cycle, not in an eviscerated, self-absorbed press, not in any construct to which the empowered America, the comfortable and comforted America, gives its limited attention. To know why city juries won't participate in the drug war any more, to know why they have opted out of our collective dysfunction, you'd have to travel to the other America – to West Fayette Street or Park Heights Avenue or East Madison Street or any other of the forgotten places. And, well, as has already been said, we are separate nations at this point. Few of us ever cross the frontier to hear voices different from our own.

The best of The Wire

The Wire top fives

STEVE BUSFIELD

By popular demand it is time for a bit of list creation. I thought we would propose a couple of top fives. And then you can debate those choices. Or ignore them and post your own lists.

TOP FIVE WIRE TRACKS

1. The Body of An American – the Pogues (wakes in Kavanagh's)

2. Way Down in the Hole – DoMaJe (season four)

3. Fast Train – Solomon Burke

4. 16 Tons – the Nighthawks (only bettered by the Redskins version)

5. I Feel Alright – Steve Earle

TOP FIVE VALCHEK MOMENTS

1. Becomes commissioner.

2. Yet another polaroid of a police van in a ship container arrives from LA/Miami/wherever.

3. Herc confides that he walked in on Royce in the act of fellatio (receiving).

4. The priest confesses that Sobotka is in competition to pay for the church window.

5. Gets decked by his son-in-law.

PAUL OWEN'S TOP FIVE SCENES:

SERIES ONE: Elastic products

SERIES TWO: Nick Sobotka meets Prop Joe

SERIES THREE: "Just a gangster, I suppose ... "

SERIES FOUR: Ruth's Chris Steak House

SERIES FIVE: "Remember that one day summer past ... "

COMMENTS

joedoone Down In The Hole: The Best Versions Thereof.

Season One. Blind Boys Of Alabama. Season Five. Steve Earle. Season Four. DoMaJe. Season Three. Neville Brothers.

Most Intense Scenes.

Kima's ambush. The shoot-out with Omar and his crew. Ziggy goes postal. Omar pays Brother Mouzone a house call. Omar and Brother Mouzone pay Stringer a house call.

JohnCooperClarke Bubbles showing an out-of-his-depth Jimmy McNulty how to tie his police boat to a pier... Lester Freamon offering to let the unit's poledancing whistle-blower room at his place, with a murmur of "To protect, and serve...!" Rawls's two-middle-finger salute to McNulty – "You have my FULL attention, Officer..." The fading MISSING posters with Frank Sobotka's bulldog face that pop up throughout Series Three and Four like a revenant... The sight of Bubbles finally walking through the cellar door to sit down with his family...

Hoppo How about Top 5 Bellends (so not the venal or vicious, just a collection of simpletons and morons):

1. Herc. While Carver learnt and developed, Herc remained a total oaf, and like all true morons was never remotely aware of the fact. What a bellend... 2. Orlando. Nice cushy job looking after the lovely Shardene and her co-workers, and threw it all away for a bit of drug money. Idiot 3. Michael Santangelo. Relied on a psychic to solve his cases for him. However, as Rawls admitted he was good at slam-dunks, clearing 6/10 of those. 4. Tony Gray. Seemed like a nice enough

chap, but no match for Carcetti's realpolitick. 5. Cheese. Must have been on a nice little earner with Prop Joe, but threw his hat in with Marlo. Ended up dead. Tool. I was going to include Poot, but then he ended up working in a shoe store, while Bodie ended up dead.

MrDarjeeling Top 5 Clay Davis moments:

1) Sheeeeeeeeee-it 2) Sheeeeeeeeeeee-it 3) Sheeeeeeeeeeeeee-it 4) Sheeeeeeeeeeeeeeeee-it 5) Sheeeeeee-eeeeeeeeeeee-eeeeeeeeeeeeeeee-it

mozwerk Top 5 tragic moments

1. Wallace getting shot by Poot and Bodie 2. Dukie shooting up down the alley way 3. Randy shouting "you gonna help me now?" to Carver 4. D'Angelo getting strangled in prison 5. Kima's girl sitting on the couch touching the stain left by Kima's felt marker after she's been shot

Top 5 Dumb Things Herc has done:

1. Told Little Kevin it was Randy who snitched on the vacant murders (ultimately causing the death of his foster mother and him going back into a home) 2. Told Maury (my most dislikable character) there was an illegal wire on Marlo 3. Assaults a church minister after wrongly accusing him of carrying drugs 4. Herc fails to answer Bubs call that gets Bubs an almightily beating at the hands of his junkie nemesis 5. Falls for bogey info provided by Marlo through a surveilance camera that he then loses

Top 5 Funniest Moments

1. Rawls in the gay bar 2. Hearing McNultys real accent 3. Omar's appearance in court dressed in a tie 4. Valchek receiving photos of his surveillance van on its world tour 5. Wilson's failure to keep a straight face when Carcetti is realising the enormity of McNultys made up serial killer

pdmalcolm I love Prop Joe's lines… Nearly all of them

"You ain't here to wave me off I take it?"

And his argument with Avon at the basketball game in Series 1

"It's 85 degrees out here"

"Look the part be the part motherfucker"

Concluding with Avon's final exasperated "Be for real!"

And my favourite moment in the whole piece? Omar selling the Co-Op their wares back hours after stealing it. And Cheese's explanation to his uncle "Shit was unseemly."

suziebee Top 5 scenes from each series (how hard is this??):

1: At the end, D'Angelo faces Bunk and McNulty and explains, heartbreakingly, about how he never had any choice. He might flip. Then later his Momma talks him out of it, and we see him in the montage, inside for the next 20... 2: Omar in court, of course. "I got the shotgun...you got the briefcase...same as you!" Love him waggling his tie at Stringer, not giving a f— about being called a faggot. Good on him. Show String isn't quite the urbane fella he fancies himself to be either. 3: Stringer wants Slim to do Clay Davis. Slim disagrees: "you talkin' 'bout some assassination shit". And Avon sums it up nicely: "he saw your ghetto ass comin'". All series we've been behind String's efforts to get out of the gangster game, and thinking Avon was holding him back..then we see Avon was right along, and Stringer was breathtakingly naive. 4: Simple. Randy to Carver: "you got my back Officer Carver? You gonna look out for me?" And when you think about it, Herc is to blame. Jeez. 5: Marlo loses his rag with his team: "my name is my NAME"...and we see some fire in his eyes at last. I, for one, don't like it (shudder). I think Jamie Hector is outstanding, matched only by Larry Gilliard Jr (who I found out is married to the woman who plays Alma Guttierriez).

Still the most shocking scene though is Ziggy going postal...

hansofoundation Bunk burning his clothes McNulty mourning the death of Stringer, gutted that Stringer would never know that McNulty had him Stringer and Avon together on the balcony reminiscing and both secretly knowing the other was out to get them Death of Wallace Bubbles at the end of season 4, inconsolable at Gerard's death in the clinic with his sponsor PrezBo photocopying the phones and working out the drug dealers code Lester whenever he was being a genius detective (which was always) Death of Stringer Bell, it took real balls for the writers to do it but keeping him alive would have compromised the series.

Cutty becoming Dennis again, that whole story was great Namond crying to Carver and Dennis about not being like his father McNulty hearing the FBI serial killer description and it being a description of him Marlo returning to the streets at the end of season 5, he's not going to be able to do what Stringer tried to do. Cheese getting shot by Slim, just a sentimental motherfucker

pdmalcolm Top five deaths you say?

1. Omar – Shocking and (at that point) completely unexpected 2. Stringer Bell – Playing the two coldest men on the eastern seaboard off against each other? Sheeeeeeeeeeeeeeeet! 3. Bodie – Knew it was coming... Went down with some dignity. Shocking to think he would be 19/20 at that point. 4. Frank Sabotka – "Did he have hands and a head?" 5. Snoop – I can't think why it stands out, it just does.

anadari top five moments when i knew i will never watch a show like this again ever in my life, and i got really sad:

1) when sobotka talks about how we no longer "make" things in america. 2) when d'angelo teaches poot and broadie chess. 3) "on a sunday morning." 4) snoop buying a nail-driver. 5) the kids at the steakhouse...

ok, and

6) the "fuck" investigation with mcnulty and buck and the bullet in the fridge door. 7) snoop saying, "we will be brief." 8) omar and buck have a little conversation on the bench. 9) when michael gives dukie a dollar for an ice cream, and then when dukie reminds him a year later, and michael doesnt remember, but oh, dukie does. 10) stringer bell in class at the community college.

i have no self-control. 11) when avon walks across the basketball in prison, and the entire game stops. you know, out of respect.

Hoppo apologies for lowering the tone, but I thought I'd have a go at Top 5 Females based on, well, attractiveness:

1. Shardene – Lester you sly old dog 2. Nerese Campbell – Not that you'd dare to do anything about it 3. Mrs McNulty – One of the more telegenic detectives later on in Homicide: LOTS 4. Alma – Extra points for resisting McNulty's charms 5. Rhonda Perlman – Because Judge Phelan gallantly commented that he'd "Love to throw a f*ck into that"

trakka D'Angelo explaining chess to Bodie and Wallace; Bubbles sat on the bench, clean for the first time in a long time, seeing the sunlight thru the trees and it taking his breath away; McNulty singing along to the Pogues before he slammed his car, twice, into the pillar; Bunk & Lester double act – both times; Bubbles, sorry, Reginald, sharing at his anniversary meeting

SaptarshiRay Justin – the corner kid who tries to sell Bunny Colvin some drugs while he's in a police car and has a conversation with Herc about baseball caps.

Herc: Hey, I been looking for those caps with the bill on the side everywhere but I could only find the ones with the bill at the front. Justin: No they're the same, you just turn it sideways. [Herc and Carver look at each other exasperated].

pdmalcolm Hoppo: I'm disappointed your list omitted both Nick Sabotka's girlfriend and Beadie Russell.

AxxB Funny Moments:

5 – Bubbles and Johnny Boy at the scrap metal merchants "You guys know you ain't got pants, right?"

4 – Bunk on Freamon "Look at how he walks, that bowlegged motherfucker... I did that to him."

3 – Season One, trying to get the desk through the door. "At this rate, we'll never get it in." (pause) "IN?"

2 – "Problems with your ex?" "A less educated man than me, a less sensitive man, a less modern man, a less civilised man... could possibly be tempted to describe her action as those of a c**t." (Kima gives McNulty the look) "What?" "You just called the mother of your children a c**t." "No I didn't!"

1 – Chris and Snoop attempt to devise a Baltimore citizenship test, to make sure they are only killing the imported New York dealers. Snoop failing any test that Chris can come up with.

jamesdlg Jay's speech at Jimmy's wake? "When you were good, you were the best we had"

pdmalcolm Rawls: "I am a reasonable guy. Jay, tell him. Everywhere I go people say to me 'Frank you are a reasonable fucking guy'"

shaggydog stringer fessing up to avon about d'angelo's murder – absolutely electric – for me this is the point where their partnership finally cracks

carver walking away from randy in the hospital.

michael, dukie and bugs splitting up.

ziggy and frank sobotka meeting in the prison waiting room.

and of course the comedy gold of snoop buying the nail gun.

henryoswald ok after a unproductive few hours at work here is shot at a list of 'best' deaths.

#1 Wallace – heartbreaking, needless, backstabbing death, my personal 'favourite' scene from all 5 season. Compounded by seeing him look after his brothers and sisters earlyer.

#2 Bodie – started with us as a young corner kid with aspirations on moving up, just like D by the time he "made it" he had realised how wrong it all was and paid the price for this knowledge.

3 one of Chris and snoops vacant kills – there was one in the vacants when the man was begging. Also when Chris killed the delivery lady to setup omar, each killing was so cold.

4 snoop – knew it was over, the game she was using to rationalise all the killings including the plan to kill Michael came back on her, and she accepted it.

5 Cheese – one that no one saw coming, and one I know I enjoyed. Slim Charles a personal favourite of mine, doing what was "right" regardless of the benjamins.

violetforthemoment Top 5 Wire Characters Who Needed A Serious Boarding Up In The Vacants

1 – An obvious number one, Maury Levy. Scum, scum, scum, scum, scum. Utterly unsympathetic, which is weird for The Wire.
2 – Namond's mother whose name I don't recall. What a horrid, objectionable woman. I am glad he got away from her and into that

damn *debating society!* 3 – Cheese. Man did not have a code.
4 – Clay Davis 5 – Bird. True, he was being set up, but still.

McNulty almost made it on there due to his conduct through most of season 5 – it was great TV and how it all got a bit out of his control was wonderful but when we settled down to watch a new episode in my house I'd remember what he was doing about 2 minutes n and start cursing him for his stupidity. It drove my other half mental.

OsakaChris (My) Most embarrassing scene …

I watched all 5 series in 2 weeks. At the height of my addiction, I was watching an episode a day, on the way to work, on a busy train. It was one of these days I jumped on the train and squeezed in between a businessman sorting through his daily affairs and an elderly lady with her shopping.

As a foreigner in Japan, you get starred at a bit on the train, and even more when you get a laptop out and start watching stuff on it. At least when your watching something though, you can forget the eyes burning in the back of your head. Anyway, this day I was salivating to see the next episode, and fired it up with the headphones on, (to the interest of my neighbours), to find the first scene was Omar in bed with his boyfriend. OK, I thought, as it looked like it was morning, so they were unlikely to be getting it on (which would have been embarrassing), only to find a full frontal Omar in his birthday suit walking around his apartment.

Anyway, not knowing what to do, I just carried on watching, and pretended that I didn't notice my neighbours pretending not to watch me. The next stop they both got off, and got on again on the next carriage.

Anyone else do that? or just me?

CodProfundity Top 5 Deaths.

Bodie going out like the soldier he was.

Stringer Bell, "get on with it motherf…"

Wallace, The incredible thing about Wallace's death is not the fact he's the most likeable of the street characters and the most vulnerable and most likley to redeem himself, though they are all important factors, no, the most incredible thing is Bodie and Poot are still likeable guys. I mourned Bodie's death and was happy that Poot was out the game when they're both cold blooded killers.

Frank Sobotka, Never have I been more angry while watching The Wire than when Agent Koutris sealed Frank's fate with a phonecall. The use of the brilliant and dramatic Turkish music builds the already tense scenes into absolute tragedy, that it striles the Sobotka's twice makes it arguably the bleakest moment of the entire series and for me, a perfect distiallation of what the show is raging against.

Omar Little, "This is Baltimore, the Gods will not save you" – Commissioner Burrell.

Top 5 Lines (this nearly could have been a top 5 Jay Landsman moments)

(Lt Marrimow)… does not cast off talent lightly, he heaves it away with great force – Jay Landsman

I'll take any man's money if they giving it away! – Namond Brice and Clay Davis

Sheeeeeeeeeeeeeeee-it – Clay Davis

What the fuck did I do? – McNulty and various others about to be f*****d by the gods of Baltimore.

Yeah, now well, thats the thing about the old days, they the old days – Slim Charles

Top 5 Holy shit this is the best show on TV moments.

DAngelo asking Stringer where Wallace is – I literally had chills running down my back.

Carver beating up on his car steering wheel after leaving Randy in the group home.

Herc's outrageous, unjust good fortune for being a ignorant traitorous bastard, specifically, Levy telling him that hes family now. At least Cheese got what he deserved.

Season 2s dockworkers storyline – this is when I first realised The Wire was far far deeper than anything on TV before and clearly better than most literature too.

Hamsterdam.

AJBee 1 – Marlo coldly and intentionally antagonising the shop security guard just to provoke a reaction so he can have him killed. All because he lost at cards methinks, bad loser 2 – Stringer quizzing his college professor on what to do when you have weak product in an agressive market. Getting an answer from somebody who has no idea how the info is being utilised. 3 – D'Angelo telling the hoppers "why do pepole get killed selling this product, why can't we do it like other things?" A repetition from McNulty and a sure sign that this is not the life for him 4 – Bunk almost puking throughout a meeting with Daniels and Beau. Her looking at him thinking, is this real POlice? 5 – Wee Bay's confused face as he hears Omars ghostly whistle as he sits with a bullet in his leg and Stinkum dead on the street. What happened? he's thinking, wasn't supposed to go down like this. At the same time a rat scuttles across the street.

rockmejoe 5. The very first scene of Season 1 – "you got to, this is America man" 4. Bunk and McNulty "you were gentle with me" 3. Landsman – "tweedy impertinence" 2. Bodie going out fighting 1. The final montage of S5 – the sweet agony of wishing it would never end..

thegirlfrommarz Top 5 "punch in the gut" moments:

Prez shooting the undercover cop. Just when you're really happy for the team, it all gets taken away. And the aftermath – when Prez wonders if he would have been so quick to shoot if the cop had been white. – McNulty in Stringer's apartment, looking at the books – "Who was I chasing?" – Herc telling Levy that Lester must be running an illegal wiretap in S5, thus handing Levy enough leverage to put Marlo back on the street as the case implodes. – D'Angelo's death in prison. I really liked D and was gutted when he was killed, even though I'd been terrified for him for ages. – Bubs trying to kill himself.

For some reason, Bunk giving McNulty the list of addresses of Marlo's lieutenants and telling him it was "from a dead stick-up boy" was more upsetting than seeing Omar die. There was a kind of gentleness in the way Bunk said it that suggested he, too, was sad about Omar's death. Or maybe I'm just reading too much into it.

Oh god, I could go on – Bodie's death. Wallace's death. Johnny overdosing in Hamsterdam. Frank Sobotka walking to his death.

Ziggy's breakdown. The whole programme was a five-series-long punch in the gut, so how do you pick a moment?

violetforthemoment McNulty going undercover in the brothel was hilarious – and his phone calls beforehand where he references the stones and the beatles. I didn't know at the time that he was really English and was taking the mick out of his rubbish "attempt" at the accent...

A drunken Bunk burning the evidence of his infidelity in the lady's bathroom was great too. Most of the guys' conversations out by the railway tracks at night, bottle of Jameson doing the rounds, were lovely moments, and anytime Lester got drunk he was marvellous.

McNulty in the lift with Daniels, when he knows Daniels knows, and Daniels knows McNulty knows *he* knows! "To be continued." Daniels is scary as hell when he's angry.

The antics of Herc and Carver and their assorted bullyboys in series 1, before Carver at least started to grow up, were quite amusing too: driving out to the towers pissed in the middle of the night to call everyone out, ffs!

One of the creepiest moments, though, had to be Stringer doing the nasty with D'Angelo's irritating ladyfriend: she was, like, three feet shorter than him, and it just weirded me out. Does that make me a bad person?

gogilesgo Wee Bey being visited by his wife in jail. "My Word will find you where ever you are" Despite the bravado in this scene and elsewhere in prison Bey is so despondent knowing he will NEVER get out of this deadend jail. Now I have no interest in ending up in Pseud's Corner but real echoes here of Odysseus' journeying to the underworld and being told by Achilles he would rather be the lowest slave on earth than the king of Hades.

First meeting of Prop Joe and Sergei – such love and respect between two old friends. Underlined at the end of season two; Joe to Vondas – "sorry to hear about my boy Sergei."

Omar in court (despite my own guilty admiration for Maury Levy).

Odell Watkins walking out (ok, wheeling out) of the mayor's office in disgust at the spoiling campaign against Carcetti.

Snoop in the hardware store "he meant the lexus of nailguns, but he ain't know it".

The Bubbles/Prezbo double take at the school.

pdmalcolm Top 5 moments of crushing inevitability?

1. Jimmy, not 1 episode after Bunk tells him he's bad for people paying Bubs $20 to go get high and bring back information about Kima's shooters. Not 1 episode after Kima had promised to help him get clean.

2. Marlo getting away with it thanks to the snake-like Maurice Levy. In fact, everyone getting away with it thanks to etc etc.

3. Dukie ending up shooting up by the end of Series 5.

4. Wallace's shooting. By his best mates.

5. The fact that Herc WILL screw something up monumentally once a series. Its a given.

Konrad 1) Nobody's mentioned the scene in S4 when the hoppers selling outside Hamsterdam are rounded up and driven off into the woods. A shockingly funny example of POlice brutality.

2) The look on McNulty's face when Carcetti's hot campaign manager kicks him out of bed.

3) Any Omar stick-up scene but the one where he was disguised as a disabled veteran was the best.

Stash house guard: "Omar, you know this is a Barksdale joint?" Omar, with a shit-eating grin on his face: "Do tell."

4) Any scene in Bunny Colvin's rowdy problem student classes. Albert to the female behaviourist: "Cheese-faced bitch!"

(Apparently this insult refers to the facial expression of a person giving head the moment their mouth fills with semen.)

5) Herc and Carver's chance meeting with Bodie and Poot at the cinema with their shorties. Excruciating...

pedro1000s Top 5 moments that have not got enough/any mentions in these comments:

McNulty at at the brothel in series 2. Then at the beginning of series 4 (I think) being asked on a stakeout if it was true, and denying it.

Omar's prison stint. Particularly when he is waiting in the holding cell, knowing that whoever joins him in there is likely to be an assasin. The way you see him readying himself for the potential fight is intense.

Daniels meeting Clay Davies' driver at the political party in the kitchen.

McNulty handing Avon the warrant with Stringer's details on it

Michael's refusal of Marlo's money at the beginning of season 4. "big paws on the puppy".

lilandy – Bernard in series three having ben nagged by his other half for most of the series is sitting in the p0lice station and says to the boy next to him "i can't wait to go to jail".

JobiasIndustries Best Wire moment: season 4, when Dookie blows that fan on the girl who attacked her classmate with a razor. The way everyone is in a panic but he is calm and seems to understand how she screwed up (like the rest of his family) is one of the saddest things I have ever seen on TV and chokes me up everytime. True televisual genius.

Surge 1) McNulty sending his kids to follow Stringer. Amusing and a moment that sums up how the man's obsession with his work conflicts with the family life part of him dearly wants.

2) Ziggy sitting in the car before taking the gun and going on the rampage. You're left to imagine for yourself the things that are running through his head. All the humiliations and frustrations that run through the season come back to you. You're left dumnstruck by what he does next.

3) Avon and Stringer's last moment together. Trying to destroy each other – yet remainng close friends. Swapping childhood anecdotes – while aquiring the information to arrange a hit. Genius.

4) Bubbles going from early morning optimism to the depths of self loathing as he discovers what happened to those hot shots he mixed... Heartbreaking.

5) Michael with shotgun. As you realise he's become Omar it gives a competely different perspective on the journey he's been on.

Marwood1974 So many great ones already mentioned here, it would be rude to repeat them. I would say one of my favourites that hasn't been mentioned is when Dennis goes to ask Avon for money for gym equipment...

"You went through all that for $10,000?!"

Anyone else think that, slowly but surely, we are going to list every single scene in the show?

cbearrun Best 5 Songs: 1. Fast Train – Solomon Burke 2. Way Down in the Hole – Blind Boys of Alabamma (so glad that was S5 ending) 3. Walk on Gilded Splinters – Paul Weller 4. Way Down in the Hole – DoMaJe (S4) 5. The Fall – Blake Leyh (Credits).

Marwelldezueew Top five you know what's going to happen no matter how much you don't want it too moments.

Kima undercover getting in that car with Orlando Randy getting police protection Omar as soon as he came back in season 5 Frank going to meet the Greeks Bubs making those pills and then meeting Sherrod...

Top five the writers did good,

Destroying the CSI's in one 4 minute scene, the motherf***ers Killing Wallace, Frank, Omar, Bodie and D'Angelo Allowing Bubs upstairs, as close as the wire was ever going to get to giving us a Hollywood ending, yet its only someone allowed upstairs for dinner with their Sister. Omar going to get some cereal. They saved the least deserving boy in series 4!!!!!!!

Things The Wire made me do

Cheer when a murdering drug deal shoots another murdering drug dealer in the head, Cry when Randy shouts after Carver You gonna look out for me, Sgt. Carver? Laugh "Know what the plural of pussy is?" with the Isley Brothers playing in the back ground. Walk up to a stranger at my friend's leaving do and say' sh*******************e' (he was wearing a McNulty t-shirt), much to the confusion of everyone else he joined in. We then didn't talk to anyone else for the rest of the night. Wish I was a cigar smoking, overweight, black homicide detective in B-more.

1morepaulcunningham This is like choosing your favourite Beatles album, depends on the time of the day and what what mood I'm in

Most heartbreaking scene for me has to be Wallace's death but then it could be Michael saying goodbye to Bug.

Most shocking scene Bubbles hanging himself in Season 4, followed by the most compassionate moment when Landsman of all people, decides to let him go knowing how much Bubs is suffering for Sherrod's death.

Favourite opening to an episode Omar and Brother Mouzane doing their "Once Upon A Time In The West" face off.

Favourite Ending – Kima's 'goodnight moon, goodnight gangbangers, goodnight po po…………. – beautiful.

Funniest scene – Bunk and McNulty – "you were gentle".

Most cinematic scene as the camera tracks the horror on Carcetti's face as he walks through Hamsterdam – compelling.

How Andre Royo has not been given an Emmy, I do not know.

DeBuoy All the scenes with Brother Mouzone were classic, and what strength of mind that the writers did not reuse him, there was a real risk of him becoming a caracature.

That same strength killed off Stringer Bell. I found myself literally holding my breath from the moment Omar appeared in the building site. Contrast the code of honour of Omar and Mouzone against the dishonour of Bell.

Snoop's death – an intensely dislikable character redeemed slightly by the calm acceptance she has for her death. A grudging respect for the decency (?????) Mike shows her. A fantastically tense scene.

Clay Davis begging for his life – "I am out there doing the Lord's work for you Irv… I've been carrying water for you Irv." Davis pleads to Burrell trying to get the idictment blocked. When he realises he is on his own, he chokes back the tears "You think I'm going down, you think I'm done, I'm going to hold on to this moment Irv…" He meant it and he didn't even have to say Sheeeeeeeeeeeeeet.

Landsman's eulogy for McNulty. Pull away the porn mag and ignore the profanities and you realise the sergeant's office is inhabited by a lard-coated poet. Who didn't want to be in that bar with a pint and a whiskey chaser in their hands?

The convenience store security guard confronting Marlo for stealing a lolly. He was truly brave. Marlo had just been hijacked by Omar at the poker table and stole the sweet in a pathetic attempt at reasserting himself. The guard lost his life. The pyschotics – Marlo, Chris and Snoop – denuded society just a little more. The scene is about moral courage and self-respect. Not enough of it around at the moment.

drumsleet Season 5: Chris Partlow sidling up to the counter at the Courts of Justice, asked if he requires "civil" or "criminal"... Chris replies, "Criminal. Definitely".

ShangoDan Top 5 meets:

1. Stringer and Crew. All about the Product

2. Marlo and Old Face Andre. Poor Andre gets robbed by Omar, and wants Marlo to give him some time to pay up, so calls Omar a terrorist who "blows up shit just to," pointing to the government cutting Delta, the insurance companies, and NASDAQ some slack after similar terrorist attacks because they know "ain't nothing they could do." Marlo takes Andre's ring off him (later the ring goes on a lord of the rings style journey), and makes him hand it over before telling him: "Omar ain't no terrorist. He's just another nigger with a gun. And you ain't no Delta Airlines neither...So bring me what you owe and talk that global economy mess somewhere else." Perhaps today the government could get the guts to tell this to our greedy bankers? I thought not.

3. Stringer at the co-op. Shamrock, Robert's Rules in hand, taking minutes. "Nigger, is you taking notes on a criminal fucking conspiracy?

4. Prop Joe at the co-op. "For a cold-ass crew of gangsters," he says to his colleagues, "y'all carried it like Republicans and shit." Brings to mind the Godfather's similar meetings, "After all, we're not Communists. But he [Don Corloene] must let us draw the water from the well."

5. Stringer and Davis. (a) Crawl, walk, run. (b) Davis takes Stringer to the Federal Building but he doesn't enter an office. Instead, the "Federal" guy comes down: "I know B&B like I know a thousand other outfits". They saw his ghetto ass coming!

Realcruelty OUT-OF-HER-DEPTH LAWYER: Mr Little, how does a man rob drug dealers for eight or nine years and live to tell about it? OMAR: Day at a time, I suppose.

Cole's wake in Season 1, from Landsman's speech ("Ray Cole stood with us. All of us. In Baltimore, working. Sharing a dark corner of the American experiment. He was called. He served. He is counted.") to "Body Of An American", to McNulty and Bunk trying to stand up.

ShangoDan Top 5 arrests (the good, the bad, the ugly, the funny, and the i make it to the list cos there's 5, man).

The Good. McNulty & Daniels take Avon – Season 1. No need to break the door down, they'll open it (not like other cop shows, eh?). Stringer shocked to find out he's not going, yet was calm as hell when he thought he was.

The Bad. Officer Walker arrests Omar, practices some usual bad cop shit, and takes the ring further on its journey – Season 4.

The Ugly. Kima joins Carver et al to practice some police brutality on poor Bodie – Season 1.

The Funny. (Ok, no body got arrested here cos they fucked it up and is it really funny?) In Season 3, chasing a 14 year old with helicopters and a dozen police cars. Herc plays Shaft. He's a complicated man, and the only one that understands him is his woman. Who's the Man that would risk his neck for his brother man? And then Carver plays Apocalypse Now. You do not get to win, shitbird, we do!

The Other One. Herc and Carver (again!) fail to find a gun on a routine stop and search in our early introduction to them in Season 1. Kima saves the day by finding the missing gun. I miss those 2 being together – let's have a herc and carver spin off – 'Herc and Carver go to Seattle and beat up the natives'!

Five Omarisms (in no particular order)

Because… In-Deed. * Oh, In-deed. * Do tell. * To Bunk: "Since you're feeling all biblical and righteous and all, you think on this: now, if

Omar didn't kill that delivery lady, then someone else did... A man got to have a code." (takes Bunk back to when he first met Omar and Omar explained he doesn't rob or kill civilians and Bunk says A man must have a code. The line saves Omar). * You mistake me for a man who me repeats himself.

AxxB If I had a number six for my funny moments that nobody else has said yet, it would be Herc, Carv and their partners coming out of the movie theatre and bumping into Bodie and Poot's crew. "So you must be the lovely Mrs Herc. Did you enjoy your movie?"

LAST WORDS:

5: "Man got to get his oats, you know what I'm saying?" (Michael's Dad).

4: "Pack of Newports. Soft pack." (Omar)

3: "Look at it. Isn't it beautiful? ... I'm a Viking, Bubs." (Johnnie Boy)

2: "How my hair look, Mike?" (Snoop)

1: Get on with it, Motherf..." (Stringer)

naomi5 Top 5 moments

1 – series one

2 – series four

3 – series five

4 – series three

5 – series two

ComfyChair The Ikea scenes: First McNulty's hilariously drunken attempt in S1 and then, years of show-time later, Kima's own attempt in S5. "Are you using the right Scotch?"

And alongside everyone's loathing of Levy, please let's loathe Scott Templeton too... The award at the end of S5 was particularly nasty icing on a disgusting cake. "Let's focus on the ..." "...Dickensian aspects?"

KingKongBassett Facial hair top five....1 – Chris Partlow 2 – Walon 3 – The Deacon 4 – Johnny Fifty 5 – Norman

mayz678 Most shocking moment is when I realised that snoop was a girl!

suziebee Top 5 sexy blokes:

1. Dominic West. He's got a louche charm as McNulty, not sure if I'd fancy him in anything else (certainly didn't in 300!)

2. Wee-Bey. VERY handsome, and has provided a few brilliant moments to boot. how upset he was when the guard fucked with his fish (albeit plastic) in prison; and when he heart-wrenchingly agrees to give Namond over to Bunny. I LOVED his line to De'Londa: "Look around you...who would wanna be that (a "sodjer") if they could be anything else?" Indeed. Bit late though...

3. Stringer. Love his hair-patting! Much preferred in a suit.

4. Cutty. The ladies of west side Bodymore are right to be making moves!

5. Chris. Though what's up with the Maoist shirts? Very sexy and dangerous (alright utterly terrifying) presence. I don't mean being a mass murderer is sexy, but he has a menacing persona that he carries off in a very masculine...oh I'll shut up now.

Surge A perv's guide to The Wire. Five best shags:

5) McNulty and the waitress. How can a man drink so much he forgets how to drive and still provide a young lady with a good servicing after just coffee and eggs? Top notch.

4) Stringer and whatsername... D'Angelo's ex. A touch of vulnerability from the big man contrasting with the brazen unzipping of the lady's leisure wear. Classy.

3) Daniels and Pearlman. A suprisingly uncomplicated, businesslike technique demonstrated by the tall one.

2) McNulty and his ex wife. Typically impassioned display by the Irish wonder... but who was using who?

1) Kima and random girl. While ignoring a text from her partner. Whats not to like?

Marwood1974 KingKongBassett – you do a Top 5 of Facial Hair and leave out Cutty and Wee-Bey?!

KingKongBassett The perv's guide to The Wire needs to include McNulty's vice three-some... "there were two of 'em, I was outnumbered..."

Surge KingKong Bassett – "Sp...Sp...Spot on!"

AJBee Top 5 Wire smokers: in ascending order:

1: Omar, his only tell of nerves was a tab 2: The Sobotka family, Frank, Nicky and Zig, loved their cigs 3: Bunk, cigar smoker of the highest order 4: Mayor Royce's secretary, smoked him like a cigar (and Herc caught em) 5; Wee Bay, Smoked motherf*kers like it aint no thang!

elraul Omar: "You were the only brother who played that stick sport."

Bunk: "Lacrosse. Yeah them prep boy muthafuckas used to run when they saw the bunk coming."

ShangoDan Five things to say in favour of Mouzone:

1. He may seem unreal and atypical, but this only reflect the fact he's an outsider from New York – NY is like Wal mart coming to town, as Fat Face Rick puts it, so I guess it is something to be feared.

2. Omar's mythological character needed a match – who better than Mouzone? Apart from Omar, he's the Western character made real in the Wild Wild West that is Baltimore, a point he reinforces by using the line "Reform – Slow Train Coming."

3. He says the line, "You know what the most dangerous thing in America is, right? N***** with a library card."

4. He has a deep discussion with Omar about guns (OK, this is a cheat since it already comes under 2).

5. He wears a bow tie, is well spoken and educated. Sure, the wire's Baltimore is real, but it's good to not get too buried up in a one sided reflection of black people. Mouzone reminds us there are great black minds out there in case we forget.

Surge Great Lester Freamon moments:

1) The first time his genius is hinted at... finding the boxing shot of Barksdale.

2) (After they interview Omar in Season 1) McNulty – Are we still Police? Lester – Hmmm, technically. McNulty – Good, I was just checking.

3) Going undercover as the throwaway cellphone salesman. Not many people could get away with that jacket.

4) "Glad this is working out for you" – meeting Prezbo again in his classroom.

5) The last time we see him. Content carving his minatures and with his much younger woman.

gogilesgo ShangoDan, to add to your appreciation of Mouzone two quotes that stay with me are one from the prison meet between Avon and Brianna, where Barksdale mentions he is bringing in extra muscle from NYC.

Brianna – "Who you got in mind?"

Avon – "The Brother from New York."

Brianna – '"The...Brother?"

...and as if that was not enough, Prop Joe cements a preceeding reputation with this timeless line – "Brother Mouzone. He's got more bodies on him than a Chinese graveyard."

verrochio Top 5 people I ought to hate but don't

Prop Joe: For it was led to Omar's downfall by informing him of Marlo's high-stakes card game. Omar robbed Marlo; Marlo got payback.

McNulty: Anyone who can walk into a diner off their head at 3am and ask for breakfast but end up with a tasty barmaid on their lap should be hated / be admired / have eggs pelted at them.

Kima: The Whistleblower Extraordinaire. But deep down I guess she *probably* did the right thing.

Rawls: A nasty piece of work this one. But always riveting anytime he was on screen (especially season 3).

Chris Partlow: Yeah, I should despise serial killers but there was something about Chris's uncaring, ruthless efficiency set against his fondness(?) of Michael which I somehow found endearing.

zephirine Eradicator: re your addict speech, I think it's this one? Opening scene of Series 5 Ep 2, written by William F Zorzi.

A young white girl with long hair:

You know how it go, right?... Gave myself all these little rules about what I wouldn't do. Like I told myself I'd do a lot of shit to get high, but I swore I wouldn't never trick. ... So after I'm trickin', I thought well, you know, this ain't so bad, I'll do this for a while, but I'm gonna make some more rules for myself like, I'm gonna use condoms and I'm never gonna go with more than one guy at the same time and.. well, let's just say there are certain things I told myself I wouldn't never do... You know what my disease did to my rules, right? Yeah. Whatever it is you tell yourself you won't do to get high, you're pretty much making a list of everything you will do as soon as your inner addict tells you to. I mean, that bitch wants to kill me. She does. Even on my way here today she was telling me not to come. She was tellin' me that I was all right on the street, that it was all good......

bettyturpin Obviously have many other profound and erudite comments to make but while I am compiling them, here's my top five Wire men:

1. Stringer Bell. ("I take an XL") But only with a B-more accent (as opposed to Hackney).

2. Ellis Carver (esp in Series 4) Loving the car roof top moment and "Round up".

3. Bodie Broadus. How does he spit like that??!! Been practising for ages...v messy...

4. Jimmy McNulty. Only in plainclothes. In uniform looks like a PlayMobil Person.

5. Omar. Indeed. That silky robe/shotgun combo is a winner every time.

6. (Know was meant to be 5 but have got to get this one off my chest) Slim Charles. Can only think it's the voice...

verrochio Top Five Character Catchphrases:

5. Chain of command, gentlemen – Various 4. Indeed! – Omar Little 3. What did I do? – Jimmy McNulty 2. Yeeerp! – Snoop

And the winner by way of knockout.... 1. Sheeeeeeeeeeeeeeeeeeeit!
– Clay Davis

mcfad Top 5 Laugh-Out Louds

1. Herc catching Royce getting an extra-marital BJ. As he beats a hasty retreat the hall paintings and sculptures are smirking at him!

2. Landsman, resplendent in his Xmas tie, shuffles through the office humming a festive song, but is stopped in his tracks at all the new unsolved murders added to the board by Freaman's nocturnal activities.

3. McNulty's face as the profile of the serial killer is read out to him

4. Clay Davis in near Sarah Palin-esque gaffe Reporter: *What are you reading there, Senator?* 'Clay' Davis: *Promethus Bound. An ancient play, one of the oldest we have. About a simple man who was horrifically punished by the powers that be for the terrible crime of trying to bring light to the common people. In the words of [hastily checks author !] Aeschylus, "No good deed goes unpunished." I cannot tell you how much consolation I find in these slim pages.*

5. Cheese, explaining to his uncle how Omar robbed their entire supply: Prop Joe: *I aint hearing about no resistance* Cheese : *Man, there werent no time for that. Omar had one of them commando squads with him, man. I mean he had this one ho pulling guns out of her pussy. The shit was unseemly. .*

Realcruelty Officer Anthony Colicchio's haircut.

CodProfundity Top 5 "you know you're addicted to The Wire when.."

1. Kima says McNulty's taking Stringer's death like he was kin, you scream "But He Was!!!" and then cry for a minute or two.

2. You notice the connection between Cutty and Carver's names and spend a whole workday trying to figure out if it means anything or if it's just coincidence. The same with the fact Omar L. and Marlo are anagrams and they both have facial scars.

3. You have nightmares about a small foul-mouthed street urchin stalking you with a huge handgun while he calls you a gump.

4. You chose between 2 equally qualified job candidates because you knew one of them was a Wire fan (only kidding, Harry *coughs*)

5. You find words and phrases like "po-po", "hoppers", "re-up" "oh, indeed" "do tell" appearing in your vernacular and confusing just about everybody who hears them.

rascal123 haha, i've started using "don't make me no never mind" recently but it just doesn't sound the same in an english accent!

PaulOwen rascal123 – don't worry. Ain't no thing.

MozzaMan What I also like about The Wire, even though it's supposed to be fiction, are the people who inspired the writers. It's great discovering the story behind the story.

So how about the top 5 cameos by people who inspire The Wire?

Various Newspaper characters William F. Zorzi – Bill Zorzi, David Simon and his wife Laura Lippman

Kurt L. Schmoke – ex-mayor of Baltimore who suggested the legalisation of drugs, to his detriment like Hamsterdam – Health Commissioner

Larry "Donnie" Andrews – part of inspiration for Omar – Donnie, Butchie's friend and muscle.

Jay Landsman – inspiration for Jay Landsman – Dennis Mello.

"Little" Melvin Williams – part inspiration for Avon – The Deacon.

ShangoDan top 5 product names (all fall variously under blue tops/red tops/yellow tops – get 'em while they're hot!):

1. WMD – as recommended by a cop: "I hear it's da bomb"...
2. Greenhouse gas – "greenhouse gas is hot" 3. Bin Laden
4. Pandemic 5. Death row (or Tec-Nine, etc)

The Wire Quiz

WRITTEN BY MCNULTY, FREAMON AND CARCETTI

Joe Wade of online magazine Don't Panic (dontpaniconline.com) organised this charity quiz about The Wire, with questions written by Dominic West (McNulty), Aidan Gillen (Carcetti), and Clarke Peters (Freamon), as well as fans of the show. The proceeds went to the *Tom ap Rhys Pryce memorial trust*, set up to provide educational and vocational training to young people in the wake of the murder of the young lawyer in London in 2006. tomaprhyspryce.com

1. Which policeman's gun goes missing in season three?

a) Dozerman's

b) Bunk's

c) Landsman's

2. Who steals Namond's stash?

a) Michael

b) Dukie

c) Kenard

3. Question set by Aidan Gillen: What kind of sandwich was Carcetti complaining to Norman about having to eat repeatedly on the mayoral campaign trail?

a) Kielbasa

b) Tuna sub

c) BLT

4. What sport connects Burrell with Marlo?

a) Golf

b) American football

c) Pigeon fancying

5. Who do Chris and Snoop give up to Cheese?

a) Proposition Joe

b) Hungry Man

c) Michael

6. What is the name of Bunk's never-seen wife?

a) Nadine

b) Nina

c) Nisha

7. What novel does D'Angelo discuss in prison?

a) The Beautiful and Damned

b) The Great Gatsby

c) Tender is the Night

8. Who wins the basketball game between East and West Baltimore?

a) East

b) West

c) Game called off due to violent dispute

9. What colour ribbon does McNulty's serial killer leave on his victim's wrists?

a) Red

b) Pink

c) Green

10. Question set by Clarke Peters: What case was Freamon working on that got him sidelined for over a decade?

a) Investigation into the Barksdale crew

b) A campaign finance investigation

c) A murder/robbery of an 80-year-old woman

11. What sport did Bunk play at Edmonson?

a) American football

b) Lacrosse

c) Rowing

12. Who does Bodie work for after Avon?

a) Marlo

b) The Greeks

c) Kintel Williamson

13. What is said to be McNulty's scent?

a) Guinness

b) Sex

c) Listerine and Jameson's

14. Which character is played by Melvin Williams, a real life drug lord arrested in the 80s following an investigation involving co-writer Ed Burns?

a) Bunny Colvin

b) Cutty

c) The Deacon

15. Question set by Dominic West: The actor who plays Omar is called Michael Williams. Which famous British actor was the other well-known Michael Williams married to?

a) Helen Mirren

b) Judi Dench

c) Barbara Windsor

16. What does BNBG stand for?

a) Baltimore Needs Building Growth

b) Bunk's Never Been Greater

c) Big Negro Big Gun

See page 296 for answers

Correct answers

1. Dozerman's

2. Kenard

3. Tuna sub

4. Golf

5. Hungry Man

6. Nadine

7. The Great Gatsby

8. East

9. Red

10. A murder/robbery of an 80 year old woman

11. Lacrosse

12. Marlo

13. Listerine and Jameson's

14. The Deacon

15. Judi Dench

16. Big Negro Big Gun